T0214208

Lecture Notes in Computer Science 12927

More information about this subseries at http://www.springer.com/series/7410

Simone Fischer-Hübner ·
Costas Lambrinoudakis ·
Gabriele Kotsis · A Min Tjoa ·
Ismail Khalil (Eds.)

Trust, Privacy and Security in Digital Business

18th International Conference, TrustBus 2021
Virtual Event, September 27–30, 2021
Proceedings

Springer

Editors
Simone Fischer-Hübner
Karlstad University
Karlstad, Sweden

Costas Lambrinoudakis 🆔
University of Piraeus
Piraeus, Greece

Gabriele Kotsis
Johannes Kepler University
of Linz
Linz, Austria

A Min Tjoa
Vienna University of Technology
Vienna, Austria

Ismail Khalil
Johannes Kepler University
of Linz
Linz, Austria

ISSN 0302-9743   ISSN 1611-3349   (electronic)
Lecture Notes in Computer Science
ISBN 978-3-030-86585-6   ISBN 978-3-030-86586-3   (eBook)
https://doi.org/10.1007/978-3-030-86586-3

LNCS Sublibrary: SL4 – Security and Cryptology

This Springer imprint is published by the registered company Springer Nature Switzerland AG
The registered company address is: Gewerbestrasse 11, 6330 Cham, Switzerland

Preface

New computing paradigms, such as cloud computing, big data, and the Internet of Things, in combination with machine learning and artificial intelligence open new horizons to businesses by making possible the provision of high quality services all over the world. While these new developments and services can improve our quality of life and ensure business competitiveness in the global marketplace, they also create challenges and concerns for the protection of data and users' privacy as well as for the trust of users in the domain of digital businesses.

In answer to these concerns, the 18th International Conference on Trust, Privacy and Security in Digital Business (TrustBus 2021), held as a virtual conference during September 27–30, 2021, at Linz in Austria, provided an international forum for researchers and practitioners to exchange information regarding advancements in the state of the art and practice of trust and privacy in digital business. As in previous years, it brought together researchers from different disciplines, developers, and users all interested in the critical success factors of digital business systems.

The conference program included five technical paper sessions covering a broad range of topics, indicatively: Trust Evaluation, Security Risks, Web Security, Data Protection and End User Aspects of Privacy. The papers were selected by the Program Committee via a rigorous reviewing process (each paper was assigned to four referees for review) and 11 out of 30 papers were finally selected for presentation as full papers at the conference. Furthermore, a keynote talk was delivered by Melek Önen (Eurecom), entitled "Towards Privacy-Preserving and Trustworthy AI."

The success of this conference was a result of the effort of many people. We would like to express our appreciation to the Program Committee members, some of them also acting as shepherds for specific papers, to the external reviewers for their hard work, and to the members of the Organizing Committee. We would also like to thank Ismail Khalil for his help in promoting the conference and for his continued support of the TrustBus conference series.

Last but not least, our thanks go to all the authors, who submitted their papers, and to all the participants. We hope you find the proceedings stimulating and beneficial for your future research.

September 2021

Simone Fischer-Hübner
Costas Lambrinoudakis

Organization

Program Committee Chairs

Simone Fischer-Hübner   Karlstad University, Sweden
Costas Lambrinoudakis   University of Piraeus, Greece

Steering Committee

Gabriele Kotsis   Johannes Kepler University Linz, Austria
A Min Tjoa   Vienna University of Technology, Austria
Robert Wille   Software Competence Center Hagenberg, Austria
Bernhard Moser   Software Competence Center Hagenberg, Austria
Ismail Khalil   Johannes Kepler University Linz, Austria

Program Committee

Cheng-Kang Chu   Huawei Singapore, Singapore
Nathan Clarke   University of Plymouth, UK
Frédéric Cuppens   Polytechnique Montréal, Canada
Sabrina De Capitani di Vimercati   Università degli Studi di Milano, Italy
Vasiliki Diamantopoulou   University of the Aegean, Greece
Josep Domingo-Ferrer   Universitat Rovira i Virgili, Spain
Prokopios Drogkaris   European Union Agency for Cybersecurity, Greece
Eduardo B. Fernandez   Florida Atlantic University, USA
Jose-Luis Ferrer-Gomila   University of the Balearic Islands, Spain
Sara Foresti   Università degli Studi di Milano, Italy
Steven Furnell   University of Nottingham, UK
Jürgen Fuß   University of Applied Sciences Upper Austria, Austria
Dimitris Geneiatakis   University of the Aegean, Greece
Dimitris Gritzalis   Athens University of Economics and Business, Greece
Stefanos Gritzalis   University of Piraeus, Greece
Marit Hansen   Unabhängiges Landeszentrum für Datenschutz, Germany
Christos Kalloniatis   University of the Aegean, Greece
Georgios Kambourakis   University of the Aegean, Greece
Farzaneh Karegar   Karlstad University, Sweden
Maria Karyda   University of the Aegean, Greece
Vasilios Katos   Bournemouth University, UK
Sokratis Katsikas   Open University of Cyprus, Cyprus
Dogan Kesdogan   Universität Regensburg, Germany
Spyros Kokolakis   University of the Aegean, Greece

Stephan Krenn	Austrian Institute of Technology GmbH, Austria
Antonio Lioy	Politecnico di Torino, Italy
Javier Lopez	University of Málaga, Spain
Fabio Martinelli	Institute of Informatics and Telematics of CNR, Italy
Vashek Matyas	Masaryk University, Czech Republic
David Megias	Open University of Catalonia, Spain
Chris Mitchell	Royal Holloway, University of London, UK
Haris Mouratidis	University of Brighton, UK
Martin Olivier	University of Pretoria, South Africa
Rolf Oppliger	eSECURITY Technologies, Switzerland
Andreas Pashalidis	Bundesamt für Sicherheit in der Informationstechnik, Germany
Ahmed Patel	National University of Malaysia, Malaysia
Günther Pernul	Universität Regensburg, Germany
Nikolaos Pitropakis	Edinburgh Napier University, UK
Joachim Posegga	University of Passau, Germany
Ruben Rios	University of Malaga, Spain
Panagiotis Rizomiliotis	Harokopio University of Athens, Greece
Carsten Rudolph	Monash University, Australia
Pierangela Samarati	Università degli Studi di Milano, Italy
Ingrid Schaumüller-Bichl	Information Security, Austria
Antonio Skarmeta	University of Murcia, Spain
Stephanie Teufel	University of Fribourg, Switzerland
A Min Tjoa	Vienna University of Technology, Austria
Aggeliki Tsohou	Ionian University, Greece
Edgar Weippl	University of Vienna and SBA Research, Austria
Christos Xenakis	University of Piraeus, Greece

Additional Reviewers

Additional Aksoy
Cristina Alcaraz
Anna Angelogianni
Thomas Baumer
Alberto Blanco-Justicia
Vaios Bolgouras
Panagiotis Dedousis
Davide Ferraris
Jesús García-Rodríguez
Sergio Martínez
Farnaz Mohammadi

Rafael Torres Moreno
Pavlos Papadopoulos
Henrich C. Pöhls
Ilias Politis
Alexander Puchta
David Rebollo-Monedero
Marc Rossberger
Daniel Schlette
Stavros Simou
George Stergiopoulos

Organizers

Towards Privacy-Preserving and Trustworthy AI (Abstract of Keynote Talk)

Melek Önen

Eurecom, France

Abstract. The rise of cloud computing technology led to a paradigm shift in technological services that enabled enterprises to delegate their data analytics tasks to third party (cloud) servers. Machine Learning as a Service (MLaaS) is one such service which provides stakeholders the ease to perform machine learning tasks on a cloud platform. This advantage of outsourcing these computationally-intensive operations, unfortunately, comes with a high cost in terms of privacy exposures. The goal is therefore to come up with customized ML algorithms that would by design preserve the privacy of the processed data. Advanced cryptographic techniques such as fully homomorphic encryption or secure multi-party computation enable the execution of some operations over encrypted data and therefore can be considered as potential candidates for these algorithms. Yet, these incur high computational and/or communication costs for some operations. In this talk, we analyze the tension between ML techniques and relevant cryptographic tools. We further overview existing solutions addressing both privacy and trust requirements.

Contents

Privacy and Users

Trust Evaluation

Monitoring Access Reviews by Crowd Labelling

Sebastian Groll[1,2(✉)], Sascha Kern[1,2], Ludwig Fuchs[2], and Günther Pernul[1]

[1] University of Regensburg, Universitätsstraße 31, 93053 Regensburg, Germany
`sebastian.groll@wiwi.uni-regensburg.de`
[2] Nexis GmbH, Franz-Mayer-Straße 1, 93053 Regensburg, Germany

Abstract. Access reviews, i.e. the periodical security audit of access privileges, are a basic compliance and IT-security requirement for medium- and large-scale organizations. Assessing the quality of the reviewer's decisions ex-post can help to analyse the effectiveness of the measure and to identify structural or organizational shortcomings. Yet, current studies merely focus on improving the decision-making process itself. This paper develops a method for assessing the decision quality of access reviews by applying a solution from the crowd sourcing research realm. In order to achieve this, the problem of assessing decision quality of access reviews is generalized. It is shown that the abstract problem can be mapped to the problem of assessing the quality of crowd tagging decisions. Subsequently, an applicable solution of this research area is applied to access reviews. Furthermore, the selected approach is optimized to meet the specific challenges of access review data.

Keywords: Access reviews · Decision quality · Crowd sourcing · Identity and Access Management · Compliance

1 Introduction

Access reviews are a crucial task for Identity- and Access Management (IAM) and a basic compliance and IT security requirement for medium- and large-scale organizations [17,18]. While security concerns like insider threats represent an intrinsic motivation, external regulations and IT security standards[1] are an important driver for access reviews in practice. As access privileges are a subject to constant change, access reviews must be performed on a regular basis. They are typically executed by reviewers that hold responsibility for either an access privilege or an entity that it is assigned to. During an access review, a responsible human being manually inspects assignments of access privileges and decides if they are legitimate. If they are not, the privilege assignments are thereupon revoked. Note that access reviews are not used to evaluate the access

---

[1] Relevant examples are the Sarbanes-Oxley Act [2], Basel III [3], the European General Data Privacy Regulation [1], ISO 27002 [4] and the BSI Grundschutz [5].

S. Fischer-Hübner et al. (Eds.): TrustBus 2021, LNCS 12927, pp. 3–17, 2021.
https://doi.org/10.1007/978-3-030-86586-3_1

to resources in real-time but rather to inspect and certify an existing structure of access privilege assignments. The effective and efficient execution of access review campaigns remains a major challenge that is leveraged by technical and organizational complexity, time pressure and the sheer amount of review subjects [20]. In fact, large organizations may have numerous user accounts assigned to hundreds of thousands of access privileges spreading over dozens of application systems [13]. As a result, the manual inspection of all assignments, and the careful assessment of their legitimacy, are a time-consuming and error-prone procedure.

In the course of this work, we propose a generalized problem formulation for the quality definition of an access review decision. We then draw a link to the field of crowd sourcing and map the defined problem instance to the research area of crowd labelling. Subsequently, we adapt a well-known approach from existing literature for evaluating the quality of crowd labelling decisions and apply it to the evaluation of access review decisions. Consequently, we present a generalized data mining algorithm that can identify access review decisions with low quality.

In order to ensure both, relevance, and rigor, we follow the principles of the Action Design Research (ADR) methodology and continuously evaluate and improve our approach working together with practitioners on a real data set. The practitioners are responsible for managing the access review campaign rather performing the access reviews themselves. We cooperate with two companies, one IT security company with an expertise in IAM data analytics, and a large European company that performs company-wide access reviews on a regular basis. This work provides four major contributions: (1) We derive an abstract definition of an access review using a conceptual IAM model, (2) we show that research and methodologies of the crowd sourcing realm can successfully be applied to access review decision making and (3) adapt and improve a crowd labelling approach to access review quality assessment, thus contributing to both, the IT security and the crowd sourcing research realm. Finally, following the principles of ADR, (4) we evaluate and improve our approach by conducting a real-life project evaluation.

2   Theoretical Background

In the following we outline the most important definitions for our work in the IAM research area. Subsequently we give an overview of the relevant literature regarding IAM, access reviews and crowd labelling.

According to Pfitzman and Hansen [31] the term identity is a set or subset of attributes or characteristics of an entity that makes this entity uniquely identifiable among other entities. Relying on this definition, we define the term employee as referring to a uniquely identifiable real-world person working for a specific company. Following Pfitzman and Hansen [31], we use the definition of digital identity to derive the term account: An (user) account is unique in a specific application system and represents its employee in this context.

In order to manage the privilege assignments, a wide range of so-called access control models have been published. Sandhu et al. [33] propose the role-based access control model (RBAC) inducing the role as intermediary between an employee and his privileges. Using roles can significantly reduce the number of assignments and therefore increase comprehensibility [14]. Fuchs and Preis [15] argue that there are multiple semantic types of roles like business roles, organizational roles or IT-roles[2]. Shortcomings of RBAC like the lack of fine-grained access control [6,36] or continuously increasing role sizes [26] and numbers [25] led to the development and improvement of attribute-based access control (ABAC) concepts [20,21].

The aim of access reviews is to inspect and certify the privilege assignments resulting from an implemented access control model. This might be done by reviewing certain permission assignments in an application or by reviewing conceptional assignments e.g. business roles which do not really exist on the application. Jaferian et al. [20] identify key challenges of access reviews and deal with the question of how to design an access review application in order to help the reviewers to make meaningful decisions. They design and implement a tool that is supposed to aid reviewers by enhancing the user interface. However, their focus lies on designing and evaluating the UI rather than evaluating the decision quality of the reviewers. Hill [17] presents a case study that showcases the introduction of software-supported access reviews and other access control management measures in a healthcare enterprise. Bobba et al. [7] discuss the design of tools that are supposed to aid domain administrators in the execution of access reviews. To the best of our knowledge, there are no scientific publications that explicitly cover the challenge of measuring access review decision quality in a structured manner.

Crowd sourcing is a collaborative and distributed problem-solving activity, where many workers join to solve various kinds of tasks. Examples for crowd sourcing projects are Galaxy Zoo[3], Amazon's Mechanical Turk[4], where users can publish tasks for crowdsourcing, or even collective projects like Wikipedia [24]. In Galaxy Zoo, for example, people work together in order to manually classify or tag different types of galaxies, like elliptical or spiral galaxies. Crowd sourcing comprises all sorts of tasks a community of crowd workers can perform.
· In the following we focus on crowd labelling, which is a part of crowd sourcing. Crowd labelling is typically used to create labels for a large amount of data, e.g. to create input for supervised machine learning algorithms [16]. For example, above-mentioned Galaxy Zoo is a crowd labelling project. While crowd labelling has become a multi-million-dollar industry, the evaluation and improvement of crowd-sourced labels remains a crucial challenge (Lease 2011). The quality of labelling decisions is influenced by the labelers' expertise [27,30,38], their motivation [19,32], organizational circumstances and other factors [11,35]. As a result, crowd labelling may suffer from poor labelling quality or "spammers" [23] and thus numerous approaches to rate the quality of labels or crowd workers

---

[2] In the following we will refer to the term business role in order to emphasize the application- and technical- independent character of roles.

[3] https://www.zooniverse.org/projects/zookeeper/galaxy-zoo/.

[4] https://www.mturk.com/.

have been published [8, 16, 22, 30]. Other approaches aim to improve the quality of labels in a generic way, e.g. by sorting out low quality labellers [10], or programmatically generating "gold labels" (i.e. correct labels that can be used to test the accuracy of labellers) [30].

2.1 Research Method

In order to design an ensemble artifact that addresses and satisfies organizational needs and ensures the rigor required for scientific contributions, we utilize the ADR method [34]. ADR relies on a close cooperation between researchers and practitioners and provides a framework for the dynamic interaction between the two parties. It defines four main stages containing principles to follow during their respective execution.

In the (1) Problem Formulation Phase the research opportunity is identified. The specific problem can be triggered by researchers, practitioners, or end-users. One crucial and challenging task is to define "the problem as an instance of a class of problems" [34]. This ensures that a solution for a more generalized problem is created and may extend the range of applicable theories. In this study the definition of a generalized problem enabled us to apply research approaches from the crowd sourcing realm on a problem of the IAM research area. Another principle of this phase is to design an artifact by utilizing theories. Finally, this phase also contains setting up an ADR team, which consists of practitioners and researchers, securing the long-term commitment of the practitioners as well as defining the roles and responsibilities of the team members. In the (2) Building, Intervention and Evaluation (BIE) phase the artifact is shaped in an iterative process. The practitioners and end-users implicitly take part in the design process by continuously evaluating the artifact. Moreover, the members of the ADR team benefit from their diverse expert knowledge. For example, our team consists of IAM researchers, IAM consultants and practitioners, respectively having different perspectives and insights on IAM and access reviews. While executing phase 1 and phase 2 the researcher simultaneously executes the (3) Reflection and Learning Phase. Thereby the researcher continuously transforms the gained knowledge to a broader class of problems. Therefore, our solution does not only improve the quality assessment of access reviews but is applicable for the broader field of crowd labelling as well. In the final phase (4) Formalization of Learning the researcher outlines the results achieved during the development of the artifact and its application to the organizational context. Due to the context-specific nature of ADR projects, a generalization of the concrete solution is necessary.

3   Problem Formulation

3.1 Practice-Inspired Research

For this study we worked together with two companies: The first one is a small IT security company, which offers tools and consulting services for mid-sized and large organizations in the field of IAM. The provided services include the tool-based preparation and execution of access reviews. The second company is a large European organization with more than 15.000 employees. This company is forced to conduct company-wide access reviews on a regular basis due to existing compliance regulations. Our research was triggered by questions raised by customers of the partnering IAM security company like "How can I detect abnormalities in the access review process?", "How can I find out if the reviewers are doing their job carefully enough?" or "How can the correctness of decisions be ensured?". Thus, summarizing the requests and discussions we had with customers of the IT security company, we formulate the initial research question as follows: *"How can low-quality review decisions in an access review be identified ex-post?"*

Defining the roles of the practitioners [9], we decided that their responsibilities contain the provision of (anonymized) realworld IAM data (i.e. the access review data), the provision of contextual knowledge, as well as the regular evaluation of the developed artifact during the execution of the BIE cycle.

3.2 Defining Access Review Decision Quality as an Instance of a Class of Problems

According to Sein et al. [34], a "critical element of the problem formulation phase is defining the problem as an instance of a class of problems" [34]. This step is necessary to draw and contribute foundations and methodologies from and to the knowledge base. Thus, a funded and more general conceptual definition of the term "decision" in the context of access reviews. To achieve this, we adapt the existing conceptual IAM model proposed by Kunz et al. [26]. Their generic IAM model is a derivation of several relevant IAM standards (including RBAC and ABAC) and technologies containing and relating, amongst other things, employees, which are called digital identities in their work, accounts, permissions and business roles (Fig. 1)). Please note that Fig. 1 represents a simplified version of the original IAM model, specifically adapted to the requirements of representing access reviews and review decisions[5]. Employees refer to the real persons working for a company. They are represented by their accounts on the specific application systems of the organization. The accounts themselves are assigned to permissions representing fine-grained authorization objects to access services offered by these systems. Permissions may be structured hierarchically, i.e. owning a parent permission leads to the possession of additional child permissions. In contrast to permissions, business roles are less technical entities within IAM environments which are typically used to represent organizational or functional roles of employees like "Accountant" or "Sales Representative" [15]. They are used to bundle permissions from different application systems to grant employees access to all application systems needed for the daily work or for executing specific tasks or business processes. In contrast

---

[5] Therefore, we removed "Context" and "Policy" from the model because these entity types do not influence access reviews. We also renamed the term "(Digital) Identity" to "Employee" in order to fit our definitions and naming conventions, however, the meaning remains the same.

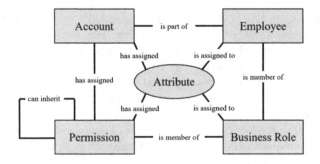

Fig. 1. Conceptual IAM model derived from Kunz et al. [26]

to accounts, business roles are directly assigned to employees, underlining their application-independent focus. Each of the entities described by Kunz et al. [26] may possess a set of attributes, which contains metadata of the respective entity. A typical attribute for an employee may be a job title or the location she is currently working at. Utilizing the conceptual IAM model of Kunz et al. [26] as well as our experiences from practical industry projects, we differentiate access reviews in two different main classes: (1) An entity itself, respectively its attributes, may be reviewed and (2) the relations between the entities, i.e. the edges in Fig. 1, may be reviewed. In the remainder of our practical analysis, we focus on the second class of access reviews (relationship reviews), however we argue that our research in general can be easily applied on the first class as well. Further generalizing, a decision d in an access review contains two entities (e.g. an account and a per-mission) and the decision whether these two entities should remain assigned to each other or not. Every entity e comprises a set of attributes x_e. Combined with the expert and contextual knowledge of the reviewer, these attributes form the foundation of the decision to be made. An access review decision by a reviewer r concerning the relation between two entities can further be expressed as $d_r(e1, e2) = \{x_{e1}, x_{e2}, y\}$ where y may be true or false, assuming the labels "keep relation" or "remove relation". Thus, an access review decision made by reviewer r comprises a set of features from the two entities and the information if these entities should remain linked or not. Finally, an access review with n decisions can be represented as a set $AR = \{d_i | i \in 1, ..., n\}$. Because we are especially interested in excessive assignments our research problem can be described as assessing the quality of every d_i with the label $y =$ "keep relation" to find suspicious and possibly wrong decisions.

4   Theory-Ingrained Artifact

According to the principles of ADR, we draw from the foundation of existing literature, to create the initial design of an artifact informed by theories. Therefore, we show that our generalized problem can be transferred to the research area of crowd sourcing and we apply selected approaches from this area. We also use well-established visualization techniques from IAM research to visualize our results.

The quality assessment problem of access reviews derived in the previous chapter can be mapped to the problem researchers are facing when assessing the labelling quality of crowd workers. In an access review campaign, every decision $d(e1, e2)$ is a labelling task, with the labels "keep relation" and "remove relation". Like our previously defined vector of entity attributes x_e, the data which must be labelled in crowd labelling comprises several features and is typically expressed as a feature vector. And like one of the main problems of crowd labelling, our aim is to assess the quality of the decisions (i.e. labels).

Visualization is a key component of data analytics that can leverage the insights gained from otherwise less comprehensible data sets and make them accessible to non-technical experts. We suggest extending the access grid that was introduced by Meier, Fuchs and Pernul [28] for this sake as it is a well-proven interactive visualization technique that is tailored for displaying IAM data in an easily understandable manner. The reviewed entities are displayed as rows, and the referenced entities are displayed as columns. Each cell hence depicts the relationship between two entities: If an assignment exists between these two entities, the cell is filled; otherwise it is left blank. An assignment that exists, but was not subject of the review, is filled grey (i.e. assignments that deliberately were not part of the access review campaign). The color of a cell indicates a reviewer's decision: If an assignment was approved i.e. a positive decision was made, the cell is green; a negative decision is marked by a orange filling. If a positive decision is detected by our algorithm's outcome and therefore potentially has low quality, then a violet border is placed around the otherwise green cell (See Fig. 2).

4.1 Designing the Initial Artifact

To design the initial artifact, we utilize theories of the crowd sourcing domain and access grid visualizations to assess the quality of a set of given access review decisions. When mapping access reviews to crowd sourcing, there are several challenges, causing access reviews to be a more specific problem in the crowd sourcing domain: (1) Access reviews, as defined in the previous section, only consist of binary decisions, while crowdlabelling may have more than one possible label e.g. more types of galaxies to classify. (2) During access reviews, one decision is usually made by one reviewer (e.g. a responsible department owner of an employee or a responsible business role owner) whereas in typical crowd labelling tasks, several reviewers label the same data. Therefore, approaches like majority vote, which are often used in crowd labelling [8,22,37], cannot be applied easily. (3) Following the principle of least privilege [12,33], the quality of positive decisions is more important in access reviews than the quality of negative decisions.

4.2 Applying Crowd Sourcing Theories to Access Reviews

Based on these assumptions, we selected the machine learning approach of Geva and Saar-Tsechansky [16] for our initial artifact design. It aims to create a ranking of decision makers based on their decision quality and is capable of handling binary decisions. One of its key assumptions is that every decision is created by exactly one reviewer. The underlying research question is: "how can we rank workers by the relative quality of their decisions without resorting to the acquisition of additional and potentially costly, peer-review by other experts?" [16]. The key idea is to generate a so-called Pseudo Ground Truth (PGT) for every decision, i.e. an estimation of the correct y. This PGT can be compared with the decisions a decision maker has made to estimate her decision quality and to create a ranking of the decision makers. In order to create the PGT, a so-called base model is generated for every decision maker. The base model is trained with decision data, i.e. all decisions $d_r = \{x, y\}$ where r is the respective decision maker. These calculated base models can predict a decision for a given feature vector x, even if the decision maker, on whom the model is based, never made this decision. In other words, the base models are able to simulate reviewers' decisions. Following this concept, it is possible to create the PGT for a decision of a certain decision maker by conducting a vote with the base models of all the other decision makers. Note that the base models are necessary because of our assumption that every decision was only carried out by one decision maker and therefore it is not possible to use the decision data of the other decision makers directly. If a decision would have been carried out by multiple decision makers, a simulation using base models would not be necessary, because we could use the concrete decisions themselves. After being generated, the PGT is used to create a decision quality score for every decision maker by dividing the decisions, where the PGT and the decision maker agree, by the total amount of decisions that the decision maker has made. Geva and Saar-Tsechansky [16] claim that the precision of the decision quality score can further be improved by introducing the concept of confidence within the PGT and applying it as weight to every decision. To calculate the confidence value, the result of the vote from the different base models is used. Finally, the calculated decision quality scores of the decision makers can be used to create a ranking of decision makers regarding their decision quality. This general approach can be adopted to our problem: Throughout the process of an access review, the reviewer represents the decision maker according to the model of Geva and Saar-Tsechansky [16]. The feature vector x is represented by the attributes of the two entities that the reviewed assignment refers to, e.g. an account and a certain permission in an application system. The actual decision ("keep relation" or "remove relation") is the label y. Usually, several attributes for different entity types (e.g. employee, permission, etc.) are available in an identity management system and it is a critical and complex task to select a meaningful set of attributes. For example, the employee's gender usually has no influence on her permissions but the function she holds within the organization might heavily influence the assignment of certain permissions.

5   Building, Intervention and Evaluation

5.1   Mutually Influenced Roles

During the design and learning process, there was ongoing knowledge and feedback communication between the ADR team and the partnering IT security company. Firstly, the IT security company provided the data analysis platform that enabled the ADR team to explore the customer data and to understand the review decisions in detail and as-a-whole. Secondly, the ADR team required contextual knowledge to understand individual review decisions in the real data set, and to determine ex-post whether a decision was erroneous or not. This context knowledge was acquired through workshops with responsible IT staff of both partnering companies. Information provided by the second industry partner regarding their organizational structures, attribute semantics, as well as responsibilities of reviewers proofed to be a valuable addition to the evaluation process.

5.2   Access Review Campaign Data

The industry partner executing the access review provided the ADR team with a real data set of a company-wide, quarterly access review campaign. The access review campaign was exclusively executed for account to permission assignments. The assignments were presented to the responsible reviewers in the form of employee to permission assignments to simplify their user interface and foster user acceptance. The delivered data set[6] comprised a total of 71.464 decisions regarding 10.891 employees and 1.623 permissions and was used both for the development of the artifact and for its evaluation. The provided decisions included 3.461 decisions that had no label (i.e. reviewer decision) asserted. This is in fact not unusual for an access review campaign of this scale due to organizational circumstances (e.g. illness of reviewers, technical challenges, etc.). Unlabelled decisions were omitted by our algorithm and did not affect the results. Table 1 shows the key figures of the data set. The ADR team used to work on various subsets of the data with a meaningful filter selection, i.e. decisions regarding employees of a single department and permissions of a single application system. This way, it was possible to use existing contextual knowledge, or to pose specific inquiries to representatives of the company to gather their expertise and to understand the origin of the observed decisions.

Table 1. Key data of the evaluation data sets.

Key data	Data set
Employees to review	10.891
Reviewers	855
Application systems	13
Permissions	1.623
Positive/Negative decisions	67.116 (93,9%)/887 (1,2%)
Not decided (reviewer did not make a decision)	3.461 (4,8%)
Total decisions to make	71.464

---

[6] The data set was gathered by using exports of the company's human resource system as well as exports of the different application systems.

5.3   Reciprocal Shaping

After implementing the initial artifact, the ADR team carried out the approach
on the real data set in a first BIE cycle. However, the generated PGT comprised
almost only positive decisions. Further analyzing the results highlighted three
major reasons: Firstly, there was a very strong bias towards positive decisions
in the data set with 93.9% of the provided decisions being positive, which was
expected because most permission assignments are correct. The second discovered limitation is that a lot of the calculated base models had to make decisions
that they were not qualified for. For example, a base model generated for a
reviewer who had only made decisions regarding employees in the marketing
department and permissions for application system "A" now was queried about
a permission from application system "B" being assigned to an employee of the
software development department. Such unqualified base models, which do not
share any attributes with the currently processed decision, tend to guess a positive decision. The reason is, that most of the decisions used to generate the
model are positive themselves. The third issue was noise that was generated by
base models that were based on very few or even only one single decision. Their
decision making was inflexible and used to overrule correct negative decisions
just as unqualified base models did. As a result of these issues, the base models
almost always voted for positive decisions, and a completely positive PGT was
generated. To address these challenges, we extended the voting process of the
base models in a way that the votes are no longer considered equally meaningful.
The underlying assumption is that a base model is more successful in identifying
errors correctly than another if it is based on more similar decisions.

We represent this qualification of a base model b(r), based on reviewer r, for a
decision d by calculating an experience score $e_{d,b}$. Consequently, a decision made
by this base model during the voting process is weighted with this experience.
Let B be the set of all base models and B_d^+ be a subset of B with all base models
that generate a positive label for decision d. Then the quality of a decision d^r
made by reviewer r is the sum of the experience scores of B_d^+ , divided by the
sum of the experience scores of B. The base model based on reviewer r itself is
excluded from this score. The quality can then be expressed as:

$$q_{d,r} = \frac{\sum_{b^+ \in B_d^+ \setminus \{b(r)\}} (e_{d,b^+})}{\sum_{b \in B \setminus \{b(r)\}} (e_{d,b})}$$

We then define a quality threshold t that represents a minimum quality score
which needs to be undercut to generate a finding for a suspected false decision.
This way it is possible to adjust the output sensitivity of the algorithm. Formally, the decision d made by reviewer r is suspicious in terms of its quality,
when $q_{(d,r)} < t, 0 \leq t \leq 1$ The quality threshold t can be adjusted to increase or
decrease the amount of generated negative decisions and hence determines the
detection sensitivity of the algorithm. While we argue that there is no determined optimum value as the amount of generated negative decisions depends
on a data set's positive decision bias, we achieved good results with a threshold

of approximately 0.6^7. As base model decisions are made based on the assigned entities' attributes x_{e1} and x_{e2}, we define that a base model has a higher experience than another if it has made more decisions on entities with equal attributes. We hence calculate a matching attribute score $attr_{d,b}$ for each base model decision by summing up all attributes of all decisions of the current base model, i.e. the decisions of the reviewer the base model is based on, that are equal to the current decision's attributes x_{e1}, x_{e2}. This matching attribute score is the basis of our introduced experience score. In order to normalize the sum of matching attributes, we used a sigmoid function, which is often used in artificial neural network research for similar normalization problems [29]. The sigmoid function ranks base models with few decisions very low, but still allows all base models with a certain "maturity" to be taken into consideration in the weighted vote. The experience score is hence defined as $e_{d,b} = $ sigmoid($attr_{d,b}$). With respect to the last ADR phase (Reflection and Learning) we emphasize that this improvement can be easily adopted to the generalized crowd labelling approach by simply enhancing the voting process of the base models with the method described in this chapter. Our approach can be helpful when dealing with data with an extreme bias. However, we argue that it might also be useful when dealing with non-biased data sets, as including the experience score decreases the influence of unqualified base models and increases the influence of qualified base models.

5.4   Evaluation

The final evaluation data set was selected by filtering the review campaign data to decisions regarding permissions of one large application system. It comprised 36.181 decisions with 34.744 positive, 383 negative and 1054 neutral labels. For the evaluation, three meaningful attributes were selected, and the quality threshold t was set to 0.6. The evaluation run yielded 33 results that indicated a false "keep relation" label. Manually investigating these findings together with our expert partners in the two companies, we were able to verify the correctness for 30 of them. This equates to an accordance of 90,9%. Please note that a higher quality threshold would have resulted in more findings and presumably also a lower accordance, while a lower threshold would have had the opposite effect. Using the selected strict parameterization and the low generated number of suspicious reviewer decisions allowed us to conduct focused review workshops with the industry partners without confronting them with a potentially large number of results (which in turn would have complicated the expert review process). Summing up, the chosen parameterization allowed us to yield a small number of likely correct results with an acceptably small error rate. As an example, Fig. 2 displays four findings discovered by the algorithm regarding two employees in an access grid. The employees are displayed in the rows of the visualization. Four positive decisions (see violet border) were made be the same reviewer, while

---

[7] Note that determining a suitable threshold must be done manually and the value highly depends on the imported data.

all other permissions of the two employees were marked for removal by another reviewer. Expert consultations revealed that the reviewer who made the negative decisions was the manager of these employees and knew that they had left the company during the past month. At the same time the positive decisions were made by a system administrator who was not informed about this fact. According to our industry partner's access review campaign experts, these findings are especially relevant, as they do not only expose possibly wrong decisions, but rather reveal structural and organizational problems concerning the quality of their overall IAM processes, e.g. lack in knowledge management or usability. Further expert evaluation revealed that reviewers had allegedly pressed a wrong button or decided too hastily.

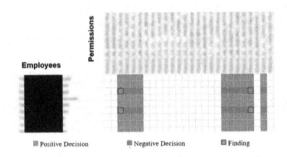

Fig. 2. Findings of the algorithm visualized with an access grid.

6   Conclusion

In the course of this work, we addressed the quality evaluation of access review decisions by answering the research question "How can low-quality review decisions in an access review be identified ex-post?". To achieve this, we firstly developed a generalized problem formulation. Subsequently, we mapped this problem and its characteristics to the research area of crowd sourcing. We facilitated an approach by Geva and Saar-Tsechansky [16] developed to assess the quality of crowd labelling decisions and consequently adapted it to the given problem formulation. Additionally, we developed a theory-ingrained artifact that allowed us to identify erroneous access review decisions automatically. During result evaluation we were able to prove the applicability of our approach for evaluating the quality of human access review decisions. We discussed interim results and considered the feedback provided by our industry partners in order to make sure that the research objectives are in line with actual practical needs. Following the ADR principle of generalized outcome, we provided both, a generalized problem, as well as a generalized solution formulation. The approach may be applied back to the original approach from the crowd labelling realm which, in turn, leads to the achievement of a general improvement and contribution to the field.

References

1. The European Parliament and the Council of the European Union: General Data Protection Regulation. https://eurlex.europa.eu/legal-content/EN/TXT/?uri=CELEX%3A32016R0679. Accessed 22 Mar 2021
2. One Hundred Seventh Congress of the United States of America: "Sarabanes-Oxley-Act (SOX)". https://www.iso.org/standard/54533.html (2002). Accessed 22 Mar 2021
3. Basel committee on banking supervision: Basel III: a global regulatory framework for more resilient banks and banking systems. https://www.bis.org/publ/bcbs189.pdf (2010). Accessed 22 Mar 2021
4. International organization for standardization. "ISO/IEC 27002: Information technology - security techniques - code of practice for information security controls". https://www.iso.org/standard/54533.html (2013). Accessed 22 Mar 2021
5. Federal office for information security (BSI): "IT-Grundschutz". https://www.bsi.bund.de/EN/Topics/ITGrundschutz/itgrundschutz_node.html (2018). Accessed 22 Mar 2021
6. Azhar, A., Amin, M., Nauman, M., Shah, S.U.: Efficient selection of access control systems through multi criteria analytical hierarchy process. In: 2012 International Conference on Emerging Technologies, pp. 1–8 (2012). https://doi.org/10.1109/ICET.2012.6375419
7. Bobba, R., Gavrila, S., Gligor, V., Khurana, H., Koleva, R.: Administering access control in dynamic coalitions. In: Proceedings of the 19th Conference on Large Installation System Administration Conference, vol. 19, p. 23, LISA 2005. USENIX Association, USA (2005)
8. Brodley, C.E., Friedl, M.A.: Identifying mislabeled training data. J. Artif. Int. Res. 11(1), 131–167 (1999)
9. Cole, R., Purao, S., Rossi, M., Sein, M.: Being proactive: where action research meets design research. In: ICIS 2005 Proceedings, p. 27 (2005)
10. Dekel, O., Shamir, O.: Vox populi: Collecting high-quality labels from a crowd. In: COLT (2009)
11. Erickson, L.B., Trauth, E.M., Petrick, I.: Getting inside your employees' heads: navigating barriers to internal-crowdsourcing for product and service innovation (2012)
12. Ferraiolo, D., Kuhn, D.R., Chandramouli, R.: Role-Based Access Control. Artech House, Boston (2003)
13. Fuchs, L., Pernul, G.: Supporting compliant and secure user handling-a structured approach for in-house identity management. In: The Second International Conference on Availability, Reliability and Security (ARES 2007), pp. 374–384. IEEE (2007)
14. Fuchs, L., Pernul, G.: HyDRo – hybrid development of roles. In: Sekar, R., Pujari, A.K. (eds.) ICISS 2008. LNCS, vol. 5352, pp. 287–302. Springer, Heidelberg (2008). https://doi.org/10.1007/978-3-540-89862-7_24
15. Fuchs, L., Preis, A.: BusiROLE: a model for integrating business roles into identity management. In: Furnell, S., Katsikas, S.K., Lioy, A. (eds.) TrustBus 2008. LNCS, vol. 5185, pp. 128–138. Springer, Heidelberg (2008). https://doi.org/10.1007/978-3-540-85735-8_13
16. Geva, T., Saar-Tsechansky, M.: Who's a good decision maker? data-driven expert worker ranking under unobservable quality (2016)

17. Hill, L.: How automated access verification can help organizations demonstrate HIPAA compliance: a case study. J. Healthcare Inf. Manag. **20**(2), 116 (2006)
18. Hummer, M., Kunz, M., Netter, M., Fuchs, L., Pernul, G.: Adaptive identity and access management-contextual data based policies. EURASIP J. Inf. Secur. **2016**(1), 1–16 (2016)
19. Ihl, A., Strunk, K.S., Fiedler, M.: The influence of utilitarian and hedonic motivation on success in crowd work (2018)
20. Jaferian, P., Rashtian, H., Beznosov, K.: To authorize or not authorize: helping users review access policies in organizations. In: 10th Symposium on Usable Privacy and Security ({SOUPS} 2014), pp. 301–320 (2014)
21. Jin, X., Krishnan, R., Sandhu, R.: A unified attribute-based access control model covering DAC, MAC and RBAC. In: Cuppens-Boulahia, N., Cuppens, F., Garcia-Alfaro, J. (eds.) DBSec 2012. LNCS, vol. 7371, pp. 41–55. Springer, Heidelberg (2012). https://doi.org/10.1007/978-3-642-31540-4_4
22. Khattak, F.K., Salleb-Aouissi, A.: Robust crowd labeling using little expertise. In: Fürnkranz, J., Hüllermeier, E., Higuchi, T. (eds.) DS 2013. LNCS (LNAI), vol. 8140, pp. 94–109. Springer, Heidelberg (2013). https://doi.org/10.1007/978-3-642-40897-7_7
23. Kittur, A., Chi, E.H., Suh, B.: Crowdsourcing user studies with mechanical Turk. In: Proceedings of the SIGCHI Conference on Human Factors in Computing Systems, pp. 453–456 (2008)
24. Kittur, A., et al.: The future of crowd work. In: Proceedings of the 2013 Conference on Computer Supported Cooperative Work, pp. 1301–1318 (2013)
25. Kuhn, D.R., Coyne, E.J., Weil, T.R.: Adding attributes to role-based access control. Computer **43**(6), 79–81 (2010)
26. Kunz, M., Puchta, A., Groll, S., Fuchs, L., Pernul, G.: Attribute quality management for dynamic identity and access management. J. Inf. Secur. Appl. **44**, 64–79 (2019)
27. Leicht, N., Rhyn, M., Hansbauer, G.: Can Laymen outperform experts? The effects of user expertise and task design in crowdsourced software testing (2016)
28. Meier, S., Fuchs, L., Pernul, G.: Managing the access grid-a process view to minimize insider misuse risks (2013)
29. Menon, A., Mehrotra, K., Mohan, C.K., Ranka, S.: Characterization of a class of sigmoid functions with applications to neural networks. Neural Netw. **9**(5), 819–835 (1996)
30. Oleson, D., Sorokin, A., Laughlin, G., Hester, V., Le, J., Biewald, L.: Programmatic gold: Targeted and scalable quality assurance in crowdsourcing. In: Workshops at the Twenty-Fifth AAAI Conference on Artificial Intelligence. Citeseer (2011)
31. Pfitzmann, A., Hansen, M.: A terminology for talking about privacy by data minimization: anonymity, unlinkability, undetectability, unobservability, pseudonymity, and identity management (2010)
32. Rouse, A.C.: A preliminary taxonomy of crowdsourcing (2010)
33. Sandhu, R.S., Coynek, E.J., Feinsteink, H.L., Youman, C.E.: Role-based access control models. Computer **29**(2), 38–47 (1996)
34. Sein, M.K., Henfridsson, O., Purao, S., Rossi, M., Lindgren, R.: Action design research. MIS Q. **35**(1), 37–56 (2011)
35. Tavanapour, N., Bittner, E.A.: The collaboration of crowd workers (2018)
36. Valecha, R., Kashyap, M., Rajeev, S., Rao, R., Upadhyaya, S.: An activity theory approach to specification of access control policies in transitive health workflows (2014)

37. Whitehill, J., Wu, T.F., Bergsma, J., Movellan, J., Ruvolo, P.: Whose vote should count more: optimal integration of labels from labelers of unknown expertise. Adv. Neural Inf. Process. Syst. **22**, 2035–2043 (2009)
38. Wöhner, T., Köhler, S., Peters, R.: Good authors = good articles?-how Wikis work. In: Wirtschaftsinformatik, pp. 872–886 (2015)

Automating the Evaluation of Trustworthiness

Marc Sel$^{(\boxtimes)}$ and Chris J. Mitchell

Information Security Group, Royal Holloway, University of London, Egham, Surrey
TW20 0EX, UK
Marc.Sel.2013@live.rhul.ac.uk, me@chrismitchell.net

Abstract. Digital services have a significant impact on the lives of many people and organisations. Trust influences decisions regarding potential service providers, and continues to do so once a service provider has been selected. There is no globally accepted model to describe trust in the context of digital services, nor to evaluate the trustworthiness of entities. We present a formal framework to partially fill this gap. It is based on four building blocks: a data model, rulebooks, trustworthiness evaluation functions and instance data. An implementation of this framework can be used by a potential trustor to evaluate the trustworthiness of a potential trustee.

Keywords: Trust · Trustworthiness · Semantics · Ontology · OWL · SPARQL

1 Introduction

Trust is important because its presence or absence can have a strong influence on what we choose to do or not do, both as individual and as a group. Trusting decisions are made by all of us, often in the context of electronic service delivery. Also automata are increasingly confronted with such decisions. The one that is trusting is commonly referred to as the trustor, the one that is trusted is referred to as the trustee. The trustee may live up to the trustor's expectation, or may let him down. Betrayal of trust is the responsibility of the trustee, not of the trustor. The negative consequences of betrayal of trust may however impact the trustor.

There is a lack of clarity and of agreement on the basic meaning of the terms trust and trustworthiness. Gambetta [4] provides a broad treatment of trust, where in the last chapter the following reasons to trust are given.

- If we do not, we shall never find out.
- Trust is not depleted through use, on the contrary.

High level definitions of trust exist but are hard to apply in practical situations. Castelfranchi and Francone [2] state that *'trust is in fact a deficiency of control that expresses itself as a desire to progress despite the inability to control'*.

© Springer Nature Switzerland AG 2021
S. Fischer-Hübner et al. (Eds.): TrustBus 2021, LNCS 12927, pp. 18–31, 2021.
https://doi.org/10.1007/978-3-030-86586-3_2

The term trust carries an ambiguous meaning, as it is used both as a positive and as a negative characteristic. In natural language, trust is perceived as a positive term, such as trust between husband and wife. However, Gollman [5] argues that trust is bad for security. It is remarkable that the European eIDAS Regulation [3], covering trust services and the provision thereof, does not include a definition of trust or trustworthiness.

In the execution of electronic transactions, there are often controls in place, based on service providers such as Trusted Third Parties (TTPs) who claim they can be trusted. However, the use of TTPs based on a Public Key Infrastructure (PKI) lacks a clear definition of trust. In this case trust is expressed through PKI policies which consist of sets of documents, including Certificate Policies and Practise Statements. Semantics is expressed in natural language and formalisms such as Object Identifiers and XML Schema Definitions, which are poor in expressing meaning. Huang and Nicol [6] state that the major PKI specification documents do not precisely define what trust means in PKIs. Rather there are implicit trust assumptions embedded, some of which may not always be true. Such implicit trust assumptions may cause relying parties to have differing understandings about the meaning of certificates and trust.

We address the aforementioned problem by defining a framework that includes a structured process to define requirements, a data model and trustworthiness evaluation functions that are based on these requirements and transformations that adapt real world data to the data model, allowing the transformed data to be stored in a graph database. The practical feasibility of the framework has been demonstrated by a partial implementation of the data model in the Ontology Web Language (OWL), of the evaluation functions in SPARQL, and of the transformations in XSLT. The resulting data was stored in a GraphDB database. The framework allows the use of the semantic interpretations specified by the data model in the evaluations and their outcomes.

The remainder of this article is structured as follows. Section 2 describes the $\mathcal{TE}$ framework and its components. Section 3 describes a partial implementation of the framework, including the creation of instance data based on real-world information and the performance of trustworthiness evaluations on this data. Section 4 presents related work. Section 5 gives conclusions and ideas for future work. The appendix contains selected results from the execution of a sample evaluation as specified in Sect. 3.

2   The $\mathcal{TE}$ Framework

The objective of the $\mathcal{TE}$ framework is to allow a potential trustor to evaluate the trustworthiness of a potential trustee. This evaluation is based on verifying whether a set of rules is satisfied by particular instance data. The framework contains four classes of components: a data model, rulebooks, trustworthiness evaluation functions, and instance data about the potential trustees and their context.

2.1 Defining Trustworthiness

The following working definition of trustworthiness is used in the remainder of the article. Trustworthiness is a characteristic of an entity, where entities include persons, ICT systems, organisations and information artefacts, with the properties given below. An entity can be qualified as being ex-ante or ex-post trustworthy, as follows.

- When an entity is qualified as ex-ante trustworthy a trustor can have reasonable expectations that future interactions and their outcomes will be consistent with what has been communicated or committed by the trustee. This is also called forward-looking trustworthiness.
- When an entity is qualified as ex-post trustworthy a trustor can have reasonable expectations that the outcome of a transaction performed in the past can be relied upon. This is also called backward-looking trustworthiness.

2.2 Requirements

The requirements for the framework were developed on the basis of a literature review and the requirements developed in the Horizon2020 FutureTrust project[1] work packages [11], [12]. Requirements from both sources were combined into the following set of integrated requirements.

- IR1 Semantic definition of trustworthiness: *As a participant in an electronic ecosystem I can understand the meaning of trustworthiness of participants I plan to engage with, so that I can make an informed decision on whom to interact with.*
- IR2 Transparency: *As a participant in an electronic ecosystem where I have access to a function that allows me to evaluate trustworthiness of other participants, I can access all information (including inputs used and operations performed) of this function in a transparent[2] way, so that I can understand the factors that contribute to trustworthiness and their mapping on evidence such as qualifications of entities.*
- IR3 Linked and unique identity: *As a participant in an electronic ecosystem where I have access to a function that allows me to evaluate the trustworthiness of other participants, I can rely on this function combining all information about participants available within the ecosystem, so that I can claim the outcome of the trustworthiness evaluation is based on all information known about the evaluated participant.*
- IR4 Competently acting in role *As a participant in an electronic ecosystem I have access to and I can demonstrate that I accept the definitions of roles, the qualifications that are required per role, and how these qualifications are demonstrated by participants, so that I can verify these arguments are suitable to support the reliance I want to take on the outcome of the reasoning.*

---

[1] http://www.futuretrust.eu.

[2] The term 'transparent' is used as defined in the Oxford English Dictionary figurative meaning, as 'frank, open, candid, ingenuous' and 'Easily seen through, recognized, understood, or detected; manifest, evident, obvious, clear'.

- IR5 Governance, security and controls: *As a participant in an electronic ecosystem I can understand the governance, security safeguards and controls that are in place within the ecosystem, so that I can claim the outcome of the trustworthiness evaluation took into consideration that the ecosystem meets good practices regarding these topics.*
- IR6 Policy choices: *As a possible participant in an electronic interaction I can determine the information and the reasoning justifying that a participant is qualified as trustworthy, so that I can verify that information and reasoning are compatible with the way I want to rely on the reasoning's outcome.*
- IR7 Obtaining credible data: *As a participant in an electronic ecosystem I can understand the origin and the type of data that is used in the evaluation of trustworthiness of participants, so that I can claim the outcome of the trustworthiness evaluation is based on credible data.*

2.3   Framework Participants

The framework positions participants within an ecosystem, structured in three planes as depicted in Fig. 1. They may invoke services provided by participants from any plane. The enabler plane consists of the participants whose role is to enable trustworthiness, and it also contains the rulebooks and the trustworthiness evaluation functions which are available to all participants. The roles in this plane are as follows.

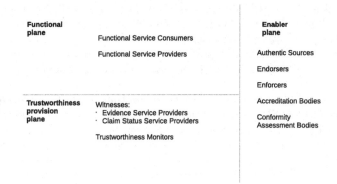

Fig. 1. Planes in a trustworthy ecosystem

- Authentic Source (AS) role. An authentic source holds a mandate to register and validate information about entities and makes this information available. The mandate can be a document that has legal validity because it is published in an official journal or because it is accepted to be binding through a contract or membership agreement.

- Endorser (EnDo) role. An endorser expresses its publicly visible approval for a rulebook through its endorsement, and makes information on responsibility, accountability, and authority to implement security governance available either itself or endorses information made available by others.
- Enforcer (EnFo) role. An enforcer is an entity with power to enforce consequences among participants. An enforcer acts as arbiter or judge and provides the possibility for redress. Enforcement is outside the proposed system[3], but information about whether enforcement is available can be captured and reasoned about.
- Accreditation Body (AB). An accreditation body[4] is an entity that performs accreditation, i.e. the independent evaluation of conformity assessment bodies against recognised criteria for their impartiality and competence. An AB accredits participants in the role of a Conformity Assessment Body.
- Conformity Assessment Body (CAB) role. A CAB assesses the conformity of participants and their services against relevant criteria, and provides assurances of conformity in the form of attestations.

The trustworthiness provision plane involves participants that provide trustworthiness services. The principal roles in this plane are as follows.

- Evidence Service Provider (EvSP) role. An EvSP creates information that serves as evidence. It includes traditional Trust Service Providers such as Certification Authorities, Identity Providers, Attribute Providers, (Remote) Signature Services, Time Stamp Services, etc.
- Claim Status Service Provider (CsSP) role. A CsSP provides status information regarding claims, e.g. verifying a response to an authentication request, or verifying an electronic commitment or signature.
- Trustworthiness Monitor (TwsMo) role. A participant in this role monitors the provision of services by EvSPs and CsSPs and attests to this.

The functional plane consists of participants that act in the role Functional Service Providers (FuSPs), that offer business services, and Functional Service Consumers (FuSCs), that interact with FuSP services.

2.4 Data Model

Predicates are used to model the data points that are used for trustworthiness evaluation. The purpose of the predicates is to represent things from the real

---

[3] One may evaluate the trustworthiness of a credit card provider in a variety of ways, for example that once all other possibilities are exhausted, potential disagreements will be settled before a court of law (an enforcer). Courts of law and all things legal are outside the credit card scheme. Nevertheless I can reason about whether the presence of such an enforcer improves the outcome of evaluation of trustworthiness. Marsh, Sect. 8.5 [13] provides a detailed discussion of the role of an enforcer.

[4] Regarding the roles of Accreditation Body and Conformity Assessment Body, the terminology of ISO/IEC 17000:2020 [7] is adhered to.

world, so that they can be reasoned with. To refer to terms within a predicate, a projection function is used. It can be distinguished from the corresponding predicate by the use of a calligraphic letter in the first position. For example $Predicatename(term_1, term_2)$ is a predicate, and $\mathcal{P}redicatename(term_1, term_2)$ is a projection function. 15 predicates were specified, of which a selection is listed below. S always refers to the Subject.

- $Actor(X)$, an entity without any attestation
- $Attestation(a_{id}, T)$, where a_{id} = the identity of the issuer of the attestation and triple $T = \{S, A, V\}$ where A refers to Attribute and V to Value
- $Participant(X)$
- *Base role* specified as $Attestation(a_{id}, (S, roleTypeBase, V)$ where V refers to an instance of a role type
- $Accreditation(a_{id}, (S, accreditedFor, N)$ where N refers to Norm
- $Conformance(a_{id}, (S, doesConformTo, N)$ where N refers to Norm
- $LegalQualification(a_{id}, (S, legalQual, L)$ where L refers to a legal qualification such as a law, regulation, act, or decree

2.5 Rulebooks

The purpose of a rulebook is to formally capture an understanding of what trustworthiness means in a particular context, where this understanding is captured in the form of constraints. A rulebook contains a mandatory and a discretionary part. The mandatory constraints verify the basis for relevant execution of the discretionary rules. The latter can be selected by a potential trustor to configure a policy for trustworthiness evaluation.

Two rulebooks were created inspired by the eIDAS Regulation [3] and according to the specification described in Sect. 2.2. Rulebook β_{AE} allows the evaluation of the trustworthiness of an ecosystem, and β_{AP} of a participant.

Both rulebooks were constructed as follows. IR1 is addressed by formulating the rules that are derived from the requirements in First Order Logic (FOL) using a taxonomy of data points that have a truth-functional interpretation. While FOL adds value by its truth-functional interpretation, the implementation refines this by using the Organization (ORG) ontology [20] and the Provenance (PROV-O) ontology [19]. This improves interpretation because the ontologies are written in OWL, which allows expression of fine-grained constraints and provides an interpretation in natural language.

Dedicated rules were elaborated, addressing the requirements IR2, IR3, IR4 and IR5 as follows. IR2 is addressed by making the data model, the rules and the trustworthiness evaluation functions publicly available, by using instance data from publicly available sources, and by the specification of IR2 rules. Mandatory rules specify requirements on existence and identification of the rulebook and naming of participants. Discretionary rules specify requirements on the existence of participants in specific roles.

IR3 is addressed by a mandatory rule regarding the uniqueness of identity. Discretionary rules specify requirements on identity attestation regarding self-attestation, increasingly stringent third-party attestation and legal attestation of identity. IR4 is addressed by a mandatory rule on role attestation regarding self-attestation, and discretionary rules specify increasingly stringent attestation requirements for the different roles, including the legal attestation of roles. IR5 is addressed by discretionary rules that cover disclosure and segregation of duty.

IR6 is addressed by keeping the number of mandatory rules minimal, and allowing the potential trustor to select discretionary rules that correspond best to its policy. IR7 is addressed by selection criteria for data sources from where the instance data will be generated.

A selection of rules is shown in Table 1. S_{pt} corresponds the set of participants and S_{abr} corresponds to the set of role attestations. Projection functions are used, e.g. $\mathcal{A}ttestation_{t_{sub}}(A)$ refers to the subject of attestation A.

Table 1. Sample rules from rulebook β_{AP}

$\beta_{IR4-M01}$	A participant's base roles must be self-attested	$\forall\, X \in S_{pt}\ \exists\, A_1,\, A_2 \in S_{abr}$ $(\mathcal{A}ttestation_{t_{sub}}(A_1) = f_{id}(X)$ $\wedge\ \mathcal{A}ttestation_{t_{att}}(A_1) = \text{roleTypeBase}$ $\wedge\ \mathcal{A}ttestation_{t_{sub}}(A_2) = \mathcal{A}ttestation_{a_{id}}(A_1)$ $\wedge\ \mathcal{A}ttestation_{t_{att}}(A_2) = roleTypeBase$ $\wedge\ \mathcal{A}ttestation_{t_{val}}(A_2) = \mathcal{A}ttestation_{t_{val}}(A_1))$
$\beta_{IR4-D027A-AP}$	If the selected participant acts in the role of an evidence service provider then this role must be attested to as conforming to the requirements of an eIDAS TSP by inclusion in a European Trusted List by a trustworthiness monitor	$\exists\, A_1,\, A_2,\, A_3 \in S_{attn}$ $(\mathcal{A}ttestation_{t_{sub}}(A_1) = f_{id}(P_1)$ $\wedge\ \mathcal{A}ttestation_{t_{att}}(A_1) = roleTypeBase$ $\wedge\ \mathcal{A}ttestation_{t_{val}}(A_1) = R_{EvSP}$ $\wedge\ \mathcal{A}ttestation_{t_{sub}}(A_2) = \mathcal{A}ttestation_{t_{sub}}(A_1)$ $\wedge\ \mathcal{A}ttestation_{t_{att}}(A_2) = isRegisteredIn$ $\wedge\ \mathcal{A}ttestation_{t_{val}}(A_2) = eIDASTrustList$ $\wedge\ \mathcal{A}ttestation_{t_{sub}}(A_3) = \mathcal{A}ttestation_{a_{id}}(A_2)$ $\wedge\ \mathcal{A}ttestation_{t_{att}}(A_3) = roleTypeBase$ $\wedge\ \mathcal{A}ttestation_{t_{val}}(A_3) = R_{TwsMo})$
$\beta_{IR4-D304-AP}$	If the selected participant is an evidence service provider or claim status provider, it must be monitored by a trustworthiness monitor attested by a legal act	$\exists\, P_1,\, P_{TwsMo} \in S_{PT}\ \exists\, A_1,\, A_2,\, A_3,\, A_4 \in S_{attn}$ $(\mathcal{A}ttestation_{t_{sub}}(A_1) = f_{id}(P_1)$ $\wedge\ \mathcal{A}ttestation_{t_{att}}(A_1) = roleTypeBase$ $\wedge\ \mathcal{A}ttestation_{t_{val}}(A_1) = (R_{EvSP} \vee R_{CsSP})$ $\wedge\ \mathcal{A}ttestation_{t_{sub}}(A_2) = f_{id}(P_{TwsMo})$ $\wedge\ \mathcal{A}ttestation_{t_{att}}(A_2) = roleTypeBase$ $\wedge\ \mathcal{A}ttestation_{t_{val}}(A_2) = R_{TwsMo}$ $\wedge\ \mathcal{A}ttestation_{a_{id}}(A_3) = f_{id}(P_{TwsMo})$ $\wedge\ \mathcal{A}ttestation_{t_{sub}}(A_3) = f_{id}(P_{TwsMo})$ $\wedge\ \mathcal{A}ttestation_{t_{att}}(A_3) = doesSupervise$ $\wedge\ \mathcal{A}ttestation_{t_{val}}(A_3) = f_{id}(P_1)$ $\wedge\ \mathcal{A}ttestation_{t_{sub}}(A_4) = f_{id}(P_{TwsMo})$ $\wedge\ \mathcal{A}ttestation_{t_{att}}(A_4) = legalQual$ $\wedge\ \mathcal{A}ttestation_{t_{val}}(A_4) = uri)$

2.6   Trustworthiness Evaluation

The trustworthiness evaluation function $twseval_{AE}$ is invoked by a trustor to assist in deciding to what extent an ecosystem represented by instance data can be regarded as trustworthy.

$$twseval_{AE}(R_{id}, \{DiscretionaryRules\}, InstanceData)$$

where

- R_{id} identifies the applicable rulebook,
- $\{DiscretionaryRules\}$ denotes the set of discretionary rules selected by the trustor, and
- $InstanceData$ identifies the instance data that is to be used.

Execution of the function includes verification of the mandatory rules of the selected rulebook. The function returns *true* when all of the evaluated rules return *true*. *True* means that the evaluated ecosystem meets the constraints specified in the rules, which is an indication of trustworthiness. The function returns *false* when at least one of the evaluated rules returns *false*. *False* means that the evaluated ecosystem does not meet the constraints specified in the rules, which is an indication of a lack of trustworthiness.

The trustworthiness evaluation function $twseval_{AP}$ is used to verify that a participant is trustworthy.

$$twseval_{AP}(RBK_{id}, P_1, target\_base\_role\_X, \{DiscretionaryRules\}, InstanceData, \{Norms\})$$

where

- RBK_{id} denotes the identification of the applicable rulebook,
- X denotes the identification of the potential trustee,
- $target\_base\_role\_X$ denotes the target base role of X, i.e. the role the trustor would expect the trustee X to act in,
- $\{DiscretionaryRules\}$ stand for the set of discretionary rules selected by the trustor, which allows to configure a trustworthiness evaluation policy, and
- $InstanceData$ denotes the reference to the instance data that is to be used,
- $\{Norms\}$ denotes the set of discretionary norms (i.e. legal acts and technical standards) the trustee is expected to provide attestations of conformity assessment to.

The function returns *true* or *false* for each of the evaluated rules.

2.7   Instance Data

For the trustworthiness evaluation to be based on credible data, such data must come from authoritative sources that allow access to data that corresponds to one or more predicates. This leads to the following selection criteria. The data source must offer data that is specified in the data model, it must be authoritative for this data, it must include a description of its meaning, and the data must be available in a machine readable format.

There are a number of data sources capable of providing data corresponding to one or more predicates. The current implementation limits itself to data sources in the public domain. On the basis of the selection criteria, the European Trusted Lists[5] and the Linked Open Data source FactForge[6] were selected as data sources for information about companies. On the same basis, a FOAF file from Elsevier's Mendeley Data Search (described by Petrovic and Fujita [16]) and one of the first author's X.509 certificates, produced by the Belgian national identity register, were used as data sources about natural persons.

3   Implementation

The framework was implemented in a front-end and a back-end layer. The front end layer contains the $\mathcal{TE}$ data model, created using Protégé [14], and transformation programs[7] that download information from the data sources and transform it according to the $\mathcal{TE}$ data model, and SPARQL queries whose answers allow to verify the satisfaction of the rules. The back end layer stores the downloaded information as instance data in an Ontotext GraphDB database[8].

The implementation was limited to the evaluation of ex-ante trustworthiness. An evaluation of an entity as a potential trustee involves the following steps. The trustor must connect to the database that holds the instance data, select the discretionary rules of its choice and execute the queries that correspond to the mandatory and selected rules. The query results allow to verify satisfaction of the rules.

Part of an evaluation of an evidence service provider is provided as example. The rules from Table 1 were used, specifying discretionary rules on role attestation. Table 3 shows the results of a query that selects evidence service providers and the provenance of their role attestation. The selection shows a.o. two role attestations for Zetes. The first is based on the Belgian Trusted List and demonstrates satisfaction of IR4-D027A-AP. The second is self-attested and derived from the Zetes website. This demonstrates satisfaction of IR4-M01. Table 4 shows the results of a query that selects participants and their legal attestation. The legal norm can be seen in the right-most column. The selection shows that the legal attestation of Zetes is based on its Certificate Practise Statement, which demonstrates satisfaction of IR4-D304-AP.

---

[5] https://ec.europa.eu/tools/lotl/eu-lotl.xml.

[6] http://factforge.net.

[7] Developed in a combination of Java and Extensible Stylesheet Language Transformations [21] (XSLTs).

[8] https://graphdb.ontotext.com/.

The implementation is available online at the following URLs.

– The data model: http://www.marcsel.eu/onto/te/te-data-model.owl.
– A set of instance data: http://www.marcsel.eu/onto/te/DBL.owl.
– The rulebook β_{AE}: http://www.marcsel.eu/onto/te/RuleBook-BAE-FOL.pdf.
– The rulebook β_{AP}: http://www.marcsel.eu/onto/te/RuleBook-BAP-FOL.pdf.
– Trustworthiness evaluation queries that verify satisfaction of the β_{AP} rulebook: http://www.marcsel.eu/onto/te/RuleBook-BAP-SPARQL.txt.

4   Related Work

The $\mathcal{TE}$ framework was compared with related work. Its model and reasoning approach are most closely related to Bernabé's SOFIC/Trust-DSS approach [1]. The main similarities are the following.

– Both use the formalisms of an ontology and rules with the aim to support trust-related decisions.
– Both import other ontologies to improve interoperability.

The main differences are the following.

– SOFIC/Trust-DSS approach focuses on decisions related to cloud service providers while the $\mathcal{TE}$ model addresses the broader setting of a potential trustor and a potential trustee.
– The SOFIC/Trust-DSS approach bases its trust-related decision support on an ontology which is security based. The $\mathcal{TE}$ model integrates security data points but does not limit itself to those.
– The SOFIC/Trust-DSS approach involves significant manual effort for the manual translation of observations about a service providers into instances of a SOFIC class, and for the manual customisation of rules in function of what needs to be assessed. The $\mathcal{TE}$ model has automated this translation by the use of XSL, and includes the concept of a rulebook which consists of pre-specified rules.
– The SOFIC/Trust-DSS approach is open to a variety of data sources and rules may be created for specific cases. The $\mathcal{TE}$ model demonstrated its working on actual data imported through the data import and transformation mechanism where the data is formalised in description logic.
– The SOFIC/Trust-DSS approach uses data aggregation and quantification. The $\mathcal{TE}$ model does not, because it is hard if not impossible to define semantics for numbers (what one person rates as 0.7 might be rated otherwise by another person).

A high-level comparison with other related work is given in Table 2.

Table 2. Trust-related ontologies in OWL

Model	Main objectives	Representation formalism	Reasoning
Bernabé [1]	Decision Support System for intercloud trust and security, to allow secure interoperability in a trusted heterogeneous multidomain	Security Ontology For the InterCloud (SOFIC) in OWL	SWRL rules over the ontology and quantification with Fuzzy logic
Karthik [8]	Trust framework for sensor-driven pervasive environments	OWL ontology	Security rules in SWRL
Karuna [9]	Trust model for on-line health information systems	Taxonomy of trust factors and a User's Trust Profile Ontology UTPO in OWL which defines trust factors as classes, taking particularly their relation to the user into account	Recommender algorithms
Kravari [10]	Internet of Things trust management (short paper with only schematic description and implementation)	ORDAIN, general-purpose ontology for trust management, OWL, using RDF/XML	Aggregation and confidence level calculations
Oltramari [15]	Information and decision fusion as a decision support system on trust for humans	ComTrustO, a composite trust-based ontology framework fusion, modelled in OWL, using DOLCE as foundation	Information-based inference and decision fusion
Sel [17]	Trust modelling based on logic	OWL DL and existing vocabularies from W3C	Inference and SPARQL
Sullivan [18]	Definition of security requirements, metrics and trust terms	Ontology for trust-terms defined in OWL, including transparency, measurability, data, accountability, auditing, identification, responsibility, liability	Inference and queries

5   Conclusions and Future Work

The proposed framework demonstrates a possible way to automate the evaluation of trustworthiness. It consists of a data model, rulebooks, a data import and transformation mechanism to create instance data, and queries that verify the satisfaction of selected rules by this data. A potential trustor can select those rules that correspond best to its policy for trustworthiness evaluation. The rules specify requirements regarding the values of a set of data points. Queries allow to verify the satisfaction of these rules. Under the $\mathcal{TE}$ framework, the interpretation of a trust claim is specified as the outcome of the verification of a rule. As a consequence, the meaning of trustworthiness and the interpretations of trust claims are well defined. Furthermore was demonstrated how information from a wide range of data sources can be selected and transformed in the format of the $\mathcal{TE}$ data model, leading to a new way to use existing information to logically reason about trustworthiness.

When compared to the use of trust in TTPs, we argue the proposed $\mathcal{TE}$ model is more precise in terms of semantics regarding the meaning of trustworthiness because it allows a potential trustor to select data points that represent specific information on a potential trustee from a qualified and distributed set of data sources.

The following are candidate topics for future research.

- The potential use of privacy-enhancing techniques to avoid the need for a single linked identity could be investigated.
- The use of legal ontologies could be studied to analyse how additional data points that address legal information could allow expression of legal effects such as presumption of validity and exemption from the burden of proof as components of the evaluation of trustworthiness.
- The possible use of trustworthy hardware and/or software for the creation of attestations could be investigated.
- How independence (or the lack thereof) of participants contributes to trustworthiness could be studied.
- How to create rulebooks for a consensus-governed society rather than for a law-governed society could be investigated. This could include the role of membership organisations such as e.g. the Kantara Initiative[9] as accreditation body and as publisher of a trust list. In such a consensus-governed society the participants must be attested by other participants using a consensus scheme. Many consensus-based schemes that are based on blockchain technology are emerging.
- Regarding the implementation, the use of additional data sources as well as the use of on-line querying rather than the current downloading could be analysed.

Finally, the development of a browser/mail client plug-in that embeds all or parts of the framework is envisaged. This would allow easier experimentation and also access for less technical users.

---

[9] https://kantarainitiative.org/.

6 Appendix

Table 3. A selection of evidence service providers and the provenance of their role attestation

	EvSP	Role attestation	wasDerivedFrom
1	te:Certipost-NV-SA	te:RoleAttestation-Certipost-NV-SA	https://tsl.belgium.be/tsl-be.xml
2	te:Zetes-SA-NV	te:RoleAttestation-Zetes-SA-NV	https://tsl.belgium.be/tsl-be.xml
3	te:Certipost-NV-SA	te:RoleAttestation-Certipost-NV-SA-self	https://www.basware.com/en-en/about-basware/legacy-of-innovation/
4	te:Zetes-SA-NV	te:RoleAttestation-Zetes-SA-NV-self	https://www.zetes.com/en
5	te:SMETS1-PKI-Service-from-SML	te:RoleAttestation-SMETS1-PKI-Service-from-SML-self	https://www.securemeters.com/
6	te:Society-for-Worldwide-Interbank-Financial-Telecommunication-SCRL	te:RoleAttestation-Society-for-Worldwide-Interbank-Financial-Telecommunication-SCRL	https://tsl.belgium.be/tsl-be.xml
7	te:DigiCert-Europe-Belgium-BV	te:RoleAttestation-DigiCert-Europe-Belgium-BV	https://tsl.belgium.be/tsl-be.xml
8	te:Portima-scrl-cvba	te:RoleAttestation-Portima-scrl-cvba	https://tsl.belgium.be/tsl-be.xml
11	te:Belgian-Mobile-ID-SA-NV	te:RoleAttestation-Belgian-Mobile-ID-SA-NV	https://tsl.belgium.be/tsl-be.xml
14	te:Kingdom-of-Belgium-Federal-Government	te:RoleAttestation-Kingdom-of-Belgium-Federal-Government	https://tsl.belgium.be/tsl-be.xml
15	te:Banco-Santander-SA	te:RoleAttestation-Banco-Santander-SA	https://sede.minetur.gob.es/Prestadores/TSL/TSL.xml

Table 4. A selection of participants legally attested in their role

	P1	Role attestation of P1	LegalRole qualification	LegalNorm
1	te:BE-BELAC	te:RoleAttestation-AB-BE-BELAC	te:BE-LegalQualification-001	te:BE-Royal-Decree-BELAC-D2014-02-07
2	te:Certipost-NV-SA	te:RoleAttestation-Certipost-NV-SA	te:BE-LegalQualification-003	te:BE-Certipost-CitizenCA-CPS-Version-1.4
3	te:FR-COFRAC	te:RoleAttestation-AB-FR-COFRAC	te:FR-LegalQualification-001	https://www.legifrance.gouv.fr/loda/id/JORFTEXT000019992087/
4	te:FPS-Economy-SMEs-Self-employed-and-Energy-Quality-and-Safety	te:RoleAttestation-TwsMo-FPS-Economy-SMEs-Self-employed-and-Energy-Quality-and-Safety	te:BE-LegalQualification-004	te:BE-LAW-FPS-ECO-BE-SIGN-establishment-2016
5	te:UK-UKAS	te:RoleAttestation-AB-UK-UKAS	te:UK-LegalQualification-001	https://www.legislation.gov.uk/uksi/2009/3155/pdfs/uksi_20093155_en.pdf
6	te:Zetes-SA-NV	te:RoleAttestation-Zetes-SA-NV	te:BE-LegalQualification-007	te:BE-Zetes-CitizenCA-ForeignerCA-CP-CPS-Version-1.1

References

1. Bernabé, J.B., Pérez, G.M., Skarmeta-Gómez, A.F.: Intercloud trust and security decision support system: an ontology-based approach. J. Grid Comput. **13**(3), 425–456 (2015)
2. Castelfranchi, C., Falcone, R.: Trust and control: a dialectic link. Appl. Artif. Intell. **14**(8), 799–823 (2000)
3. EU: EU 910/2014 Regulation of the European Parliament and of the Council of 23 July 2014 on electronic identification and trust services for electronic transactions in the internal market, OJ L 257, 28 August 2014, pp. 73–114 (2014)
4. Gambetta, D.: Can we trust trust? In: Gambetta, D. (ed.) Trust: Making and Breaking Cooperative Relations, pp. 213–237. Basil Blackwell, Oxford (1988)
5. Gollmann, D.: Why trust is bad for security. Electron. Notes Theor. Comput. Sci. **157**(3), 3–9 (2006)
6. Huang, J., Nicol, D.M.: An anatomy of trust in public key infrastructure. Int. J. Crit. Infrastruct. **13**, 238 (2017)
7. ISO/IEC 17000: Conformity Assessment - Vocabulary and general principles. Technical report, International Organization for Standardization (2020)
8. Karthik, N., Ananthanarayana, V.S.: An ontology based trust framework for sensor-driven pervasive environment. In: AlDabass, D., Shapiai, M.I., Ibrahim, Z (ed.) AMS 2017, pp. 147–152 (2017)
9. Karuna, P., Purohit, H., Motti, V.: UTPO: user's trust profile ontology - modeling trust towards online health information sources. CoRR abs/1901.01276 (2019)
10. Kravari, K., Bassiliades, N.: ORDAIN: an ontology for trust management in the internet of things. In: Panetto, H., et al. (eds.) OTM 2017. LNCS, vol. 10574, pp. 216–223. Springer, Cham (2017). https://doi.org/10.1007/978-3-319-69459-7_15
11. Sel, M., Üstündağ Soykan, E., Fasllija, E.: Deliverable 2.5 on trust and trust models. https://www.futuretrust.eu/deliverables (2017). Accessed 20 June 2020
12. Sel, M., Dißauer, G., Zefferer, T.: Deliverable 2.6 evaluation scheme for trustworthy services. https://www.futuretrust.eu/deliverables (2018). Accessed 23 June 2020
13. Marsh, S.P.: Formalising trust as a computational concept. Ph.D. thesis, University of Stirling (1994). d.Phil. thesis
14. Musen, M.A.: The Protégé project: a look back and a look forward. AI Matters **1**(4), 4–12 (2015)
15. Oltramari, A., Cho, J.: ComTrustO: composite trust-based ontology framework for information and decision fusion. In: 18th International Conference on Information Fusion, FUSION 2015, Washington, DC, USA, 6–9 July 2015, pp. 542–549 (2015)
16. Petrovic, G., Fujita, H.: SoNeR: social network ranker. Neurocomputing **202**, 104–107 (2016)
17. Sel, M.: Improving interpretations of trust claims. In: Habib, S.M.M., Vassileva, J., Mauw, S., Mühlhäuser, M. (eds.) IFIPTM 2016. IAICT, vol. 473, pp. 164–173. Springer, Cham (2016). https://doi.org/10.1007/978-3-319-41354-9_13
18. Sullivan, K., Clarke, J., Mulcahy, B.P.: Trust-terms ontology for defining security requirements and metrics. In: 4th European Conference Software Architecture, ECSA 2010, Copenhagen, pp. 175–180. ACM (2010)
19. W3C: PROV-O: The PROV Ontology W3C Recommendation 30 April 2013. https://www.w3.org/TR/prov-o/ (2013). Accessed 1 Dec 2020
20. W3C: The Organization Ontology W3C Recommendation 16 January 2014. https://www.w3.org/TR/vocab-org/ (2014). Accessed 1 Dec 2020
21. W3C: XSL Transformations (XSLT) Version 3.0 W3C Recommendation 8 June 2017. https://www.w3.org/TR/xslt-30/ (2017). Accessed 9 Dec 2020

Security Risks

At Your Service 24/7 or Not? Denial of Service on ESInet Systems

Zisis Tsiatsikas[1,2](✉) ⓘ, Georgios Kambourakis[3] ⓘ,
and Dimitrios Geneiatakis[4] ⓘ

[1] Atos, 14122 Athens, Greece
[2] University of the Aegean, 83200 Karlovasi, Greece
`tzisis@aegean.gr`
[3] European Commission, Joint Research Centre (JRC), 21027 Ispra, Italy
`georgios.kambourakis@ec.europa.eu, gkamb@aegean.gr`
[4] European Commission, Directorate-General for Informatics,
1000 Bruxelles/Brussel, Belgium
`dimitrios.geneiatakis@ec.europa.eu`

Abstract. Emergency calling services are a cornerstone of public safety. During the last few years such systems are transitioning to VoIP and unified communications, and are continuously evolving under the umbrella of organizations, including NENA and EENA. The outcome of this effort is NG911 or NG112 services operating over the so-called Emergency Services IP network (ESInet). This work introduces and meticulously assesses the impact of an insidious and high-yield denial-of-service (DoS) attack against ESInet. Contrariwise to legacy SIP-based DoS, the introduced assault capitalizes on the SDP body of the SIP message with the sole purpose of instigating CPU-intensive transcoding operations at the ESInet side. We detail on the way such an attack can be carried out, and scrutinize on its severe, if not catastrophic, impact through different realistic scenarios involving a sufficient set of codecs. Finally, highlighting on the fact that 911 or 112 calls cannot be dropped, but need to be answered as fast as possible, we offer suggestions on how this kind of assault can be detected and mitigated.

Keywords: Emergency services · ESInet · NENA · EENA · NG9-1-1 · NG1-1-2 · DDoS · VoIP · SIP · SDP · Transcoding · Codec

1 Introduction

During the last two decades, the Session Initiation Protocol (SIP) has dominated the Voice over IP (VoIP) market as the prevalent means for session management. In this context, SIP has been selected by the 3rd Generation Partnership Project (3GPP) as the fundamental protocol in the IP-Multimedia Subsystem (IMS). No less important, the National Emergency Number Association (NENA) has adopted SIP for the Next Generation 9-1-1 (NG911) architecture in the United

© Springer Nature Switzerland AG 2021
S. Fischer-Hübner et al. (Eds.): TrustBus 2021, LNCS 12927, pp. 35–49, 2021.
https://doi.org/10.1007/978-3-030-86586-3_3

States and Canada [1]. Specifically, NENA introduced the concept of Emergency Services IP network (ESInet), currently in ver. i3 [1]. The signaling inside ESInet is delivered via SIP. This means that opposite to legacy emergency calling services that operate over Public Switched Telephone Network (PSTN), and thus, thanks to their closed nature, show a reduced attack surface, ESInet is integrated with the Internet, and therefore is far more vulnerable.

Emergency calling services are continuously evolving in different continents. For instance, based on the NG911 project, the non-governmental European Emergency Number Association (EENA) presented an equivalent one called NG112 [2]. In fact, NENA and EENA have declared their intent to increase cooperation and efforts on international standardization of emergency calling systems and, in essence, the corresponding standards inherit the same core architecture [3]. Therefore, SIP comprises the basis for EENA NG112 too.

This broad adoption of SIP also in emergency services was mostly due to the protocol's open text-based nature and flexibility. Nevertheless, this benefit does not come without a price, as SIP is inherently insecure. Indeed, thus far, a significant number of works have scrutinized the security and privacy issues of SIP and relevant protocols, including Session Description Protocol (SDP), from both an offensive and defensive viewpoint [4–10]. Among the different attacks, Denial of Service (DoS) along with its Distributed (DDoS) form is one of the most calamitous and difficult to defend. And even there is a growing interest in SIP-powered DDoS assaults, to our knowledge, there is a discernible lack of works that abuse SIP and associated session profile protocols, namely SDP, to assault emergency architectures.

Due to the critical nature of 911 or 112 calls, Telcos must offer uninterrupted access to the emergency service on a twenty-four seven basis. For instance, according to the Federal Communications Commission (FCC), this stems also from their legislative obligation about serving any incoming emergency call [11]. In this direction, Border Control Function (BCF), most often combined with a Session Border Controller (SBC) component, offers a first level of protection against DDoS inside the Emergency Services IP Network (ESInet). Usually, this is limited to the filtering of messages in the application layer, say, through blacklisting techniques and the detection of known malware attacks. The requirements to classify a packet as normal or attack traffic, is most often related to the number of messages received from specific IP addresses within a time window. That is, most protection schemes put emphasis on volumetric assaults, i.e., the number and size of received messages, and not the media conveyed over the signaling. For example, a legacy product will most probably not raise any alarm in case it receives a limited number of signaling requests for the initiation of High Definition (HD) video streams, due to the low volume of the signaling messages. Still, as explained in the next sections, these messages are enough to hit the limits of a Digital Signal Processing (DSP) video transcoder [12], in case they are received malevolently. Recall that ESInet supports a variety of sources including audio, video, and data, either in a recorded or live form.

As illustrated in Fig. 1, the core network elements for successfully routing an emergency call in ESInet include the Emergency Services Routing Proxy (ESRP), and the Public Safety Answering Point (PSAP). The first is responsible for selecting the appropriate answering point, based on the caller location, while the latter is the last frontier of the ESInet, namely the entity which hosts the call-takers. The PSAP always offers the possibility to connect a caller with an Interactive Voice Response (IVR) system, in case a call-taker is not readily available. The network topology is not the same in each ESInet installation, and thus the number of the ESRP and the PSAP elements typically varies between different deployments. From a security viewpoint, the aforementioned network elements are protected by the use of BCF. Additionally, a number of gateways (GW), located outside of the ESInet borders, ensure the interoperability with non-IP networks. For example, a PSTN user can access the emergency calling service only through a GW. The latter translates the analog voice signals to IP and vice versa. The same holds true for all the different networks which are connected to ESInet. Based on this architecture, calls can stem from anywhere in the internet and interconnected IP networks, including cellular ones.

Our Contribution: We focus on the exploitation of specific fields (session descriptors) of SDP bodies, which are carried by SIP INVITE requests, to launch powerful DDoS attacks against ESInet. As detailed next and vis-à-vis the current literature, this novel type of attack is not volumetric, but instead capitalizes on the CPU-expensive bidirectional media transcoding process when placing a call. We experimentally assess the impact of the attack and show that even with a small number of attack instances its effect is immense. We also propose countermeasures towards mitigating this threat.

The next section elaborates on relevant to the attack components of the ESInet architecture and sketches the adversarial model. Section 3 details on the testbed and the experiments performed to assess the impact of the attack, while Sect. 4 puts forward possible countermeasures. Section 5 overviews the related work. The last section concludes and offers pointers to future work.

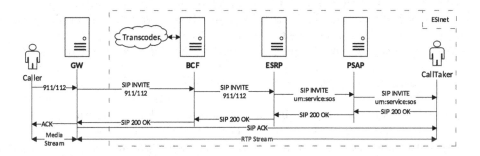

Fig. 1. The basic components of ESInet

2   Preliminaries and Adversarial Model

A VoIP communication channel comprises real-time Transport Protocol (RTP) packets which traverse the network between two or more endpoints, namely the caller and callee(s). As already mentioned, SIP is the predominant method to negotiate the parameters for generating, and delivering these packets. Precisely, during session establishment, SIP messages typically carry in their SDP body the media parameters, which instruct the endpoints on how to generate the bidirectional RTP media stream[1].

A SDP body carries information regarding the (a) network data, including the IP addresses and ports per endpoint, (b) proposed codecs (also known as vocoders) that will be used for compressing and decompressing the digital media. The latter information is the result of capturing analog sound or video with a microphone or camera at the caller's side. In further detail, the SDP exchange mechanism is based on the offer/answer model [14]. Typically, the session initiator advertises the codecs which are supported by the caller's device. The callee answers with the codecs of preference, either those included in the offer or not. If the devices cannot reach an agreement, the session establishment is terminated with a "488 Not Acceptable here" response. To avoid that, the NG911/NG112 architecture is equipped with special DSP that can transcode in real-time virtually any kind of well-formed RTP packet, i.e., any codec [15]. Figure 3 depicts the upper part of a common SDP body as generated by the MicroSIP client [16], where the descriptors of interest are marked in red font. Precisely, the m descriptor designates a media name and transport address, while the a descriptors contain zero or more media attribute lines in order of preference [13], in this case, the Opus, G723 and Speex audio codecs. This means that a SDP body may contain more than one codecs, one or many per media type.

Moreover, in the event of an emergency call, the PSAP agent, i.e., the call-taker needs to obtain a complete and accurate view of the emergency scene. To this end, as mentioned earlier, the NG911 and NG112 architectures are continuously evolving to maturate to a robust system supporting different types of media, namely text, audio, and video [1]. Thus far, there is no restriction on the type (and quality) of media the callers need to convey for establishing an emergency call. And as highlighted earlier, Telcos are obliged by the relevant legislation to connect every emergency call [11], even if the caller requests to establish the most expensive in terms of both codec and bandwidth communication stream [17].

Given the text-based nature of the protocol, SIP messages [18] can be crafted even by script kiddies. Capitalising on this fact, to our knowledge, this work is the first to explore and assess the effects of crafting the SDP body of SIP INVITE requests to force expensive real-time transcoding operations, namely codec conversion, at the ESInet side. Simply put, the sole thing the evil-doer has to do

---

[1] In rare cases, say, due to the use of a "recvonly", or "sendonly" call flow attribute in the SDP body [13], the communication will be unidirectional, thus, if transcoding is required, its cost will be associated with the translation of one stream.

is to offer a single, preferably wideband[2], super-wideband or fullband quality codec for audio and another for video, which however are not supported by the call-taker's equipment. This inevitably leads to CPU-expensive operations at the BCF or PSAP side, depending on where the transcoder lies [1]. Naturally, any wideband-encoded RTP stream is bandwidth-hungry as well, potentially leading to a double negative effect on the ESInet infrastructure. This is true only in case the transcoder is placed in the PSAP [19]; if so, the ESInet network legs from BCF to ESRP will experience high bandwidth utilization. Given however that typically the transcoder is placed in the BCF [20], bandwidth consumption may only affect external to ESInet networks. For this reason, and because this work concentrates on the non-volumentric aspect of this attack, bandwidth consumption remains outside our scope.

We focus only on outsiders, either malevolent individuals or groups of nefarious actors. They can range from script kiddies and polarized groups with a targeted agenda, to all kinds of cybercriminals, including cyberterrorists, hacktivists, and nation-state actors. The motivation and goals of each of the aforementioned actors vary; from simple curiosity and just causing commotion, to orchestrated cyberattacks causing havoc, confusion, and even bringing the emergency services down to its knees. Thinking about the arsenal and dexterity of the potential opponents, things are worst. Simple and freely available open-source software tools, namely a softphone, and little skillfulness, i.e., editing the softphone's code to make it offer only high-quality codecs for audio and video, which at the same time are not supported by the callee, are the sole prerequisites. From this point on, the impact of the attack depends on the number of attack instances impersonating legitimate emergency callers. For instance, as we demonstrate in Sect. 3, a script kiddie having a medium-grade off-the-shelf laptop at hand can easily unleash as much as 4 attack scripts. On the other hand, a botherder, or someone who rents their services, can hurl a myriad of attack bots at the service. The same effect can be achieved by harnessing the power of social networking sites; a myriad of users can be unwittingly launch attacks against any service [21], and incentivized users forming a group may coordinate toward causing havoc. Under the perspective of unified networks, and assuming the case of a botnet assembled by legacy VoIP, WebRTC, and cellular-network bots, Fig. 2 abstractly depicts the way this attack can be unleashed against ESInet.

So far, a typical PSAP deployment comprises a set of hardware deskphones, which are usually controlled via a web application. The Computer-Supported Telecommunications Applications (CSTA) [2] is a common protocol for this purpose. The web application only caters for remote control to the deskphones, meaning that the audio and video streams solely rely on the capabilities of the

---

[2] Narrowband codecs offer a simple voice quality of 8 kHz, which most of the times is enough for a typical PSTN voice communication. Wideband, super-wideband, or fullband codecs offer an increased sound quality and improved compression technology, thus reducing the required bandwidth and preserving sound fidelity. Their main drawback is related to the DSP cycles which are consumed in the compression process.

latter. For example, the Avaya J100 Series IP Phones [22] does not support the wideband Speex audio codec, while the Grandstream GXV3275 device does not support the VP8 video codec [23]. The same holds true for the Cisco 8800 Series Multiplatform Phone [24]. On the other hand, the Yealink SIP-T58V supports VP8, but it does not provide H.263 [25]. This means that if these modern devices were part of a PSAP deployment, and an emergency caller offered only one of the aforementioned codecs, the transcoding process would be inevitable. This also means that a smart assailant will first perform a reconnaissance round by means of robocalls against the targeted PSAP [26] to learn the supported codecs, and then employ any other, preferably high-quality, during the attack. While vendors continuously improve their deskphone capabilities through software and/or firmware upgrades, it is almost impractical to implement all the possible codecs. And even if this happens sometime in the future, it should be mandatory for any PSAP device.

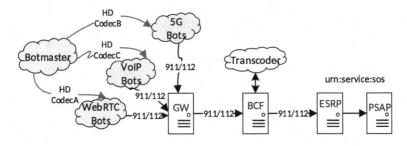

Fig. 2. The BCF element receives an increased number of streams which require transcoding. Note that the transcoder may reside in the PSAP instead of BCF.

```
v=0
o=- 3816215169 3816215169 IN IP4 192.168.xx.xx
s=pjmedia
b=AS:84
t=0 0
a=X-nat:0
m=audio 4000 RTP/AVP 96 4 97 101 102 103
c=IN IP4 192.168.xx.xx
b=TIAS:64000
a=rtcp:4001 IN IP4 192.168.xx.xx
a=sendrecv
a=rtpmap:96 opus/48000/2
a=fmtp:96 maxplaybackrate=24000;sprop-
maxcapturerate=24000;maxaveragebitrate=64000;useinbandfec=1
a=rtpmap:4 G723/8000
a=rtpmap:97 speex/16000
...
```

Fig. 3. The upper part of a representative SDP body

3   Evaluation

3.1   Test-Bed Setup and Attack Scenarios

To assess the impact of the described attack, we created the testbed topology shown in Fig. 4. Specifically, the deployment consists of two Virtual Machines (VM), managed by a VirtualBox hypervisor, hosted under the same physical master machine. The latter is equipped with an Intel i5-8365U CPU clocked at 1.60 GHz, and 16 GB of RAM. Both the VMs afford 4 vCPU cores, but with different slices of RAM, namely 4 and 5GB, respectively. The first VM runs Debian Ubuntu in v20.04.1 along with *Kamailio* [27] in v5.3.7, and a *rtpengine* [28] instance executed as a Kamailio module in v8.4.0.0. With reference to Fig. 4, in addition to the SIP server, this VM represents the transcoder in the ESInet architecture. The second VM runs on MS Windows 7 32bit, hosting at most 8 instances of the MicroSIP softphone in v3.19.30. Obviously, this VM emulates the attack instances and the PSAP deskphone devices, i.e., 4 callers and 4 call-takers.

As depicted in Table 1, we experimented with a set of 7 unique codecs and 4 attack scenarios representing a diverse number of attack instances, from 1 to 4. The audio codec septet used comprises the following widely-used vocoders: G.729 8 kHz, G.722 16 kHz, OPUS 24 kHz, Speex 16 kHz, PCMU 8 kHz, PCMA 8 kHz, and GSM 8 kHz. The first 3 have been used for both the caller and callee endpoints. PCMU was used only by the caller, while the rest only by the callee. These codecs are typical for a real-life installation [29] and also meet the limitations of the software we exploited in our testbed, i.e., rtpengine [28] and MicroSIP [16]. The rightmost columns of the table present the CPU overhead induced by the transcoding process for a specific pair of caller versus callee codecs, with a call duration equal to 145 secs. This duration is reasonable, given that an attack instance will most likely occupy the service for a limited amount of time, probably through pre-recorded media streams, and then leave. The scenarios per septet are ordered based on the average CPU utilization, from lesser to greater.

We argue that the implemented scenarios offer a sufficient understanding of the transcoding cost between narroband and wideband encoded packets. That is, for each such codec combination, we trigger a bi-directional transcoding operation, namely the codec of the caller is transcoded to that supported by the callee and vice versa. For instance, in Sn11, the Speex encoded RTP packets stemming from two different attack instances (callers), will be bidirectionally transcoded to G.722 RTP packet on-the-fly, so that the two ends are in position to understand and decode the packets.

3.2   Results

The experiments attempt to estimate the CPU overhead introduced in the system due to the stressing of the transcoding engine. Bear in mind that SIP signaling is not an issue here; only a handful of INVITE messages are sent. For instance, in Sn27 the CPU of the transcoding engine reaches an instantaneous peak load equal to 185.7%. This is however achieved with a negligible signaling volume composed of only 4 SIP INVITE requests. Put simply, although the signaling attack traffic is negligible, the information carried by SDP bodies lead to RTP streams which induce an overpowering CPU overhead. Also, as expected, in all the attack scenarios the memory utilization at the call-taker side was negligible $\approx 1\%$.

With reference to the left part of Fig. 5 and Table 1, the maximum mean value perceived across the most stressing set of scenarios, namely Sn22 to Sn28, equals to 143.7%, which is clearly overwhelming for the vCPU used. At the same time, for the same septet, the minimum instantaneous value perceived in Sn22, which is the least demanding scenario, is $\approx 80\%$ followed by $\approx 92\%$ of Sn27. Even more, the standard deviation metric for this septet of scenarios has a mean value of $\approx 11.5\%$, meaning a rather small dispersion of values around the mean. More or less, the same observation can be deduced for the rest of the scenarios. For instance, the right part of Fig. 5 depicts the CPU overhead for scenarios Sn6, Sn11, Sn16, and Sn24. While the codec parameters remain the same for these scenarios, the number of media (attack) streams varies between 1 and 4. From the figure it becomes apparent that as the number of streams increases, the CPU utilization is also significantly augmented. Based on the same subfigure, as expected, the largest difference among the plotted curves is perceived between scenarios Sn6 and Sn24. That is, while Sn6 presents a peak overhead of 87.7% with an average of $\approx 55\%$, the corresponding scores for Sn24 are almost doubled or over-doubled, namely 151% and $\approx 127\%$, respectively. This proportional to the number of attack streams augmentation in CPU utilization holds true also for the rest of the scenarios employing the same pair of codecs, even if in some cases it is considerably lower. For instance, among the Sn7, Sn13, and Sn19, Sn27 couples, the perceived difference for the same metrics are +51.1%, +50.6% and +12.4%, +8.4%, respectively. Generally, from 3 attack instances and above is obvious that the CPU has already reached its limits, and thus the aforementioned differences tend to decrease or disappear. For instance, when focusing on Sn20, Sn26 and Sn21, Sn27 pairs, one can discern close enough average and peak CPU values. Actually, after scaling up the number of attack streams to 5 the system has crashed.

Overall, as already explained in Sect. 2, the numbers in Table 1 clearly indicate that an attacker could exploit an expensive wideband codec like OPUS, with the aim to initiate multiple CPU-intensive emergency streams to the ESInet. Another, more clever, strategy could be the assailant to initiate the 911 or 112 calls with a narrowband codec, like PCMU, and then at any time re-negotiate a wideband one, due to low audio quality. The same tactic can be followed to insidiously force the caller-taker to re-negotiate the codec. Say, for example, that the parties establish a session using the PCMU codec. Then, the call-taker realizes that the voice/video quality is poor, and thus dispatches a re-INVITE towards the caller for updating the SDP parameters. After that, the attacker will offer a wideband codec, which however the call-takes does not support. In any case, the process of upgrading the quality of a media stream is something trivial, because the call-taker needs to obtain a clear view of the emergency incident right away.

Taking into account all the above, it is obvious that the transcoding cost for a quite strong vCPU is overburdening, even for a handful number of streams. In case of large scale emergency incidents, say, a flood, earthquake, or wildfire, the PSAPs will receive a surge of calls. Most of them will stuck on the call queue due to unavailable call-takers. Even in this case, the PSAP will need to deliver an automated message to the emergency caller, using an IVR system. As already said, and given that providers have a legal obligation to connect every emergency call [11,30], in case of incompatible media between the caller and the PSAP, the media stream must be transcoded. Naturally, the situation may be worse if one assumes an assault involving an army of infected SIP devices (bots), which may be triggered in parallel to a real emergency incident or at any time.

One may argue that a hardware-based transcoder would be able to cope against such an multi-source attack. However, even the most robust modern and powerful products, like for example a Mediant 9080 SBC cluster, can transcode up to 30K concurrent audio streams [31]. Also, a hardware-based video transcoder introduces business limitations due to the complexity of the processing that needs to perform. For example, the Codensity T432 Massif Video Transcoder [12], supports 128 sessions for the transcoding between H.264 AVC and H.265 HEVC. This means that for a relatively small botnet comprised of 6K infected devices [30], an emergency deployment would need at least 46 installed T432 modules for handling incompatible, high resolution, video streams. In case of a multitudinous army comprised of 493K bots [32], an emergency architecture would need to be equipped with 3,851 modules, which is obviously infeasible and futile. Given this situation, it is apparent that via a much smaller-scale attack comprised of high resolution video streams, an attacker can achieve the same result in terms of CPU utilization.

A last observation is that even with narrowband codecs, which are not supported by the call-taker, and a small number of attack instances an assailant can consume a significant amount of CPU resources, yet such an attack can fly entirely under the radar. For instance, Sn1 alone, scored a mean CPU utilization of ≈45%. While this single RTP stream demonstrates a tiny attack footprint, if repeated using a well thought-out time plan can result to a hard to detect and defend against low-and-slow DoS.

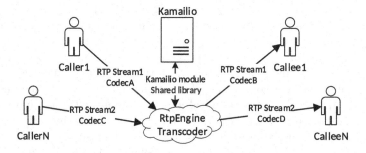

Fig. 4. Test-bed setup

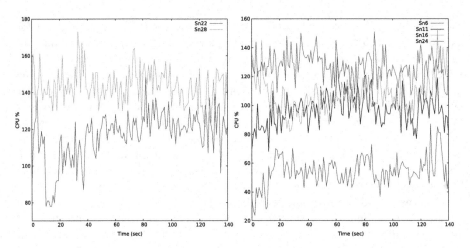

Fig. 5. Zoom on CPU overhead for Sn22 and Sn28 (left), and Sn6, Sn11, Sn16, and Sn24 (right)

4 Detection and Remedies

DDoS attacks are considered a plain sailing even for inexperienced malicious individuals. This holds true for two reasons. First and foremost, there is a rise in new armies of infected devices, which are broadly available for rent in the dark web [33]. Second, there is a blooming on communities which develop corresponding offensive tools for research [34], or simply for fun and coding [35]. The same also applies to the defenders' side, which occupies a substantial share in the research area of DDoS prevention or detection. Indeed, several solutions have been hitherto proposed in the literature towards detecting non-volumetric DDoS [36–38]. These may include rule-based methods to block the attack flows, statistical-driven methods, or even approaches to exploit software-defined infrastructure to combat this kind of assaults.

Detecting the attack presented in this work would require one to deploy a statistical scheme to monitor the number of SIP messages which carry expensive codecs in their SDP body. For example, time series analysis can offer an overview of the codec deviations in 911/112 emergency calls over specific time intervals. In case the BCF or the PSAP element detects a significant increase in the mean value of the total bandwidth that is requested by the emergency calls, then an alert could be raised. The mitigation of this attack could also rely on a mechanism in charge of generating an automated announcement to the emergency caller, say, from an IVR. The announcement could offer information about the emergency incidents taking place in the caller's geographical location, or the calls directly related to the incident reported by the caller. This alternative could significantly lessen the transcoding time. Other approaches may also be applied, similar to those for the detection of robocalls [26], including puzzles, behavioral analytics, and caller ID authentication [39]. This may be of service even if the detection of a bot that ini-

Table 1. Transcoding cost for diverse codec translations and different number of callers. Values in the next to last column are represented as a 95% confidence interval over 145 measurements. Peak mean and max values are shown in boldface.

Scen.	Caller codec	Callee codec	Attack instances	CPU%			
				Min	Max	Mean	St. Dev.
Sn1	G.729 8 Khz	PCMA 8 Khz	1	26.7	67.3	45.2 ± 1.2	7.4
Sn2	Speex 32 Khz	OPUS 24 Khz	1	18.8	66.7	45.8 ± 1.3	8.3
Sn3	PCMU 8 Khz	OPUS 24 Khz	1	29.7	79.2	46.4 ± 1.4	8.7
Sn4	G.722 16 Khz	GSM 8 Khz	1	28.7	68.9	48.7 ± 1.2	7.6
Sn5	OPUS 24 Khz	G.729 8 Khz	1	27.5	**103.9**	54.2 ± 2.2	14.1
Sn6	Speex 16 Khz	G.722 16 Khz	1	24.5	87.7	54.8 ± 1.6	10.2
Sn7	OPUS 24 Khz	Speex 16 Khz	1	35.3	96.2	**62.0 ± 2.3**	14.3
Sn8	G.722 16 Khz	GSM 8 Khz	2	36.3	101.0	71.8 ± 2.1	13.4
Sn9	G.729 8 Khz	PCMA 8 Khz	2	48.0	102.9	72.7 ± 1.8	11.3
Sn10	PCMU 8 Khz	OPUS 24 Khz	2	46.5	122.3	91.2 ± 2.4	14.8
Sn11	Speex 16 Khz	G.722 16 Khz	2	68.9	134.3	97.4 ± 1.7	10.9
Sn12	OPUS 24 Khz	G.729 8 Khz	2	38.5	138.5	107.3 ± 3.0	18.8
Sn13	OPUS 24 Khz	Speex 16 Khz	2	65.7	143.3	112.6 ± 2.4	14.8
Sn14	Speex 32 Khz	OPUS 24 Khz	2	74.3	**152.9**	**123.1 ± 2.0**	12.8
Sn15	G.729 8 Khz	PCMA 8 Khz	3	74.8	129.1	98.3 ± 1.6	10.1
Sn16	Speex 16 Khz	G.722 16 Khz	3	82.4	153.8	108.3 ± 2.0	12.5
Sn17	G.722 16 Khz	GSM 8 Khz	3	83.8	134.0	109.2 ± 1.5	9.8
Sn18	PCMU 8 Khz	OPUS 24 Khz	3	89.4	152.4	120.5 ± 2.1	13.5
Sn19	OPUS 24 Khz	Speex 16 Khz	3	101.9	173.3	130.1 ± 2.5	15.8
Sn20	OPUS 24 Khz	G.729 8 Khz	3	107.7	159.6	131.7 ± 1.6	10.5
Sn21	Speex 32 Khz	OPUS 24 Khz	3	105.8	**175.5**	**136.5 ± 2.2**	13.9
Sn22	G.729 8 Khz	PCMA 8 Khz	4	78.0	160.8	117.0 ± 2.2	13.7
Sn23	G.722 16 Khz	GSM 8 Khz	4	94.4	156.7	120.0 ± 1.7	11.0
Sn24	Speex 16 Khz	G.722 16 Khz	4	100.0	151.0	127.2 ± 1.6	10.2
Sn25	PCMU 8 Khz	OPUS 24 Khz	4	104.9	163.8	129.1 ± 2.0	12.5
Sn26	OPUS 24 Khz	G.729 8 Khz	4	110.5	163.2	132.8 ± 1.4	9.2
Sn27	OPUS 24 Khz	Speex 16 Khz	4	92.3	**185.7**	138.5 ± 2.2	14.0
Sn28	Speex 32 Khz	OPUS 24 Khz	4	121.0	173.8	**143.7 ± 1.5**	9.6

tiates emergency calls by exploiting an infected device, would not be as straightforward as with a bot that places robocalls for advertisement reasons.

Generally, however, the emergency call nature and the associated legislation requirements, create a complex environment which needs a deeper look on the detection and/or prevention mechanisms that will be deployed in the NG911 or NG112 ecosystem. For instance, one could say that in case the caller offers a high-quality video codec not supported by the PSAP, the latter should transcode it to a lower-quality codec for the sake of possibly lightening CPU load, especially if the system is overstressed or under attack. Nevertheless, this is not a simple decision to make, because, say, the call-taker may indeed need to inspect a HD video to fully comprehend the emergency situation reported by the caller. In a similar mindset, callers asking codecs that require transcoding could be placed in the waiting queue for sometime; at least, this may make dump bots to self-disconnect. However, such a caller may be actually in an utmost need, say, a life-and-death situation.

5   Related Work

The general security and privacy issues regarding NG911 and NG112 ecosystems have been already emphasized in different reports by the corresponding organizations [40,41]. For instance, the document in [40] highlights on the DDoS threat posed by botnets, mentioning however only SIP INVITE/REGISTER message floods. Also, the report in [41] points out general risks in the NG911 architecture, including Telephony DoS (TDoS) and DDoS, from a volumetric perspective. On the other hand, the so far relevant scientific literature on ESInet security is scarce. Actually, we were able to find only two works which touch on this topic [30,42]. Both of them concentrate on DDoS assaults on NG911, only from a volumetric viewpoint, without drawing attention to the media details. Specifically, the first work explores general threats with respect to the 911 architecture, while the latter introduces a new, unblockable according to the authors DDoS attack, which relies on the anonymization of the cellular identifiers that reside on the user's device.

6   Conclusions and Future Directions

With more than 320M emergency calls made every year in the European Union [40], emergency services comprise a highly delicate and critical public safety asset. Nevertheless, in today's interconnected world, the developmental highway towards NG911 and NG112 entails opening emergency services access to the internet. While this openness caters for greater communications efficiency and contributes to the unified communications ecosystem, also opens the door to evil-doers to among others disrupt or cut off communications and the underlying services.

This work explored a novel attack against ESInet, which comprises the keystone of modern emergency services. Backed up by the fact that ignoring or dropping a 911 or 112 call is out of question, the introduced attack perniciously crafts specific descriptors of the SDP body carried by SIP INVITE messages to force CPU-hungry operations in terms of transcoding at the ESInet side. In simple terms, the assailant preferably offers high quality codecs, which however are unsupported by the call-taker's equipment. This inevitably begets transcoding. Through small-scale experiments, we argue that the upshot of this attack, especially if exercised by an abundant army of bots and the use of fullband voice or

HD video codecs, can drive the emergency services into paralysis. More stealthy flavors of the attack are also very possible depending on the codec used, the number of attack instances, and the assault scheduling plan. Even worse, the attack can be mounted using off-the-self equipment and open source software, while the mastery of the opponent can be as little as that of a script kiddie. A certain amount of reconnaissance is required as well.

Given that the attack has been evaluated on a single physical machine, and thus employed only voice codecs, a certain direction is to further assess it using video codecs and a greater number of powerful workstations and attack instances. The implementation of a robust scheme to detect the attack and possibly nip it in the bud is also left for future work.

References

1. NENA: NENA detailed functional and interface standards for the NENA i3 solution (2016). https://cdn.ymaws.com/www.nena.org/resource/resmgr/standards/NENA-STA-010.2_i3_Architectu.pdf. Accessed 21 Nov 2020
2. EENA: EENA operations document, 112 PSAPs technology (2014). https://eena.org/document/112-psaps-technology/. Accessed 21 Nov 2020
3. Kumar Subudhi, B.S., et al.: Performance testing for VoIP emergency services: a case study of the EMYNOS platform. Procedia Comp. Sci. **151**, 287–294 (2019)
4. Geneiatakis, D., et al.: Survey of security vulnerabilities in session initiation protocol. IEEE Comm. Surv. Tutorials **8**(3), 68–81 (2006)
5. Keromytis, A.D.: A survey of voice over IP security research. In: Information Systems Security, pp. 1–17 (2009)
6. Tsiatsikas, Z.: Detection and prevention of denial of service attacks in SIP and SDP. Ph.D. dissertation, University of the Aegean (2019)
7. Karopoulos, G., Kambourakis, G., Gritzalis, S., Konstantinou, E.: A framework for identity privacy in SIP. J. Net. Comp. Appl. **33**(1), 16–28 (2010)
8. Karopoulos, G., Kambourakis, G., Gritzalis, S.: PrivaSIP: ad-hoc identity privacy in SIP. Comp. Stand. Int. **33**(3), 301–314 (2011)
9. Karopoulos, G., Fakis, A., Kambourakis, G.: Complete SIP message obfuscation: PrivaSIP over Tor, pp. 217–226 (2014)
10. Fakis, A., Karopoulos, G., Kambourakis, G.: OnionSIP: preserving privacy in SIP with onion routing. J. Univ. Comp. Sci. **23**(10), 969–991 (2017)
11. FCC wireless 911 requirements. https://transition.fcc.gov/. Accessed 21 Nov 2020
12. T432 massif^{TM} ultra-dense video transcoder. https://netint.ca/product/t432_transcoder/. Accessed 21 Nov 2020
13. Handley, M., et al.: SDP: "Session Description Protocol," RFC 4566 (Proposed Standard), Internet Engineering Task Force, July 2006
14. Okumura, S., et al.: "Session Initiation Protocol (SIP) Usage of the Offer/Answer Model," RFC 6337, August 2011
15. Reaves, B., et al.: AuthentiCall: efficient identity and content authentication for phone calls. In: USENIX Security 2017, 16–18 August 2017, pp. 575–592 (2017)
16. MicroSIP - Open source portable SIP softphone for Windows based on PJSIP stack. https://www.microsip.org/. Accessed 21 Nov 2020
17. Bandwidth calculator. https://www.asteriskguru.com/tools/bandwidth_calculator.php. Accessed 21 Nov 2020

18. Tsiatsikas, Z., et al.: The devil is in the detail: SDP-driven malformed message attacks and mitigation in SIP ecosystems. IEEE Access **7**, 2401–2417 (2019)
19. NENA: Understanding NENA's i3 architectural standard for ng9-1-1 (2011). https://cdn.ymaws.com/www.nena.org/resource/collection/2851C951-69FF-40F 0-A6B8-36A714CB085D/08-003_Detailed_Functional_and_Interface_Specification_ for_the_NENA_i3_Solution.pdf. Accessed 21 Nov 2020
20. Liberal, F., et al.: European NG112 crossroads: toward a new emergency communications framework. IEEE Commun. Mag. **55**(1), 132–138 (2017)
21. Athanasopoulos, E., et al.: Antisocial networks: turning a social network into a Botnet. In: Wu, T.-C., Lei, C.-L., Rijmen, V., Lee, D.-T. (eds.) ISC 2008. LNCS, vol. 5222, pp. 146–160. Springer, Heidelberg (2008). https://doi.org/10.1007/978-3-540-85886-7_10
22. Avaya. Avaya j100 series IP phone overview and specifications. https://downloads. avaya.com/css/P8/documents/101054321. Accessed 21 Nov 2020
23. Gxv3275 IP multimedia phone for android, user guide. http://www.grandstream. com/sites/default/files/Resources/gxv3275_user_guide.pdf. Accessed 21 Nov 2020
24. Cisco 8800 series. https://www.cisco.com/c/en/us/td/docs/voice_ip_comm/ cuipph/MPP/8800/english/AG/p881_b_8800-mpp-ag_new.pdf. Accessed 21 Nov 2020
25. Yealink SIP-T58V. https://www.yealink.com/upfiles/products/201707/150036535 4909.pdf. Accessed 21 Nov 2020
26. Tu, H., Doupé, A., Zhao, Z., Ahn, G.: SOK: everyone hates robocalls: a survey of techniques against telephone spam. In: IEEE Symposium on Security and Privacy, SP 2016, San Jose, CA, USA, 22–26 May 2016. IEEE Computer Society, pp. 320–338 (2016). https://doi.org/10.1109/SP.2016.27
27. Kamailio SIP Server. http://www.kamailio.org/w/. Accessed 21 Nov 2020
28. What is RTPengine? https://github.com/sipwise/rtpengine. Accessed 21 Nov 2020
29. Gibson, J.D.: Challenges in Speech Coding Research, pp. 19–39. Springer, New York (2015)
30. Guri, M., Mirsky, Y., Elovici, Y.: 9-1-1 DDoS: attacks, analysis and mitigation. In: EuroS&P. IEEE 2017, pp. 218–232 (2017)
31. Audiocodes session border controllers. https://www.audiocodes.com/. Accessed 21 Nov 2020
32. Kolias, C., Kambourakis, G., Stavrou, A., Voas, J.: DDoS in the IoT: Mirai and other botnets. Computer **50**(7), 80–84 (2017)
33. Robertson, J., et al.: DarkWeb cyber threat intelligence mining. In: CUP, USA (2017)
34. Stanek, J., et al.: SIPp-DD: SIP DDoS flood-attack simulation tool. ICCCN **2011**, 1–7 (2011)
35. DDoS attack tools: seven common DDoS attack tools used by hackers. https:// security.radware.com/ddos-knowledge-center/ddos-attack-types/common-ddos-attack-tools/. Accessed 21 Nov 2020
36. Hong, K., et al.: SDN-assisted slow HTTP DDoS attack defense method. IEEE Commun. Lett. **22**(4), 688–691 (2018)
37. Shtern, M., et al.: Towards mitigation of low and slow application DDoS attacks. In: IEEE International Conference on Cloud Engineering 2014, pp. 604–609 (2014)
38. Tripathi, N., Hubballi, N.: Slow rate denial of service attacks against HTTP/2 and detection. Comput. Secur. **72**, 255–272 (2018)
39. Combating Spoofed Robocalls with Caller ID Authentication. https://www.fcc. gov/call-authentication. Accessed 21 Nov 2020

40. EENA Technical Committee: Security and Privacy Issues in NG112 (2017). https://eena.org/document/ng112-security-privacy-issues. Accessed 21 Nov 2020
41. Cybersecurity and I.S. Agency: Cyber risks to ng9-1-1 (2019). https://www.cisa.gov/sites/default/files/publications/NG911CybersecurityPrimer.pdf. Accessed 21 Nov 2020
42. Quaddi, C., et al.: Hacking 911: Adventures in Disruption, Destruction, and Death. https://www.defcon.org/images/defcon-22/dc-22-presentations/Quaddi-R3plicant-Hefley/DEFCON-22-Quaddi-R3plicant-Hefley-Hacking-911-UPDATED.pdf. Accessed 21 Nov 2020

Impact of False Positives and False Negatives on Security Risks in Transactions Under Threat

Doncho Donchev[1], Vassil Vassilev[1,2(✉)], and Demir Tonchev[1]

[1] Sofia University "St. Kliment Ohridski" - GATE Institute, Sofia, Bulgaria
{doncho.donchev,demir.tonchev}@gate-ai.eu
[2] London Metropolitan University - Cyber Security Research Centre, London, UK
v.vassilev@londonmet.ac.uk

Abstract. This paper presents a theoretical model, algorithms, and quantitative assessment of the impact of false positives and false negatives on security risks during transaction processing. It is based on analysis of the effect of the parameters of the optimal strategy for planning countermeasures in Partially Observable Markov Decision Processes. The paper reveals the dependency between the false positives and false negatives of the analytics and their impact on the efficacy of the algorithms for detection. Such an analysis is an important component of cybersecurity frameworks, planning countermeasures for mitigating the risks from security threats, but it can be applied to many other business processes which experience device malfunctions or human errors.

Keywords: Transactional models · Intrusion detection and information filtering · Risk assessment · Markov Decision Process

1 Introduction

Contemporary Intrusion Detection Systems (IDS) are widely used in cybersecurity for detecting and classifying potential security threats of unauthorised intrusions [1]. Such intrusions are particularly dangerous during transaction processing because they can lead to significant financial losses. There are a number of security measures which can be used to counteract this, but their success is contingent on the precision of the detection and the time of the counteraction. In both network-based IDS, which use signature information [2], and host-based IDS, which use behavioral information [3] the data analysis utilizes a variety of methods for Machine Learning (ML). More complex frameworks typically combine logical analysis of security policies, AI Planning and data analytics using ML within hybrid architecture.

The terms *false positives* and *false negatives* in data science denote errors in the detection, identification, classification and prediction of data patterns during the analysis [4]. In this paper, we will present the results of a quantitative assessment of the impact of false negatives and false positives on the security

© Springer Nature Switzerland AG 2021
S. Fischer-Hübner et al. (Eds.): TrustBus 2021, LNCS 12927, pp. 50–66, 2021.
https://doi.org/10.1007/978-3-030-86586-3_4

risks. The risks in our approach are calculated on the basis of the optimal strategy for control of the transactions under security threats, modelled as Partially Observable Markov Decision Processes (POMDP) [14].

2   Importance of False Positives and False Negatives

The false positives/false negatives in intrusion detection and in threat intelligence in general, are parameters, which together with the moments of counteracting, have an impact on the security risks along transactions. They characterize the methods for detection and knowing their impact on the risks, would allow us to devise an optimal strategy for controlling the transactions in real-time, as well as to chose appropriate detection methods at the design stage.

Basic analysis of the false positives/false negatives in ML can be found in abundance in the literature [6]. Unfortunately, it is not appropriate for controlling the security risks in transaction processing. Relatively detailed analysis of the security risks dependent on the counteractions is given in [7], but the dependency of the risks on the precision of the methods is practically eliminated. In [8] the risks are modelled using Markov chains, but the analysis looks for prediction rather than for protection from attacks. There is some research on how to reduce the rate of false negatives [10] and false positives [11] by taking into account prior classification of the malicious activities and by learning from historical data, but without estimating their direct impact on security risks [12].

Our approach goes further in this direction. Firstly, the use of POMDP allows us to distinguish between unpredictable, but partially observable security events, and predictable, but uncontrollable effects of malicious actions. The solution of the decision making problem in such a case is given by the optimal strategy for counteracting which can be calculated analytically. Secondly, since the false negatives and false positives are parameters of this model, the variations of the risk thresholds can reveal the dependency between the prior probabilities for detecting threats and the risks of diverting the transactions from their normal execution, under the influence of security threats. Since the false negatives and false positives characterise the ML algorithms applicable to the specific data, we can account their impact in order to devise suitable planning heuristics.

3   Security Countermeasures and Risks in Transactions

Our method for risk assessment using POMDP was introduced in [14] to integrate the decision making with the stochastic planning of security countermeasures in digital banking. To make the paper self-contained, here, we will provide a brief description of the POMDP model and its use for assessing the security risks by computing the optimal strategy for applying countermeasures.

3.1 Applying Security Countermeasures and Decision Making

The decisions to execute diagnostic actions and to apply counteractions are essential parts of any cybersecurity framework. A natural criterion for choice of counteractions is the security risks. Considering data analytics and ML methods for diagnostics as black boxes allows to develop purely deterministic model of the transactions, but the risk assessment requires non-deterministic formalization. The asynchronous events in transactions can be either unpredictable, but anticipated, like many malicious interventions, or unexpected, but predictable, such as human or technical errors. This determines the model of transaction processing under threats as POMDP, rather than Markov Decision Process (MDP) with full information. Our POMDP model has the following elements:

1. **State space** $S = \{safe, danger, deadend\}$ – corresponds to the different types of situations from the point of view of the risk they pose:
   (a) $safe$ Situations along the transactions in absence of any threats;
   (b) $danger$ Situations in which the system is under the influence of security threats but still able to recover, and
   (c) $deadend$ Situations in which the system experiences severity and crashes completely under the security threats.
2. **Control space** $C = \{noact, respond\}$ – corresponds to the two types of actions from risk perspective:
   (a) $noact$ – no control intervention, the system goes straight to the next situation according to the recommended action and continues the normal track of execution of the current transaction, and
   (b) $respond$ – counteraction, which brings the system back to a safe situation after malicious action deviating the transaction from its normal course.
3. **Observation space** $Z = \{nothreat, threat, crash\}$ – corresponds to the different types of events from risk viewpoint:
   (a) $nothreat$ – asynchronous event, which is non-threatening and does not require counteraction;
   (b) $threat$ – detection of malicious intervention which requires counteraction, and
   (c) $crash$ – losing control of the system without chance for recovery.
4. **Transition kernel** $q(s_{n+1}|s_n, c_{n+1})$ – probability of the transition from situation s_n to situation s_{n+1} under control c_{n+1}, calculated as follows:
   – $q(safe|safe) = p$, p is the probability for absence of threats after transition from a safe situation;
   – $q(danger|safe) = 1 - p$, $1 - p$ is the probability for presence of threats after transition to from safe situation;
   – $q(safe|danger, respond) = 1$ because the counteraction in dangerous situation eliminates the threat;
   – $q(deadend|danger, noact) = 1$ because the absence of counteraction in dangerous situation leads to inevitable crash of the system, and
   – $q(deadend|deadend) = 1$ since there is no way out of the crash.
5. **Occurrence kernel** $t(z_n|s_n)$ – probability of the occurrence of event z_n in situation s_n, calculated as follows:

- $t(nothreat|safe) = p_{11}$ – probability of not observing threat occurrence in a safe state (*true negative*);
- $t(nothreat|danger) = p_{12}$ – probability of not observing threat occurrence in a dangerous stage (*false negative*);
- $t(threat|safe) = p_{21}$ – probability of observing threat occurrence in a safe state (`false positive`);
- $t(threat|danger) = p_{22}$ – probability of observing threat occurrence in a dangerous state (*true positive*), and
- $t(crash|deadend) = 1$ – probability of observing the system crash under threat.

If we denote the matrix with entries $p_{ij}, i, j = 1, 2$ by P its transpose P^T is a stochastic matrix since

$$p_{11} + p_{21} = p_{12} + p_{22} = 1.$$

6. **Costs** – quantitative measures of the costs of taking actions which can be interpreted differently, depending on the needs; we are considering it to be the delay caused by the additional counteractions to neutralize the detected threats:
   (a) Current cost $r(c)$ calculated as follows: $r(noact) = 0$, $r(respond) = -c$ where $c > 0$ is the cost for executing counteraction *respond*;
   (b) Final cost $R(s)$ calculated as follows: $R(safe) = R(danger) = 1$ if either the transaction terminates normally or the threat occurs after finalizing it, and $R(deadend) = 0$ if the crash occurs during the transaction.
7. **Horizon** N – length of the transaction, measured by the number of safe situations along the transaction.

Definition 1. *Security decision $\phi(s)$ is a function, which for each state $s \in S$ chooses either noact or respond.*

The security decisions may modify the transactions by enforcing *respond* actions in some situations. Therefore, they can extend the path of the transactions. If the security decisions are wrong, the transactions may end in a *deadend* situation. To maximize the chances of making the right decisions, we will account all information available at the time of decision making, which will turn the security decision into a stochastic function of the parameters of the POMDP model.

Definition 2. *Decision policy $\pi = (\phi(1), \phi(2), ..., \phi(N))$ is a collection of security decision functions such that on each step n of the transaction, $\phi(n)$ depends only on the past history till time n, and the prior probabilities of the states at time 0, that is before the transaction has begun.*

We assume that the prior probability of state *deadend* is 0, since otherwise any policy makes no sense. Therefore, the sum of the prior probabilities of the other two states is equal to 1, and the prior distribution of the states at time 0 is determined by the prior probability x of state *safe*.

We consider a decision problem with the following criterion:

$$v^\pi(x) = E_x^\pi(R(state_N) - cK), \tag{1}$$

where E_x^π is the expectation, corresponding to the policy π and the prior probability x, and K is the total number of times when we apply the action *respond*. $R(state_N)$ is the final income which we get on the last step of the transaction.

Definition 3. *A value function of the POMDP model is the function*

$$v(x) = \max_\pi v^\pi(x). \tag{2}$$

A policy π such that $v(x) = v^\pi(x)$ is an optimal policy. In our framework the optimal policy certainly exists, since there are only a finite number 2^N of possible policies. Evidently $0 < v(x) < 1$, since $R(x) \le 1$, $c > 0$, and the policy which does not recommend using the action *respond* at all yields a positive income, equal to the probability to avoid observing *crash* during the transaction. This allows us to define the risk, corresponding to the prior probability x as $1 - v(x)$.

The main difference between an MDP and POMDP is the introduction of the **Observation Space** and the **Occurrence Kernel**. These two components of the model reflect the non-predictability of the asynchronous events, which can happen in different situations at arbitrary times during the transactions. Although they make the POMDP model more complex, as we will show later, its complexity can be reduced by statistical methods.

3.2   Risk Assessment Based on Optimal Strategy for Counteracting

The problem for controlling the transactions under threats, formulated as POMDP, can be reduced to a problem for a fully observed MDP [14]. In this section we will sketch the reduction procedure which enables the analysis of the impact of false negative and false positive rates on security risks.

In order to find both the value function and the optimal strategy, we will follow the standard procedure for reducing the POMDP model with partially observable states to a MDP model with fully observable states, which would allow us to apply the standard dynamic programming algorithm. The reduction can be done by following the steps bellow:

1. Constructing sufficient statistics for the POMDP model by solving the filtration equations
2. Building a model with fully observable states using the sufficient statistics from step one
3. Solving Bellman's equation for the MDP model, built in step two, using the dynamic programming algorithm

Sufficient Statistics for the POMDP Model. Let f_n (resp. g_n), $n = 0, 1,...,N - 1$, be 3×1-vectors with elements equal to the prior (resp. posterior) probabilities of the states *safe, danger* and *deadend* during the transaction. We assume that $f_n(1)$ and $g_n(1)$ correspond to state *safe*, $f_n(2)$ and $g_n(2)$ – to state *danger*, and $f_n(3)$ and $g_n(3)$ – to state *deadend*. We can think of these vectors as points belonging to the two-dimensional simplex in $\mathbf{R}^3$. In order to exclude the trivial case of a system's breakdown before any transaction has begun, we assume that $f_0(3) = 0$. Thus, we have $f_0(1) = x$, $f_0(2) = 1 - x$, where x is the same as in (1). The other vectors f_n and g_n satisfy the following relations:

- Since the state *deadend* is absorbing, $g_n(3) = 0$ or 1. If $g_n(3) = 1$, then $f_m(3) = g_m(3) = 1$ for all $m > n$.
- Making use of the Bayes formula, the coordinates of the vector g_n can be calculated as follows:

$$g_n(1) = \frac{f_n(1)p_{21}}{f_n(1)p_{21} + f_n(2)p_{22}} := \Gamma^1(f_n(1), f_n(2)), \tag{3}$$

$$g_n(2) = \frac{f_n(2)p_{22}}{f_n(1)p_{21} + f_n(2)p_{22}}, \quad g_n(3) = 0, \tag{4}$$

if $z_n = threat$;

$$g_n(1) = \frac{f_n(1)p_{11}}{f_n(1)p_{11} + f_n(2)p_{12}} := \Gamma^2(f_n(1), f_n(2)), \tag{5}$$

$$g_n(2) = \frac{f_n(2)p_{12}}{f_n(1)p_{11} + f_n(2)p_{12}}, \quad g_n(3) = 0, \tag{6}$$

if $z_n = nothreat$;

$$g_n(1) = 0, g_n(2) = 0, g_n(3) = 1, \tag{7}$$

if $z_n = crash$.

On the other hand, if $g_n(3) = 0$ then the coordinates of f_{n+1} are

$$f_{n+1}(1) = pg_n(1), f_{n+1}(2) = (1 - p)g_n(1), f_{n+1}(3) = g_n(2), \tag{8}$$

whenever $c_n = noact$;

$$f_{n+1}(1) = p, f_{n+1}(2) = 1 - p, f_{n+1}(3) = 0, \tag{9}$$

if $c_n = respond$.

The last equations show that if we consider the vectors $g_n, n = 0, 1, \dots, N-1$, as points in the two-dimensional simplex, they are located either in the vertex of the simplex, corresponding to state *deadend*, or on the edge, connecting the vertices corresponding to states *danger* and *safe*. On the other hand, the location of the points on this edge is determined by a single coordinate, equal to the posterior probability of the state *safe*. This observation plays an important role for reducing the POMDP model to a MDP model with fully observable states.

Building a Model with Fully Observable States. According to the general theory of POMDP (see [13]), the sufficient statistics allow us to reduce the initial POMDP problem to a fully observed MDP problem on the basis of posterior probabilities $g_n, n = 0, 1, ...N - 1$. We consider such a model with state space - the set $S = (0, 1) \cup \{*\}$, where $*$ is an isolated point. The controlled process in the model with complete information is defined by

$$x_n = \begin{cases} *, & \text{if } g_n(3) = 1 \\ g_n(1), & \text{if } g_n(3) = 0 \end{cases}, \quad n = 0, 1, ...N - 1.$$

Let us note, that in view of (3), (5), and the total probability formula, the initial distribution of x_0 is the following:

$$x_0 = \begin{cases} \Gamma^1(x, 1 - x) \text{ with probability } p_{21}x + p_{22}(1 - x) \\ \Gamma^2(x, 1 - x) \text{ with probability } p_{11}x + p_{12}(1 - x) \end{cases}.$$

The fact that P^T is a stochastic matrix implies that the distribution of x_0 is a proper probability distribution. The same holds for all distributions that appear in the definition of the transition kernel $t(\{y\}|x, c)$ of the model with fully observable states. The filtration equations (3)–(7), and the total probability formula motivate us to define it as follows:

$$t(\{y\}|x, c) = \begin{cases} pxp_{21} + (1 - p)xp_{22}, & \text{if } y = \Gamma^1(px, (1 - p)x) = \Gamma^1(p, 1 - p) \\ pxp_{11} + (1 - p)xp_{12}, & \text{if } y = \Gamma^2(px, (1 - p)x) = \Gamma^2(p, 1 - p) \\ 1 - x, & \text{if } y = * \end{cases},$$

provided that $c = noact$,

$$t(\{y\}|x, c) = \begin{cases} pp_{21} + (1 - p)p_{22}, & \text{if } y = \Gamma^1(p, 1 - p) \\ pp_{11} + (1 - p)p_{12}, & \text{if } y = \Gamma^2(p, 1 - p) \end{cases},$$

provided that $c = respond$,

$$t(*|*, \cdot) = 1.$$

In all other cases we set $t(\{y\}|x, \cdot) = 0$. The final reward is $R(x) = 1, x \in (0, 1), R(*) = 0$. The other elements of the model —the action space C, the running reward r as well as the horizon N remain unchanged after the reduction.

Solving Bellman's Equation for the Fully Observed MDP Model. Consider the functions

$$V_n(x) = \max_\pi E_x^\pi(\Sigma_{k=n}^{N-1}r(c_{k+1}) + R(x_N)), n = 0, 1, ...N - 1. \quad (10)$$

They satisfy the Bellman's equation

$$V_n(x) = \max(V_n^{'}(x), V_n^{''}(x)), \quad (11)$$

and the final condition

$$V_N(x) = R(x). \quad (12)$$

In (11), $V_n'(x)$ and $V_n''(x)$ are one-step ahead estimates of *noact* and *respond*:

$$V_n'(x) = (pxp_{21} + (1-p)xp_{22})V_{n+1}(\Gamma^1(p, 1-p))$$
$$+ (pxp_{11} + (1-p)xp_{12})V_{n+1}(\Gamma^2(p, 1-p)),$$
$$V_n''(x) = -c + (pp_{21} + (1-p)p_{22})V_{n+1}(\Gamma^1(p, 1-p))$$
$$+ (pp_{11} + (1-p)p_{12})V_{n+1}(\Gamma^2(p, 1-p)).$$

Let us note that since after action *respond* the system instantly falls into a *safe* state ($x = 1$), the right-hand side of the last formula does not depend on x, but still depends on n. Now the optimal strategy φ_{n+1} at any moment in time $n = 0, 1, ..., N - 1$ is the following:

$$\varphi_{n+1}(x) = \begin{cases} noact, & \text{if } V_n(x) = V_n'(x) \\ respond, & \text{if } V_n(x) = V_n''(x) \end{cases}.$$

These equations can be solved backwards, starting with the state of successful completion of the transaction. For example, for $n = N - 1$ we get:

$$V_{N-1}(x) = \max(1 - c, x),$$

$$\varphi_N(x) = \begin{cases} noact, & \text{if } x \geq 1 - c \text{ (above the threshold)} \\ respond, & \text{if } x < 1 - c \text{ (bellow the threshold)} \end{cases}.$$

The remaining calculations until reaching the beginning of the transaction can be performed recursively, taking the previously calculated solution as terminal. It is worth noting that not only φ_N but all φ_n, $n = 1, 2, ...N - 1$ are determined by thresholds $(y_n), n = 0, 1, ..., N - 1$, $y_{N-1} = 1 - c$, and the optimal policy recommends using of a corrective action only if $x_n < y_n$. Finally, the connection between the value functions in both models is given by

$$v(x) = (xp_{21} + (1-x)p_{22})V_0(\Gamma^1(x, 1-x)) \qquad (13)$$
$$+ (xp_{11} + (1-x)p_{12})V_0(\Gamma^2(x, 1-x)).$$

Now, following the optimal policy, we can describe the optimal behavior:

1 At the beginning of transaction ($n = 0$), depending on whether we detect a threat or not, we calculate the posterior probability x_0 of the state *safe* by the formula

$$x_0 = \begin{cases} \Gamma^1(x, 1-x), \text{ if } z_0 = threat \\ \Gamma^2(x, 1-x), \text{ if } z_0 = nothreat \end{cases}.$$

If x_0 is greater than the threshold y_0, then we do not apply the corrective action, x_0 remains unchanged, and with probability $1 - x_0$ we fall into a state *deadend*. Otherwise, we use *respond* after paying the cost c, and the posterior probability becomes 1 since we certainly know that we are *safe*;

2 In the next step, we start with a prior probability equal to the just found posterior probability (x_0 or 1), multiplied by p, observe again if there is detection of a threat, calculate the posterior probability x_1, compare it with the threshold y_1, and so on till the end of the transaction.

The above equations form the algorithmic foundation for risk assessment in transaction processing under threats. In the next section we will use it for analysis of the impact of the false negatives/false positives on the security risks.

4   Measuring False Positives and False Negatives

In the POMDP model *false negatives* and *false positives* are represented by the prior probabilities p_{12} and p_{21}, respectively. They depend only on the method for detection of the potential threats and, as such, are input parameters for our analysis. The *horizon* N depends on the particular transaction and it is another input parameter for the analysis. The parameter p measures how often we can expect attacks during the transaction. Finally, the last parameter of the model, which may have an impact on the risk, is the *cost* for using mitigating counteractions, c. At a first glance it looks like another parameter of the model, but in fact without taking into consideration the impact of both p and N, we can face extreme situations:

- **Case 1:** c is too small. Then the optimal policy may recommend applying mitigating action *respond* permanently, without considering any observations;
- **Case 2:** c is too large. Then we would not be able to neutralize all threats even if we know exactly when they occur, i.e., when both the false positives and the false negatives are equal to 0. This could happen because the total cost of the mitigating actions may exceed 1, which is the maximum reward for a successful transaction.

In order to avoid such extremes, we will make c depend on both p and N.

Let M be the max number when the action *respond* can be used. Then, we have $Mc < 1$ and $(M+1)c > 1$ and therefore,

$$\frac{1}{M+1} < c < \frac{1}{M}. \tag{14}$$

On the other hand, the number of potential threats during the transaction is a random variable which has a binomial distribution with parameters $1 - p$ and N. Taking M to be an $1 - \alpha$–quantile of this distribution, for α small enough, we guarantee that we can face Case 2 only with a probability less than α. In view of (14), $1/(M+1)$ is a lower bound for c which mitigates the risks more than M times by executing *respond*. Thus, Case 1 will not take place either.

5   Impact of False Positives/Negatives on Security Risks

In this section we provide experimental results about the impact of the false negative (p_{21}) and false positive (p_{12}) rates on the security risks, based on the optimal strategy for control of the transactions under threats using the method of dynamic programming. The additional input parameters of the model are:

- N - the length of the transaction;
- p - the probability of attack on each step of the transaction. In this section we fix this parameter to be equal to 0.1. We consider the prior probability x as a probability of attack which occurs not during the transaction but before it, and take it to be equal to 0.1, too;
- c - a penalty for applying a corrective action. We make c depend on both p and N as explained in Sect. 4.

In the calculations, we varied the input parameters within the interval of typical precision of detection algorithms. All results concern the risk $1-v(x)$, $v(x)$ being the value function of the model. The numerical calculations have been performed according to Eqs. 11 and 13, as described at the end of Sect. 3.

5.1   Dependence of the Security Risks from Detection Precision

The 3D plot of the dependence of the security risks from the rate of false negatives and false positives is shown on Fig. 1 in the Appendix. We used several combinations of input parameters as follows:

- for the false negatives p_{12} within the interval 0.01–0.4, i.e. detection in up to 60%, adequate as an estimation of the precision of a variety of methods and
- for false positives p_{21} within the same range, which is also adequate.

The 3D plot in Fig. 1 is based on the calculations in Table 1. It has a regular shape with monotonous dynamics, without extremes or inflection areas. This allows more convenient single factor analysis instead of simultaneous variation of both false negatives and false positives.

Table 1. Risk in function of false negatives/false positives ($N = 10$, $p = 0.1$, $c = 0.292$)

p12 p21	0.01	0.05	0.10	0.15	0.20	0.25	0.30	0.35	0.40
0.01	0.26490	0.34798	0.45190	0.52604	0.55737	0.56926	0.57152	0.57156	0.57039
0.05	0.28062	0.36173	0.46836	0.53355	0.55973	0.57060	0.57085	0.57117	0.57161
0.10	0.30599	0.38422	0.48614	0.53993	0.56390	0.57092	0.57045	0.57117	0.57125
0.15	0.32487	0.40617	0.50181	0.55006	0.56778	0.57117	0.57212	0.57029	0.57326
0.20	0.34341	0.42234	0.51571	0.55538	0.57060	0.57094	0.57067	0.57241	0.57045
0.25	0.36716	0.44334	0.52447	0.56019	0.57128	0.57029	0.57241	0.57060	0.57212
0.30	0.38485	0.45882	0.53555	0.56377	0.56953	0.57153	0.57106	0.57031	0.57067
0.35	0.40217	0.47885	0.54599	0.56730	0.57203	0.57239	0.57170	0.57220	0.56991
0.40	0.41912	0.49361	0.55429	0.56922	0.57060	0.57020	0.57052	0.56953	0.56983

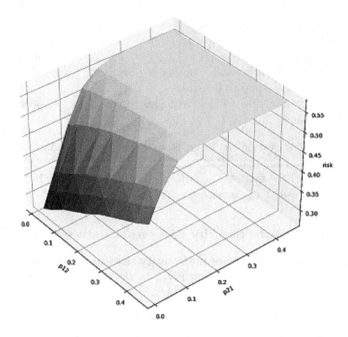

Fig. 1. 3D plot of the risk in function of the false negatives and false positives

The dependence of the risks from the false negatives p_{12} under a fixed rate of the false positives p_{21}, is shown on Fig. 2. It is linear for all fixed rates of false positives, but for the lowest rate of $p_{21} = 0.05$ it increases at the fastest rate. This means that when the detection captures the actual threats, the risk depends only on the false negatives rate. In addition, the risk for false positives around and more than 50% remains practically constant. This can be explained by the fact that although the false positives enforce unnecessary responses to non-existing threats, they also neutralize some of the misses of existing threats.

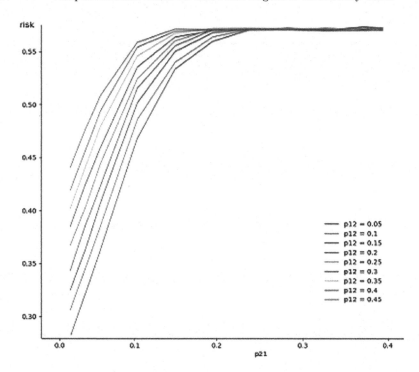

Fig. 2. Risk in function of the false negatives at fixed false positives

The dependence of the risk from the false positives p_{21} under a fixed rate of the false negatives p_{12} is shown on Fig. 3. The striking observation is, that the risk saturates around a 20–25% rate of the false positives for all rates of the false negatives. This means that the algorithms for detection, which produce more than 25% false positives, practically have the same effect on the risk. In addition, the quality of detection does not increase when lowering further the rate of false negatives under 25%. The almost parallel initial curves for different false negatives rates also show, that the quality of the detection algorithms is nearly proportional to the false positives rate within the interval 0–25%.

The results meet the expectation about the quality of detection algorithms in the two boundary cases of high/low false positives and high/low false negatives. They determines the most risky and the least risky choices of detection method, respectively. Of more interest are the results concerning the combination of low rate of false negatives with high rate of false positives. The diagram shows that the high rate of false positives tend to neutralize the low rate of false negatives in some methods. This means that some methods which are less precise in the detection of existing threats can be actually less risky than methods which are more precise just by being overprotective. This again signifies the importance of the false positives for the choice of detection method. The above analysis shows that the choice of methods for detection does not need to examine only the

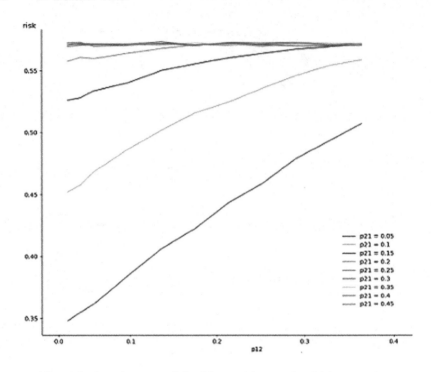

Fig. 3. Risk in function of the false positives at fixed false negatives

minimization of the rates. Beyond a certain rate of false negatives, their further minimization does not reduce the risks; beyond a certain rate of false positives, the risk does not depend on the false negatives, whatsoever. Therefore, there is no need to look for minimization of both the false negatives and the false positives simultaneously, since the quality depends on their combination, and any further minimization may be too costly, without having any significant effect on the reduction of security risks.

5.2 Dynamics of the Security Risks Along the Transactions

Intuitively, the lower the rates of the false negatives and false positives, the lower the risks are. However, this does not account for the moment of executing the counteractions in response to the threats. Table 2 contains calculations based on the optimal strategy which helps analyzing this dependence in more detail.

Table 2. Change of security risks as a function of the length of the transaction N

N	p12 = 0.05 p21 = 0.05	p12 = 0.30 p21 = 0.30	p12 = 0.05 p21 = 0.30	p12 = 0.15 p21 = 0.15	p12 = 0.30 p21 = 0.05	c
5	0.189638093	0.271971568	0.271838029	0.272796722	0.22716054	0.417
10	0.361736347	0.571060961	0.57085112	0.550062678	0.458826459	0.292
15	0.580335931	0.747278141	0.747077204	0.735406971	0.677226803	0.292
20	0.631718964	0.851101596	0.847870525	0.824268906	0.768704437	0.225
25	0.669172001	0.911364804	0.903965426	0.879386462	0.834110451	0.183
30	0.70195926	0.946130333	0.937595461	0.916204114	0.882486834	0.155

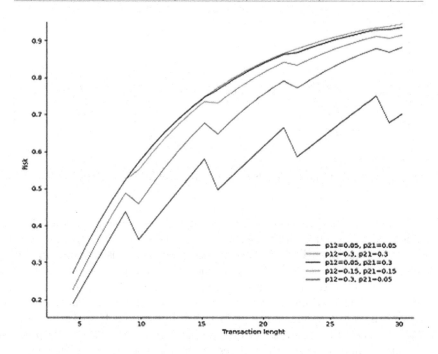

Fig. 4. Risk in function of the remaining situations of the transaction

The risk calculations account representative combinations of p_{12} and p_{21}:

– Low rates for both false negatives and false positives: $p_{12} = 0.05$ and $p_{21} = 0.05$;
– Low rate of false negatives/high rate of false positives: $p_{12} = 0.05$ and $p_{21} = 0.30$;
– Close average rates of both false positives and negatives: $p_{12} = 0.15$ and $p_{21} = 0.15$;
– High rate of false negatives/low rate of false positives: $p_{12} = 0.30$ and $p_{21} = 0.05$;
– High rates for both false negatives and false positives: $p_{12} = 0.3$ and $p_{21} = 0.3$.

Figure 4 shows the dynamics of the risks along the transactions for these combinations. All curves are nearly aperiodic, which means that the earlier you counteract, the lower the risks of crashing the transaction are.

5.3 Dependency of the Cost from the Moment of Counteracting

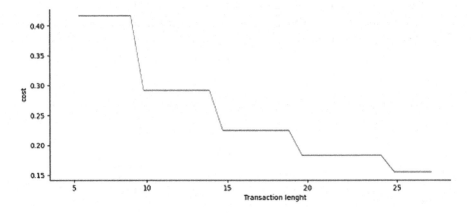

Fig. 5. Estimations of the cost c in function of the horizon N

The parameter c, which measures the costs of executing counteractions for neutralizing threats, depends on the horizon N and the probability of threat occurrence p, as discussed earlier. This dependency can be translated in terms of a relative delay of the actual transaction, due to the need to execute additional counteractions to neutralize the threats along the horizon N. The diagram shown in Fig. 5 depicts the estimated costs for executing counteractions in the remaining situations before reaching the end of the transaction. It looks like a step function, because it is based on analytical estimation of the interval of possible values rather than on the actual values of the costs according to formula 14. It still shows a linear trend of decreasing the costs, however - the longer the transaction is, the lower the cost is since earlier countermeasures may require repeating them at a later stage.

6   Discussion and Future Development

The estimation of security risks within the POMDP model is based on the optimal strategy for controlling the transactions. It minimizes only the integral risks, without accounting for any specific information about the particular transaction. The experimental results validate the theoretical model but more detailed estimation of the impact of false negatives/false positives can be done only if we know in which situation the different threats may occur. In such a case the optimal strategy can be fine-tuned to support better-informed security decision making. For this purpose, the prior probabilities should be functionally dependent on both the false negative and false positive rates of the detection algorithms and situations in which the malicious activities take place. We are also considering using risk assessment for analyzing the vulnerability of transaction processing systems by identifying dangerous situations. In a more distant future, we are additionally planning to explore the potential of reinforcement learning for increasing the precision of assessment by additional analysis of historical data. The same methodology can be used for analyzing the safety problems in other application domains in which asynchronous events may occur, such as faults, caused by machine failure, or human errors in autonomous devices and production lines.

Acknowledgments. The research presented in this paper is a result of collaboration between the Cyber Security Research Centre (CSRC) of London Metropolitan University and GATE Institute of Sofia University (GATE). GATE has received funding from the EU H2020 WIDESPREAD-2018-2020 TEAMING Phase 2 programme under Grant Agreement No. 857155 and BG Operational Programme "Science and Education for Smart Growth" under Grant Agreement No. BG05M2OP001-1.003-0002-C01. CSRC has received funding from the university Rescaling Fund. The opinions presented are, however, of the authors only and do not reflect the official policies of these organisations.

References

1. OWASP Foundation Inc. "Intrusion Detection". https://owasp.org/www-community/controls/Intrusion_Detection. Accessed 20 Jan 2021
2. Kulariya, M., Saraf, P., et al.: Performance analysis of network intrusion detection schemes using Apache Spark. In: Proceedings of 2016 International Conference on Communication and Signal Processing (ICCSP), Melmaruvathur, pp. 1973–1977 (2016)
3. Parmar, J.: A classification based approach to create database policy for Intrusion Detection and Respond anomaly requests. In: Proceedings of Conference on IT in Business, Industry and Government (CSIBIG), Indore 2014, pp. 1–7 (2014)
4. Liang, F.: Evaluating the Performance of Machine Learning Models. https://towardsdatascience.com/classifying-model-outcomes-true-false-positives-negatives-17c1e702810. Accessed 20 Jan 2021
5. Ho, C., Lai, Y., Chen, I., Wang, F., Tai, W.: Statistical analysis of false positives and false negatives from real traffic with intrusion detection/prevention systems. IEEE Commun. Mag. **50**(3), 146–154 (2012)
6. Ho, C., Lin, Y., Lai, Y., et al.: False positives and false negatives from real traffic with intrusion detection/prevention systems. Int. J. Future Comput. Commun. **1**(2), 87–90 (2012)
7. Kreidl, O.: Analysis of a Markov decision process model for intrusion tolerance. In: International Conference on Dependable System and Networks (DSN 2010), pp. 156–161. IEEE Xplore (2010)
8. Liu, Q., Xing, L., Zhou, C.: Probabilistic Modeling and Analysis of Sequential Cyber-attacks, pp. 1–19. Wiley, Hoboken (2019)

9. Chawla, N., Bowyer, K., et al.: SMOTE: synthetic minority over-sampling technique. J. Artif. Intell. Res. **16**, 321–357 (2002)
10. Pietraszek, T., Tanner, A.: Data mining and machine learning - towards reducing false positives in intrusion detection. Inf. Secur. Tech. Rep. **10**(3), 169–183 (2005)
11. Mezic, A.: How AI is solving the false positives problem in network security. MixMode Inc (2020). https://mixmode.ai/blog/how-ai-is-solving-the-false-positives-problem-in-network-security. Accessed 24 Jan 2021
12. Jean-Baptiste, E., Rotshtein, P., Russell, M.: POMDP based action planning and human error detection. In: 11th IFIP International Conference AI Applications and Innovations (AIAI 2015), Bayonne, France, pp. 250–265, September 2015
13. Dynkin, E., Yushkevich, A.: Controlled Markov Processes. In: Adaptive Markov Control Processes. Applied Mathematical Sciences, vol. 79. Springer, New York (1979). https://doi.org/10.1007/978-1-4419-8714-3_1
14. Vassilev, V., Donchev, D., Tonchev, D.: Risk assessment in transactions under threat as a partially observable Markov decision process. In: Proceedings of International Conference on Optimization in AI and Data Sciences (ODS 2021). Springer (in print)

Web Security

Launching Adversarial Label Contamination Attacks Against Malicious URL Detection

Bruno Marchand[1], Nikolaos Pitropakis[1(✉)] (ID), William J. Buchanan[1] (ID),
and Costas Lambrinoudakis[2]

[1] School of Computing, Edinburgh Napier University, Edinburgh, UK
40445877@live.napier.ac.uk, {n.pitropakis,B.Buchanan}@napier.ac.uk
[2] Department of Digital Systems, University of Piraeus, Piraeus, Greece
clam@unipi.gr

Abstract. Web addresses, or Uniform Resource Locators (URLs), represent a vector by which attackers are able to deliver a multitude of unwanted and potentially harmful effects to users through malicious software. The ability to detect and block access to such URLs has traditionally been enabled through reactive and labour intensive means such as human verification and whitelists and blacklists. Machine Learning has shown great potential to automate this defence and position it as proactive through the implementation of classifier models. Work in this area has produced numerous high-accuracy models, though the algorithms themselves remain fragile to adversarial manipulation if implemented without consideration being given to their security. Our work aims to investigate the robustness of several classifiers for malicious URL detection by randomly perturbing samples in the training data. It is shown that without a measure of defence to adversarial influence, highly accurate malicious URL detection can be significantly and adversely affected at even low degrees of training data perturbation.

Keywords: Malicious URL · Detection · Adversarial machine learning

1 Introduction

The technological advancements have reshaped our every day life in every way possible, ranging from the way we shop and socialize to our working routines. The arrival of the Internet of Things (IoT) devices and 5G infrastructures assisted this technological uprising by introducing a range of different devices that are willing to make our life easier and more convenient. However, at the same time they made the attack surface broader, offering the opportunity to malicious parties to become more effective by launching social engineering attacks to people with low situational awareness. The common ground for all the attacks is the internet.

The resources available through the internet are voluminous and tend to be accessed through the use of Uniform Resource Locators (URLs). While this

© Springer Nature Switzerland AG 2021
S. Fischer-Hübner et al. (Eds.): TrustBus 2021, LNCS 12927, pp. 69–82, 2021.
https://doi.org/10.1007/978-3-030-86586-3_5

system provides a semantic and recognisable means for users to navigate pages and media on the web, it can also be subverted by malicious actors for nefarious purposes [1]. The rate at which new URLs are generated makes it problematic to rely on any defensive measure which is static in nature and unable to predict the form previously unseen malicious URLs might take. Machine Learning (ML) presents a means by which algorithms can be leveraged to classify URLs as benign or malicious with high certainty [2,3]. However, as good a solution as this appears to be, the attackers trying to compete with the defenders in this arms race have started targeting these same algorithms to degrade their accuracy and therefore the trust in the entire mechanism [4]. Hence there is a need to not only strive toward implementing ML in such a way that it performs well in terms of correct classification, but also does so even under adverse conditions such as targeted attacks.

Our work explores the topic of malicious URL classification and shows how several ML algorithms trained on datasets to produce highly accurate classification results, can be severely affected by even a mild form of attack when no defensive measures are built into their implementation. Our contributions can be summarised as follows:

- We mount label noise adversarial attacks against C4.5/J48, KNN and RF models that detect malicious URLs using the SCX-URL2016 dataset [5].
- We analyse and critically evaluate the experimental results.
- Finally, we discuss potential mitigation techniques that can increase the classifier's robustness against our attacks.

The structure of the rest of the paper is organized as follows: Sect. 2 builds the background on adversarial ML and presents the related literature, while Sect. 3 consists of the methodology and implementation used to conduct the main experimental activity of our work. Section 4 presents and discusses the results of the experimental activity, while Sect. 5 presents potential methods of mitigating attacks on ML. Finally Sect. 6 draws the conclusions, giving some pointers for future work.

2   Background and Related Work

2.1   Machine Learning and Attacks Against It

ML is a subset of Artificial Intelligence (AI) primarily concerned with enabling computers to make predictions and decisions based on data inputs, and is theoretically underpinned by computational statistics and mathematical optimization [6]. The mechanism by which this is achieved is through using ML algorithms, otherwise referred to as models or classifiers. Such algorithms allow machines some capacity to generalise, which is especially useful as is drastically reduces the need for writing code to instruct in such tasks as classification, prediction, and decision-making. These capabilities have enabled such technologies as spam detection, computer vision, stock market analysis, and speech recognition amongst many others.

Much of the effectiveness of a ML implementation hinges on the quantity and quality of data used as input. Once features are identified, individual entries can be labelled for supervised learning, which is the paradigm of most interest in this work. Supervised learning is an approach within ML which uses data points that are labelled prior to the training of a classifier. This allows a model to be trained, validated, and have its accuracy measured, thus allowing for comparisons to be made between different algorithms on the same dataset [7].

Results given by a classifier are measured by several metrics including precision, recall, accuracy, false prediction rate, and f1-score. A breakdown of results is often represented through a confusion matrix which shows how many samples were labelled as malicious and correctly classified as malicious (True Positive), how many were labelled benign and classified as malicious (False Positive), how many were labelled malicious but classified benign (False Negative), and how many were labelled benign and correctly classified as benign (True Negative). Of concern to this work are precision and recall. The former refers to all samples labelled as malicious and benign and expresses as a percentage of this total how many were correctly classified as malicious. The latter gives a percentage of how many samples labelled as malicious were correctly classified as such. These metrics are calculated as shown in Eq. 1 and 2. It is additionally useful to use a measurement called f1-score, or f-measure, in order to compare the harmonic average or mean of Precision and Recall across classifiers. Equations 1,2 and 3 illustrate how this is calculated.

$$precision = \frac{(TP)}{(TP + FP)} \quad (1) \qquad recall = \frac{TP}{(TP + FN)} \quad (2) \qquad F1 - score = \frac{2 \times Pr \times Re}{(Pr + Re)} \quad (3)$$

C4.5 is a decision tree algorithm created by Ross Quinlan in the early 1990s, and is referred to as **J48** in the ML software suite Weka. A decision tree algorithm can be described as a classification process which begins with a binary conditional test at its *trunk* in reference to the properties of features. This process is repeated with different subsequent conditional tests to a specified depth, filtering through numerous branches until final categories are arrived upon. The nodes at the output level are referred to as the leaves of the decision tree [8]. **Random Forest** (RF) algorithm implements an ensemble of decision trees trained independently, each of which contributes its output as a *vote* to the prediction of a target label by seeing how frequently member trees agree on classification of a given data point. **Nearest Neighbour** (KNN) is a pattern recognition algorithm based on a distance function that classifies data points according to the most frequently observed class among its neighbours [8].

As useful and powerful as ML classifiers can be, they are unfortunately quite vulnerable to attacks out-the-box. Depending on if the attack is performed during the training phase or the testing phase of a classification they are called either poisoning or evasion attacks. These attacks are broadly classed as being either blackbox, graybox or whitebox depending on the knowledge an adversary has of the target [4].

Training data can be poisoned by altering the values of features or the labels of samples [9]. Label Contamination Attacks are particularly relevant to our work and involve the changing of labels, often in a binary fashion, referred to as label flipping. In the case of malicious URLs that may mean changing a label from *benign* to *malicious* or vice versa. Labels can be randomly flipped up to a set threshold, or the attack can be crafted by calculating the impact of labels which when flipped cause the maximum degradation in classifier performance [10]. The term adversarial label noise can also refer to this attack, although it should be noted that the presence of noise is often normal to a degree in datasets and simply a reflection of the complexities of the real-world settings from which data is derived. Another notable property of adversarial techniques is that they can be generalised or transferred across different models and retain effectiveness in reducing the accuracy of the classifier.

2.2 Related Work

The relationship between the development of new information technologies (IT) and threats to the security of those technologies has aptly been described as an arms race [11]. As innovative products and services emerge so do attacks against them, most often facilitating some form of fraud, theft, or extortion. The central concern of our work are URLs which can be weaponised with the intent to deliver malicious content to a user and facilitate unwanted adverse effects [3,12]. A malicious URL takes advantage of the convention of having string-based addresses for content made available through the internet, typically through hyperlink references (links) and domain names. It can be difficult for a person to detect indicators within a URL which might mark it as malicious. In light of the COVID-19 pandemic adversaries have ramped up their deployment of malicious URLs. Trend Micro reported that between February and March of 2020 malicious URL hits increased 260% [13]. This upward trend is also reflected in the 1st Quarter Phishing Activity Trends Report which shows an overall increase in detected unique phishing websites between January and March 2020 [14]. These reports show a sustained need for improved malicious URL detection capabilities in the face of relentless efforts by attackers, who leverage uncertainty to their advantage in a time of global crisis.

Security practitioners have implemented protective measures against malicious URLs in the form of blacklisting and heuristic techniques using reputation systems [2]. ML has been recognised as a technology that can facilitate the scalability of security solutions, as well as having the potential to adaptively detect novel attacks [15]. URLs are either benign or malicious and are labelled as such in the datasets that exist in literature. ML can be an effective and efficient means of detecting malicious URLs, however, all models are vulnerable to attacks that can drastically reduce classification performance and therefore the usefulness of these classifiers.

Xiao et al. [16] used a white-box approach to demonstrate an attack on Support Vector Machines (SVM) through the worst-case label noise. Adversarial examples were chosen by determining which labels, when flipped, resulted in the

Table 1. Description of the contents of the uncontaminated datasets

Dataset	Features	Benign samples	Malicious samples
All/Multi-class	12	7776	28641
Malware	9	7780	6707
Phishing	13	7586	7781
Defacement	12	7781	7930
Spam	6	7781	6698

maximum loss of accuracy to the model. It was determined that by computing the most impactful data points on which to flip labels, the performance of their novel attacks was roughly twice as effective as random label flipping. Zhao et al. [10] sought to address the optimisation of an adversarial attack in a blackbox scenario. They achieved their goal by developing an algorithm dubbed Projected Gradient Ascent (PGA) which was instrumental in constructing a label flipping strategy. Leveraging the transferability phenomenon, they noted that by training a substitute for the target model, an adversary can effectively then reduce a target's classification accuracy.

Zhou et al. [17] showed that it is possible to degrade the accuracy of a RF classifier by introducing random label noise into the training set. Their main focus though is on developing tolerance to such noise through an augmented version of the algorithm they name Noise Robust Random Forest. According to their results, their improved model maintains an accuracy of above 90%, while the classic RF implementation degrades to an average 75% accuracy. Our work differs from all the previous approaches as to the best of our knowledge is the first to evaluate the effect of a poisoning attack on the models and dataset produced by Mamun et al. [5] which were designed to perform malicious URL detection with high accuracy.

3 Methodology and Experimental Design

3.1 Dataset Overview

In order to demonstrate the effect of label contamination on ML classifier performance, an experimental example was identified from the literature in which the authors demonstrated malicious URL classifiers from a feature-engineered dataset [5]. We decided to use their study as the *target* for the experimental activity, as the classifiers produced therein showed high accuracy across several classes of malicious URLs. The dataset associated with the study was freely available from the University of Brunswick website at https://www.unb.ca/cic/datasets/url-2016.html. Downloadable as a compressed archive file, four categories of malicious URLs in single-class datasets were present in CSV format, as well as one multi-class dataset. Table 1 depicts the contents of each dataset according to the number of features contained, as well as a count of benign and malicious samples.

3.2   Experimental Design

The primary aim of our experiments was to determine the point at which the most damage could be done to a classifier with the least effort on the part of an attacker. As using label noise is known to have a greater detrimental effect on the learning ability of a classifier compared to feature noise, we used random label flipping as it required no computationally expensive calculations to be performed, while being significantly impactful. We decided to use a percentage-based threshold as a realistic constraint, also referred to as the noise budget, with one percent incremental steps in contaminated labels in the training data from 1%–10%. Experimental activity was performed on a Clevo PB50RC notebook with 16GB RAM and a CPU clock speed of 2.6 GHz running Windows 10. Following Mamun et al. (2016), the ML suite Weka (version 3.8.4) was installed for use in Graphical User Interface (GUI) mode. This suite would be used to train and test classifiers on both clean and contaminated datasets. The contaminated datasets were produced via a purpose-written script in Python 3.8.2.

The random method of contaminating data was chosen under the assumption that the dataset was not designed with robustness in mind and that the models trained would be susceptible to even small amounts of perturbation. Demontis et al. [9] state that a random label flip attack is often considered as a means of baselining the susceptibility of a classifier to error, thus in this case it was deemed appropriate to use this method. Leveraging the principle of transferability, it was anticipated that if one classifier was substantially degraded the others would show a similar effect. One multi-class and four single-class datasets in Comma Separated Value (CSV) format were used as input to a script written in Python, designed in order to produce sets of training data with contaminated labels while preserving a portion of clean data for testing. A high-level description of the entire methodology is illustrated in Fig. 1.

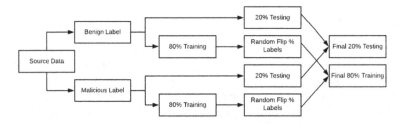

Fig. 1. High-level depiction of the methodology

Unique label values were extracted and were counted to determine whether the dataset was single or multi-class. Single-class datasets had only two labels, whereas the multi-class dataset had five. For each percentage point step provided in the setup of the script, the contents were split in this way to isolate samples with a given label into batches, making the flipping of labels more reliable. The resulting dataset were then divided into two parts, one containing 20% of instances that remained clean and were destined to be used for testing, and the other 80% were to be contaminated and used for training.

Soon afterwards, a number of instances had their labels flipped based on the percentage-step value. For single-class datasets this flipping was done by swapping the *benign* with the *malicious* label, whereas for the multi-class dataset the same was true for only the *malicious* labels. For the benign labelled data in the multi-class dataset an equal distribution of each malicious label was used instead. For example, at 1% of total labels to be flipped in the training data of benign instances 0.25% of labels would be flipped to Malware, 0.25% to Phishing, 0.25% to Defacement, and 0.25% to Spam.

Once training and testing files were ready, the original uncontaminated dataset was loaded in Weka. Then, a classifier was selected, and the Percentage Split option was set to 80, meaning that 80% of the data would be used for training with the remaining 20% used for testing. This was done to establish a baseline and replicate the results reported in [5]. For the RF classifier, various numbers of trees were used in accordance with their method. Having successfully replicated baseline Precision and Recall figures, each contaminated training file for each percentage step was loaded instead to train the classifier.

4   Results

For each of the three candidate classifiers (C4.5/J48, KNN and RF), results were obtained from training at one of two percentage ranges. The first range was from 1% to 10% and produced significant results on all classifiers for all datasets except the Spam dataset. For this dataset, unusually high resilience was observed and thus a new range of percentage steps was used exclusively for this single-class dataset. It was noted that around the 50% label contamination mark all models trained on this dataset with contaminated labels were degraded significantly and suddenly thus the percentage steps were set at: 35, 45, 47, 49, 51, 53, 55, 65, and 75%. This was chosen to give a better view of the initial robustness up until the sharp drop across the 50% threshold. All sets of graphs generated include a representation of f1-score so that the results on the three classifiers of interest can be observed in comparison.

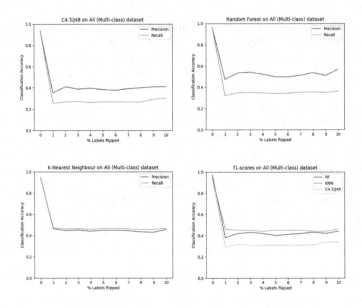

Fig. 2. Classification degradation on the Multi-class dataset (All)

Label contamination on the All/Multi-classthis dataset is illustrated in Fig. 2 and resulted in the most pronounced drop in Precision and Recall on C4.5/J48, dropping from 0.94 in both scores to 0.35 and 0.25 respectively at 1% of contaminated labels. The other decision-tree classifier, RF, dropped to 0.47 Precision and 0.32 Recall at 1% label contamination. Although all three ML models were significantly degraded in their classification capability, KNN was the least affected with the lowest scores for Precision and Recall recorded at 4% of labels contaminated, yielding 0.42 and 0.45 respectively.

All models performed similarly on the malware dataset, with the optimal percentage of labels flipped affecting C4.5/J48 at 4%, dropping Precision and Recall to 0.68 and 0.61 respectively. KNN showed 0.68 Precision and 0.60 Recall at 6%, costing slightly more for the adversary and resulting in only a slight improvement in classifier degradation over C4.5/J48. RF dropped to 0.69 Precision and 0.61 Recall at 7% of labels flipped. These results are depicted in Fig. 3.

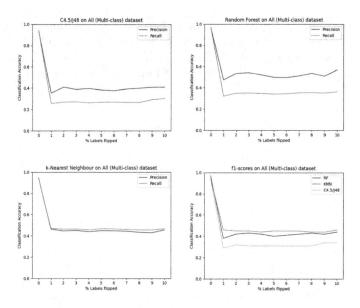

Fig. 3. Classification degradation on the Malware dataset

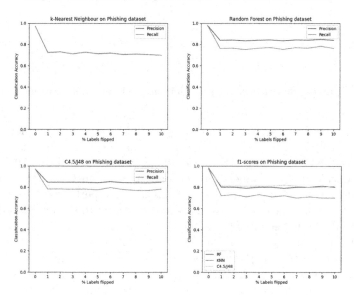

Fig. 4. Classification degradation on the Phishing dataset

The results of experimental activity on the phishing (illustrated in Fig. 4) showed similar degradation between the decision-tree classifiers, whereas the Precision and Recall of KNN was significantly more degraded. Both scores for KNN followed each other almost identically on every percentage step up to

10% with the optimal degradation observed at 3% of labels flipped, resulting in
0.71 for both metrics. RF was most efficiently degraded at 3% of labels flipped
resulting in 0.83 Precision and 0.75 Recall. At 5% of labels flipped, C4.5/J48 was
slightly less degraded than RF showing 0.84 and 0.77 for Precision and Recall
respectively.

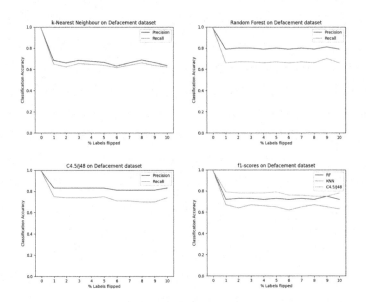

Fig. 5. Classification degradation on the Defacement dataset

All three classifiers performed with some variation on the defacement dataset
(depicted in Fig. 5) with KNN showing the greatest degradation at 6% of labels
flipped with 0.63 Precision and 0.61 Recall. RF was degraded to 0.79 Precision
and 0.66 Recall at 4% of labels flipped, and training on C4.5/J48 resulted in
0.81 and 0.70 at 8%. On this dataset the classification performance of C4.5/J48
degraded the least which is interesting when compared to the previous datasets
where both decision-tree models showed similar performance.

The spam dataset yielded an unexpected result (see Fig. 6) in the form of
what appeared to be exceptional resilience to label contamination, especially
from C4.5/J48 which held Precision and Recall scores of greater than 0.95 up
until 49% of labels flipped. RF and KNN showed similar robustness up until
around 45% of labels flipped and thereafter performance was seen to taper off
sharply and at a matching gradient. Due to the distinctive nature of the results
from this dataset, the percentage steps for flipped labels were adjusted to give
a better view of the point where classification performance dropped off. Instead
of a window of 1–10% steps were set at 35%, 45% then every 2% until 55%
and thereafter at 65% and 75%. This gives a more specific view of the point at
which degradation occurred and better illustrates the rate at which performance
dropped.

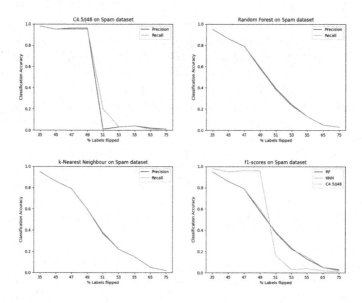

Fig. 6. Classification degradation on the Spam dataset

5   Discussion

The significant degradation observed in the majority of the datasets above is congruent with the detrimental effect of label noise on classifiers observed in the literature. In the specific case of the multi-class dataset, this may be attributable to the increased complexity of the task the classifier was directed to perform. While in the multi-class dataset each category of malicious URL shared the same number of features, in single-class form the datasets contained a varying number of features. This may have impacted the variation in degradation observed when contrasting their performance after having been trained on contaminated data.

As a measurement, Precision was affected by the number of false positives, in other words the number of malicious URLs erroneously classified as benign, while Recall was affected by false negatives, or the number of benign URLs classified as malicious. A low Recall score is least desirable as it indicates bad URLs being misclassified as good, which would have a cascading effect in a real-world scenario. Taking a closer look at the two decision-tree classifiers, RF and C4.5/J48, it can be observed that in all datasets the Precision score is visibly higher than the Recall score, indicating that these algorithms were more susceptible to incorrectly classifying malicious URLs as benign. Bearing in mind that during the process of poisoning the datasets equal percentages of benign and malicious labels had their labels flipped, this difference in Precision and Recall is not due to an imbalance in one label having more poisoned samples than the other. As a result, the overall accuracy of these classifiers is degraded further than it otherwise might have been had robustness in Recall been greater.

With regard to KNN, both metrics show generally very similar scores with the exception being the Malware dataset. This dataset has 9 features, the second lowest number with only Spam using fewer features, which may be the cause of this difference in scores as the algorithm appears to learn better with more descriptive data. The Phishing and Defacement datasets, which use 13 and 12 features respectively, resulted in much closer Precision and Recall scores on this algorithm and perhaps support the assertion that more features make KNN slightly more congruent in the way it classifies true positives and false negatives. However, in all single-class datasets the decision-tree classifiers still outperformed KNN in terms of overall robustness. In the multi-class dataset they appear to be less robust though, and it can be seen by the f1-score of KNN performing marginally better than RF. This is likely due to the fragility of decision-tree classifiers when presented with a more complex classification task, in this case a multi-class dataset.

The results seen on the Spam dataset may have been caused by several factors. Of all the single-class datasets Spam contained the fewest features, possibly leading to a lack of descriptiveness and distorting results. By contrast, the scores resulting from classification using RF on the Spam label in the multi-class dataset at 1% of labels flipped are 0.35 Precision and 0.02 Recall, perhaps indicating that the greater number of features contained in this dataset give a more realistic indication of robustness. Overall, the results presented here show that an attacker with knowledge of chosen models and access to training data, can cause highly destructive effects through even slight perturbations. This was evident for the multi-class dataset as well as all but one of the single-class datasets even at only 1% of labels flipped. If the attacker is able to flip more labels, in this case up to 10%, it has been shown that further deterioration in classification performance can be achieved.

The results presented here echo the need to employ security by design and default in ML classifiers. This is at no time truer than when the adversary might have knowledge of the model used and access to the training and test data. One approach to defending against contaminated labels is to augment or improve classifiers themselves, giving rise to variations on classic models. These are referred to as robust classifiers as they are designed with robustness to adversarial noise in mind [17]. Seen to be popular as a defence technique for Neural Network-based classifiers, often using image-based datasets, adversarial training involves crafting adversarial examples in training and/or testing data with the aim of having the model learn to tell the difference between the two. It has been noted though that even after training a model with adversarial examples the resulting classifier can still be vulnerable to adversarial samples crafted for it [18] There are also various means of performing label sanitisation, the aim of which is to identify samples which appear to be adversarial and either remove them or correct their labels [16].

6   Conclusions and Future Work

ML has become necessary in all aspects of the modern society and at the same time the primary target for malicious parties. A widely-used technique for baselining the robustness of a model to label contamination, is label flipping up to a set percentage threshold of labels in a training set. We demonstrated degradation the effect of random label flipping on the accuracy of three classifiers and associated data in a white-box scenario. These results indicated a need for mitigation against poisoning and thus a need of defensive techniques.

As future work, we aim to perform the same label flipping attack in different datasets and classifiers of the literature to observe their performance. Additionally we plan to investigate the effects of defensive measures against adversarial label contamination. The choice of attack complexity would determine which defensive measures would be appropriate and potentially most efficient for the defender.

Acknowledgments. This work has been partly supported by the University of Piraeus Research Center.

References

1. Kintis, P., et al.: Hiding in plain sight: a longitudinal study of combosquatting abuse. In: Proceedings of the 2017 ACM SIGSAC Conference on Computer and Communications Security, pp. 569–586. ACM (2017)
2. Antonakakis, M., Perdisci, R., Dagon, D., Lee, W., Feamster, N.: Building a dynamic reputation system for DNS. In: USENIX Security Symposium, pp. 273–290 (2010)
3. Christou, O., Pitropakis, N., Papadopoulos, P., McKeown, S., Buchanan, W.J.: Phishing URL detection through top-level domain analysis: a descriptive approach. arXiv preprint arXiv:2005.06599 (2020)
4. Pitropakis, N., Panaousis, E., Giannetsos, T., Anastasiadis, E., Loukas, G.: A taxonomy and survey of attacks against machine learning. Comput. Sci. Rev. **34**, 100199 (2019)
5. Mamun, M.S.I., Rathore, M.A., Lashkari, A.H., Stakhanova, N., Ghorbani, A.A.: Detecting malicious URLs using lexical analysis. In: Chen, J., Piuri, V., Su, C., Yung, M. (eds.) NSS 2016. LNCS, vol. 9955, pp. 467–482. Springer, Cham (2016). https://doi.org/10.1007/978-3-319-46298-1_30
6. Xin, Y., et al.: Machine learning and deep learning methods for cybersecurity. IEEE Access **6**, 35365–35381 (2018)
7. Pattewar, T., Mali, C., Kshire, S., Sadarao, M., Salunkhe, J., Shah, M.A.: Malicious short URLs detection: A survey (2019)
8. Michie, D., Spiegelhalter, D.J., Taylor, C.C.: Machine learning, neural and statistical classification (1994)
9. Demontis, A., Biggio, B., Fumera, G., Giacinto, G., Roli, F.: Infinity-norm support vector machines against adversarial label contamination. In: 1st Italian Conference on Cybersecurity, ITASEC 2017, vol. 1816, pp. 106–115. CEUR-WS (2017)
10. Zhao, M., An, B., Gao, W., Zhang, T.: Efficient label contamination attacks against black-box learning models. IJCA **I**, 3945–3951 (2017)

11. Biggio, B., Roli, F.: Wild patterns: ten years after the rise of adversarial machine learning. Pattern Recogn. **84**, 317–331 (2018)
12. Xuan, C., Nguyen, H., Nikolaevich, T.: Malicious URL detection based on machine learning. Int. J. Adv. Comput. Sci. Appl. **11**(1), 148–153 (2020)
13. Andrade, R.O., Ortiz-Garcés, I., Cazares, M.: Cybersecurity attacks on smart home during Covid-19 pandemic. In: 2020 Fourth World Conference on Smart Trends in Systems, Security and Sustainability (WorldS4), pp. 398–404. IEEE (2020)
14. Pranggono, B., Arabo, A.: Covid-19 pandemic cybersecurity issues. Internet Technol. Lett. **4**(2), e247 (2021)
15. Ford, V., Siraj, A.: Applications of machine learning in cyber security. In: Proceedings of the 27th International Conference on Computer Applications in Industry and Engineering., vol. 118. IEEE Xplore, Kota Kinabalu (2014)
16. Xiao, H., Biggio, B., Nelson, B., Xiao, H., Eckert, C., Roli, F.: Support vector machines under adversarial label contamination. Neurocomputing **160**, 53–62 (2015)
17. Zhou, X., Ding, P.L.K., Li, B.: Improving robustness of random forest under label noise. In: 2019 IEEE Winter Conference on Applications of Computer Vision (WACV), pp. 950–958. IEEE (2019)
18. Hein, M., Andriushchenko, M.: Formal guarantees on the robustness of a classifier against adversarial manipulation. arXiv preprint arXiv:1705.08475 (2017)

Neither Good nor Bad: A Large-Scale Empirical Analysis of HTTP Security Response Headers

Georgios Karopoulos[1]([✉]) [ID], Dimitris Geneiatakis[2] [ID],
and Georgios Kambourakis[1] [ID]

[1] European Commission, Joint Research Centre (JRC),
Via E. Fermi 2749, 21027 Ispra, Italy
{georgios.karopoulos,georgios.kampourakis}@ec.europa.eu
[2] European Commission, Directorate-General for Informatics,
1000 Bruxelles/Brussel, Belgium
dimitrios.geneiatakis@ec.europa.eu

Abstract. HTTP security-focused response headers can be of great aid to web applications towards augmenting their overall security level. That is, if set at the server side, these headers define whether certain security countermeasures are in place for protecting end-users. By utilising the curated Tranco list, this work conducts a wide-scale internet measurement that provides timely answers to the following questions: (a) How the adoption of these headers is developing over time?, (b) What is the penetration ratio of each key header in the community?, (c) Are there any differences in the support of these headers between diverse major browsers and platforms?, (d) Does the version of a browser (outdated vs. new) affects the support rate per key header?, and (e) Is the status of a header (active vs. deprecated) reflected to its support rate by web servers? Setting aside the use of the more robust Tranco corpus, to our knowledge, with reference to the literature, the contributions regarding the third and fifth questions are novel, while for the rest an updated, up-to-the-minute view of the state of play is provided. Amongst others, the results reveal that the support of headers is somewhat related to the browser version, the penetration ratio of all headers is less than 17% across all platforms, outdated browser versions may be better supported in terms of headers, while deprecated headers still enjoy wide implementation.

Keywords: HTTP · Response headers · Web application security · Internet measurement · Network security

1 Introduction

Web application (app) security is of paramount importance to businesses as well as to individuals, given that the World Wide Web (WWW) is one of the most

© Springer Nature Switzerland AG 2021
S. Fischer-Hübner et al. (Eds.): TrustBus 2021, LNCS 12927, pp. 83–95, 2021.
https://doi.org/10.1007/978-3-030-86586-3_6

popular Internet services. According to a report from a leading global content delivery network (CDN) and cloud security provider [6], assaults on web apps rose by 800% in the first half of 2020 compared to the same period in 2019. To provide web apps with a uniform and generic way of defending against such attacks, the concept of HTTP security headers seems to be highly relevant.

Apart from recent elevated web app attack statistics, the present study was further motivated by the fact that well-known OWASP Top 10 Application Security Risks [12] such as sensitive data exposure, security misconfiguration, and cross-site scripting (XSS) can be straightforwardly prevented by the deployment of HTTP security headers. Notably, in the XSS case, this approach protects users against execution of malicious code that appears to belong to trusted origins, subversion of the intended structure of documents, exfiltration of sensitive user information and unauthorised actions on behalf of victims. Simply put, HTTP security headers can be used for minimising the attack surface on the end-user's side. Furthermore, the multitude of platforms used nowadays to access the WWW, including PCs, mobile phones, and game consoles, increases the diversity of web browsers. On the one hand, this may affect the way browsers choose to enforce the actions suggested by the HTTP security headers, while on the other, certain browsers may be treated differently by web servers when it comes to HTTP headers.

As detailed in Sect. 3, although the topic of HTTP security headers has been already addressed in the literature to some extent [4, 18], this work contributes a fresh view of the state of play, specifically focusing on a triad of matters: (a) It reports on the HTTP security headers adoption by web servers; this not only offers an updated snapshot of the penetration of these headers to the community, but also draws an over time view of the developments in this ecosystem when seen jointly with the related work, (b) it examines how the browser type and version influence the enforcement of such headers, and (c) investigates whether HTTP services and browsers keep up with the latest security best practices. To this end, using the curated Tranco list, we query the top one million (1M) websites with the purpose of instigating a HTTP response header analysis. HTTP requests have been send though a custom-made web crawler and the response headers received were stored in a database.

Overall, our results are comparable to other relevant works and demonstrate that higher-ranked websites implement HTTP security headers much more often. Interestingly, with reference to data from past studies, it seems that the usage of HTTP security headers from websites follows an increasing trend over time; nonetheless, generally, the usage of headers is low, namely below 17% for the considered headers. A paradox which was also observed is that the browser and the platform used affect the HTTP security header usage, while it was surprising to discover that older browsers receive responses with HTTP security headers more frequently. Another striking outcome is that deprecated headers show a high support rate even though backward compatibility cannot justify this choice.

The rest of the paper is structured as follows. The next section provides background details on HTTP functionality and succinctly reviews major HTTP security headers. The related work is addressed in Sect. 3. Section 4 presents the scanning infrastructure, the conducted experiments, and the results. Section 5 discusses our findings, while the last section concludes.

2   Background

In the WWW setting, a web browser acts as the client that visits a website hosted on a computer, which has the role of the server. This exchange is initiated by the client by sending an HTTP request message to the server, who returns back an HTTP response message containing the requested content, say, HTML files. Together with the request, a User-Agent string is sent, which identifies the client software, i.e., the web browser. The User-Agent is then examined by the server to determine the capabilities and limitations of the client and send back an appropriate response.

Among others, the response message includes response header fields, which indicate to the client how to handle the response or pass additional information. There are diverse categories of response headers that depend on their functionality, including a category dedicated to security. Comprised mainly of metadata, HTTP security headers are an additional security layer that instruct the client how to process the received response for possibly mitigating attacks and security vulnerabilities. In this work, we study 6 of the most important security-related headers; their selection is based on current adoption rates as well as what is used in related work on the same topic. The selected headers are described below, while more details are provided in [13].

X-Frame-Options (XFO) does not allow a user agent to render a page in a frame, like <frame>, <iframe>, <embed> or <object>. This header is used against clickjacking attacks by ensuring that no transparent or opaque layers, which lead to malicious domains, appear on top of legitimate buttons or links.

X-Content-Type-Options (XCTO) forces the user agent to use the Multipurpose Internet Mail Extensions (MIME) types advertised in the Content-Type headers. This disables MIME sniffing used by some browsers to identify the content of websites, which is a practice that could lead to XSS attacks.

HTTP Strict-Transport-Security (HSTS) requests a client to access the web site using HTTPS. This basically forces the session to be carried out under the protection of a Transport Layer Security (TLS) tunnel and also blocks TLS-Stripping attacks.

Content-Security-Policy (CSP) indicates what kind of resources the user agent can load in the page carrying this header. Typically, policies specify server origins and script endpoints. This header is a measure against assaults like Cross-Site Scripting (XSS) and data injection attacks used for data theft, site defacement, and malware distribution.

X-XSS-Protection (XXP) instructs the client to stop loading the page if a reflected XSS attack is detected. This way, the execution in the client software of inline scripts inserted by an attacker can be avoided. The use of this header is deprecated by contemporary browsers and implementations should rely on CSP instead.

Referrer-Policy controls the information contained in the Referrer header. Using this header, a site can protect against the security risks related to the Referrer header.

3   Related Work

This section reviews research works devoted to general security measures taken at the server side for protecting the end-user. It also embraces contributions capitalising on HTTP response headers for safeguarding against attacks at the client side. Works focusing on other service types, such as email [7,19] are out of the scope of this paper.

Generic Security Measures: The first work that studies the overall status of the so-called declarative security is [17]. The authors concentrated mainly on the HTTP security headers that are supported by different web servers; their analysis considered the top 1K Alexa web sites. More recently, Buchanan *et al.* [4] explored HTTP response headers with emphasis on CSP, HSTS, XFO, and Public-Key-Pins, which enables the (obsolete) HTTP Public Key Pinning (HPKP) security feature. They demonstrated that only a few sites take into account the implementation of these measures in their provided services. The work in [18] conducted a thorough study paying attention on the developments of web client security since the late 90's; they observed a steady adoption of easy to deploy security mechanisms, including XFO. In the same direction, Lavrenovs *et al.* [9] delivered a more extended analysis considering HSTS, CSP, XXP, XFO, Set-Cookie, and XCTO response headers for the top 1M Alexa web sites. Moreover, Mendoza *et al.* [11] elaborated on implementation inconsistencies observed between mobile and desktop browsers, showing how such flaws can be manipulated for mounting well-known attacks. The Mozilla HTTP Observatory run the latest analysis of the Alexa top 1M sites in April 2019 [3]. Mozilla checks whether the appropriate HTTP headers are in use or not but also if they are being used correctly; this justifies the low numbers observed. The work by Scott Helme covers a period of 5 years, where the last scan was on March 2020 [15]. Initially, this "Top 1 Million Analysis" of websites was based on Alexa, but the last 2 reports used the Tranco list [10] for reliability reasons.

Secure Transport Communication: Transport layer security is basically enforced by means of HSTS and Public-Key-Pins. The authors in [8] contributed an empirical study on both these headers, which revealed that developers and administrators did not use the provided features properly. Petrov *et al.* [14] demonstrated several misconfigurations that an attacker may attempt to exploit to penetrate the system, while the authors in [2] investigated the diffusion of different countermeasures related to HTTPS, including the HSTS and Public-Key-Pins headers. The authors in [1] explored HTTPS security inconsistencies under a cross-regional prism. That is, they scanned the 250K most visited domains on the Internet using clients located at five diverse geographic regions. They exhibited that the client region does influence the security provisions, and HTTPS variances at the application layer (e.g., URLs and HTTP headers) are higher than those at the transport layer (e.g., selected TLS version, ciphersuite, and certificate).

Client-Side Injection Attacks: Weissbacher *et al.* [20] are among the very first to examine the adoption of CSP for protecting clients against injection attacks, while Somé *et al.* [16], demonstrated security micsonfigurations due to CSP and Same Origin Policy (SOP) conflicts. In the same context, Calzavara *et al.* [5] examined the XFO and CSP enforcement on diverse browsers, exhibiting implementation inconsistencies that expose end-users to clickjacking attacks.

4   Experimental Evaluation

4.1   Testbed

We have built a network scanning testbed to collect the HTTP(S) responses from the top 1M websites. This infrastructure comprises two Virtual Machines (VMs); VM1 has a 2×2.10 GHz CPU, 4 GB RAM and runs Windows Server 2012 64-bit, while VM2 has a 4×2.60 GHz CPU, 16 GB RAM and is based on Windows Server 2016 64-bit. We used NetBeans v8.1 for the development of a custom scanner in Java, and the results were saved in a MySQL v5.7.30 database. Both VMs performed network scanning operations, which were performed in the period Dec. 2020 to Jan. 2021.

The list of top 1M websites was obtained from the Tranco list [10], dated 16 Nov. 2020[1]. Tranco is the result of the aggregation of three well-known lists, namely Alexa, Cisco Umbrella, and Majestic. The reasons of selecting Tranco instead of one of the other lists is that the latter disagree on the popularity of each domain, the ranking changes significantly from day to day, and they are open to manipulation by malicious perpetrators. For each domain, four requests were made: http://domain, https://domain, http://www.domain and https://www.domain, while redirections were enabled.

Our software scanned the top 1M websites utilising diverse user agents from different platforms, namely desktop, mobile, and game console; the whole list was scanned once with each user agent. The selection of user agents was based on their popularity by statcounter.com. A quartet of desktop browsers were employed, namely Chrome v84, Chrome (old) v63, Edge v84 and Firefox v78. The mobile browsers selected were Chrome v84, Safari v604, and Samsung Internet v10. Finally, a PlayStation 4 Browser v5.55 was chosen as a representative browser from a game console. The user agent strings were acquired from WhatIsMyBrowser.com.

The HTTP security response headers considered were XFO, XCTO, HSTS, XXP, CSP, and Referrer-Policy. Although the XXP has been deprecated by modern browsers and it is recommended to use CSP instead [13], we chose to include it in our study to check if and to what degree a deprecated header is supported. It is also worth noting that this header is assumed to provide protection to older web browsers that do not support CSP, even though nowadays such browser versions are considered to be severely outdated.

---

[1] Available at https://tranco-list.eu/list/5QWN.

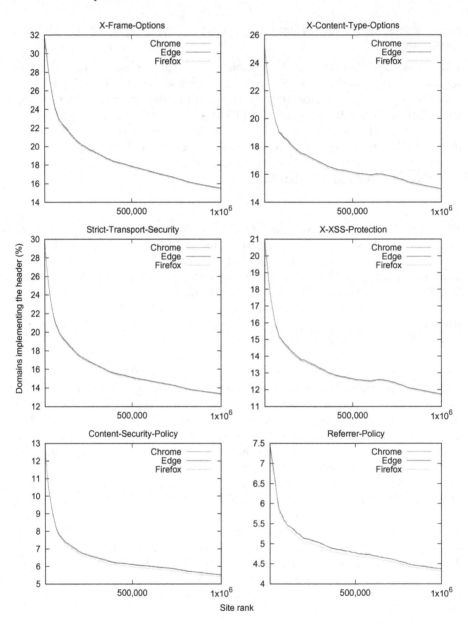

Fig. 1. Usage of HTTP security headers in top 1M websites using desktop Chrome, Edge, and Firefox browsers

4.2   Results

The first set of experiments considered the most popular desktop browsers, namely Chrome, Edge, and Firefox; a comparison among them is shown in Fig. 1. For juxtaposition reasons, we have used the same representation as in [9], where each

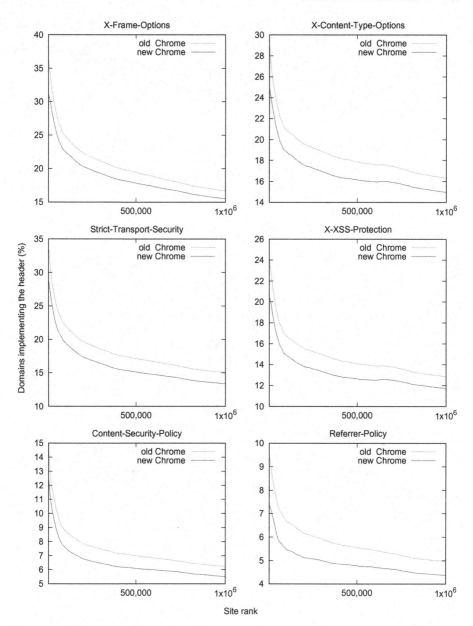

Fig. 2. Usage of HTTP security headers in top 1M websites using an old (2017) and a new (2020) desktop version of Chrome browser

graph depicts one of the above mentioned 6 HTTP security headers and the percentage of the top 1M domains that send it back in their HTTP responses. The graphs are ordered from top left to bottom right according to the support rate per header. The domains are ordered according to their rank in the Tranco list.

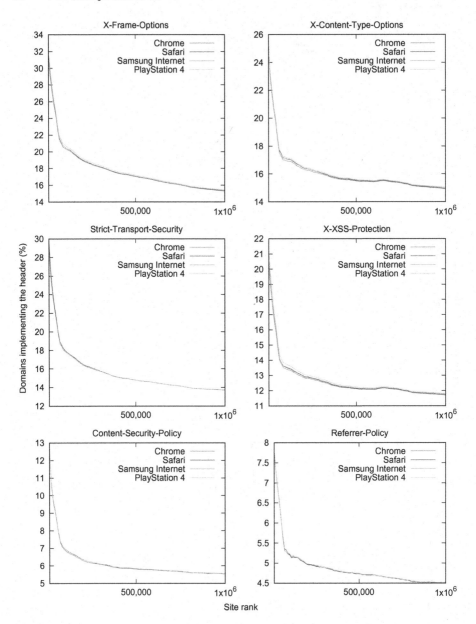

Fig. 3. Usage of HTTP security headers in top 1M websites using mobile and console browsers

Table 1. HTTP header support (%) of top 1M websites per browser (highest values in boldface)

Platform	Browser	XFO	XCTO	HSTS	XXP	CSP	Referrer-policy
Desktop	Chrome	15.50	14.95	13.36	11.71	5.51	4.37
	Chrome (old)	**16.68**	**16.31**	**15.05**	**12.85**	**6.23**	**4.97**
	Edge	15.53	14.96	13.38	11.73	5.52	4.38
	Firefox	15.44	14.89	13.30	11.66	5.41	4.33
Mobile	Chrome	15.30	14.93	13.71	11.70	5.53	4.50
	Safari	15.32	14.95	13.72	11.71	5.54	4.50
	Samsung	15.38	15.00	13.73	11.77	5.56	4.51
Console	PlayStation 4	15.44	15.03	13.74	11.80	5.54	4.52

In the next set of experiments, we utilised two different versions of the Chrome desktop browser: an old one released in 2017 and a new one released in 2020. A comparison between the two versions of Chrome is shown in Fig. 2.

The last series of experiments concerns three mobile browsers and one used in a video-game console: Chrome, Safari, Samsung Internet, and PlayStation 4 browser. The support of these browsers on HTTP security response headers is shown in Fig. 3.

Table 1 provides a comparison among all utilised user agents. For each agent, the percentage of the top 1M websites supporting each HTTP header is presented. A detailed comparison and discussion of the results is given in the next section.

5   Discussion

Catholic Overview: Considering the results presented in the previous section, it can be argued that the support of HTTP headers is affected by the browser used. Simply put, the service responds back to the corresponding browser based on its type and version. With reference to Table 1 and considering all the results, it seems that the top 1M websites tend to offer HTTP security response headers more frequently to the old version of Chrome, followed by the browser used by Playstation 4 in all headers but two. Although the difference in the numbers is small, and in some cases may be considered insignificant, the browser with the less frequent offers is the desktop version of Firefox. Another observation is that the platform (desktop, mobile or console) does not seem to play a noteworthy role; the first and the last places in header support belong to desktop browser versions and the rest of the positions are mixed. As is presented in Table 1, in any given header, the differences in the number of websites offering the header to each browser range from 0.01% or 100 websites (CSP in mobile Chrome and mobile Safari) to 2.2% or 22K websites (HSTS in the old desktop Chrome and desktop Firefox).

An overall observation is that the top ranked websites are implementing more frequently the HTTP security headers; this is in line with the related work [9]. Also, for all platforms, the order of the headers in terms of support is XFO, XCTO, HSTS, XXP, CSP, and finally Referrer-Policy. In this point, we should mention that the reason we chose not to consider other security headers, like the ones used in [13], is due to their low adoption rate. Indeed, according to our experiments (not presented in the results above) and considering the top 1M domains, for desktop Chrome these rates range from 0.01% for Cross-Origin-Opener-Policy and Cross-Origin-Resource-Policy to 1.79% for X-Permitted-Cross-Domain-Policies. While for Expect-CT the rate reaches 11.72%, this header will soon be deprecated (June 2021). Roughly the same rates were observed for mobile Chrome, apart from Expect-CT that was 11.31%.

Desktop Browsers: The three desktop browsers have comparable results, although it can be seen in Fig. 1 that Chrome and Edge are better supported than Firefox. This, once more, reveals that the responses of websites regarding HTTP security headers at some degree are related to the browser creating the request. Taking into account the total results for the top 1M websites, it is a constant observation that Edge is better supported. Chrome is very close with an insignificant difference ranging from 0.01 to 0.03%; the biggest difference is in the XFO header with 0.03%, which is 300 out of the 1M websites. The difference between Firefox and Edge is larger, ranging from 0.05 to 0.11%; the latter percentage is observed in the CSP header and equals 1.1K websites.

Old vs. New Desktop Browser: The comparison between an old and a latest version of the same desktop browser (Chrome) revealed that the old version is better supported in terms of HTTP security headers. This is evident by the graphs in Fig. 2; the situation in more detail is as follows. Taking into account the overall results for the top 1M websites, the differences of websites offering the same HTTP header between the old and the new browser version range from 0.6% or 6K websites (for Referrer-Policy) to 1.69% or 16.9K websites (in the case of HSTS). Although not presented in the results, we performed a similar set of experiments with an old and new version of Firefox for verifying our findings. The outcome was analogous to the results we present for Chrome, that is, range from 0.66% or 6.6K websites (for Referrer-Policy) to 1.79% or 17.9K websites (in the case of HSTS). Interestingly, these results are inline with recent related work [11].

Mobile and Console Browsers: The observation that the user agent plays a role in the HTTP headers that are offered by web servers is further supported by the trends observed in the graphs of Fig. 3. In desktop browsers there seems to be a more gradual drop in the usage of HTTP headers by websites; in mobile and console browsers there is a more steep drop up to the first roughly 100K websites.

Obsolete Headers: From Table 1, it becomes obvious that while the XXP header has been deprecated (e.g., Edge retired the XSS Filter in July 2018[2], Google did the same in 2019 from Chrome 78 onward[3], and Firefox just ignores this header[4]), the support for this protection is still high, ranking fourth among all the 6 examined headers. Put simply, it is pointless for a web server to advertise support for this header, while all major browsers will ignore it. This discrepancy can be also translated to a reluctance or even disregard from the administrators or the security teams managing web servers to keep up with the latest developments in the field. Although one can argue that backing this header serves as a means to protect older browsers that do not support CSP, such browsers are outdated long ago (for example, Edge supports CSP since 2016, Chrome since 2013 and Firefox since 2013) and their use would probably entail more serious security issues than the lack of CSP support.

Comparison with Related Work: Table 2 includes the results of the latest scans of related works from Sect. 3 regarding the usage of HTTP security response headers. Note that we only included contributions that report results for the top 1M websites. It is worth mentioning that works that focus on misconfigurations or inconsistencies on the deployment of HTTP security headers do not report numbers related to implemented security response headers for the examined dataset. Also, different sources for the top 1M websites are used: all works from 2014 to 2019 use the Alexa list, while [15] employs the Tranco list in his latest scans; we also use the Tranco list for reliability reasons. The effect of using a different list is demonstrated in related work results: between 2019 and 2020 there is a small drop because the last two works utilise the Tranco list. In the works utilising the Alexa list there is an incremental trend from 2014 to 2019; a similar tendency is witnessed from 2020 to 2021 for Tranco. This shows that our results are consistent with those in related work. Overall, these trends show that the global adoption rate of HTTP security headers is constantly growing over time.

As user agent for the results of Table 2 we used the Chrome desktop browser since it is the most popular by far, according to statcounter.com. The same user agent, although in an older version, is used by [4]. In [8,9,20] Firefox is used; [14] does not provide information on which user agent was used, although this does have an impact on HTTP header support as it is evident by our results.

---

[2] https://blogs.windows.com/windows-insider/2018/07/25/announcing-windows-10-insider-preview-build-17723-and-build-18204/.

[3] https://developers.google.com/web/updates/2019/09/chrome-78-deps-rems.

[4] https://developer.mozilla.org/en-US/docs/Web/HTTP/Headers/X-XSS-Protection.

Table 2. Related work on usage of HTTP security headers in the top 1M websites (highest values in boldface, §Approximate results calculated from data in [9], *a site is counted only if the header is implemented correctly)

	HTTP security headers support (%)							
Publication year	2014	2015	2017	2018	2018	2019	2020	2021
Header	Work							
	[20]	[8]	[4]	[9]§	[14]	[3]	[15]	Our
XFO	2.5	–	9.3	11.44	–	**16.42**	13.49	15.5
XCTO	4.4	–	8	11.2	–	**16.27**	12.71	14.95
HSTS	0.2	0.51	4	7	4.12	8.68	11.28	**13.36**
XXP	4.5	–	–	8.4	–	**11.74**	9.98	11.71
CSP	0.08	–	1.3	1.6	–	0.03*	4.54	**5.5**
Referrer-Policy	–	–	–	0.16	–	–	3.9	**4.37**

6   Conclusions

HTTP security response headers are a cornerstone of contemporary website security, helping to mitigate most common assaults and security vulnerabilities. This work aspires to offer a timely, full-blown, large-scale empirical analysis on the adoption of these headers in the community. Verifying the results of the previous literature in the topic, we demonstrate that while significant, the penetration of these headers in the WWW is evolving at a rather slow pace. On the other hand, we pinpoint on several novel results, showing that the support of headers slightly varies based on the browser and the platform used, but the endorsement per examined header across all browsers and platforms remain uniform, and the patronage for deprecated headers are unjustifiably high. Another unexpected result is that very obsolete browser versions enjoy significantly higher percentages of header support vis-à-vis newest versions. As a future work, we intend to cross-check these results with reported security incidents against major websites to investigate the actual effectiveness of HTTP security headers in counteracting real-life attacks.

References

1. Alashwali, E.S., Szalachowski, P., Martin, A.: Exploring HTTPS security inconsistencies: a cross-regional perspective. Comput. Secur. **97**, 101975 (2020)
2. Amann, J., Gasser, O., Scheitle, Q., Brent, L., Carle, G., Holz, R.: Mission accomplished? HTTPS security after diginotar. In: Proceedings of the 2017 Internet Measurement Conference, IMC 2017, New York, NY, USA, pp. 325–340. ACM, November 2017
3. April King: Analysis of the Alexa Top 1M sites, April 2019. https://pokeinthe.io
4. Buchanan, W.J., Helme, S., Woodward, A.: Analysis of the adoption of security headers in HTTP. IET Inf. Secur. **12**(2), 118–126 (2017). Publisher: IET Digital Library

5. Calzavara, S., Roth, S., Rabitti, A., Backes, M., Stock, B.: A Tale of Two Headers: A Formal Analysis of Inconsistent Click-Jacking Protection on the Web, pp. 683–697 (2020)
6. CDNetworks: State of the Web Security, H1 (2020). https://www.cdnetworks.com
7. Kambourakis, G., Draper-Gil, G., Sanchez, I.: What email servers can tell to Johnny: an empirical study of provider-to-provider email security. IEEE Access **8**, 130066–130081 (2020). https://doi.org/10.1109/ACCESS.2020.3009122
8. Kranch, M., Bonneau, J.: Upgrading HTTPS in mid-air: an empirical study of strict transport security and key pinning. In: Proceedings 2015 Network and Distributed System Security Symposium, Internet Society, San Diego, CA (2015)
9. Lavrenovs, A., Melón, F.J.R.: HTTP security headers analysis of top one million websites. In: 2018 10th International Conference on Cyber Conflict (CyCon), pp. 345–370, May 2018
10. Le Pochat, V., Van Goethem, T., Tajalizadehkhoob, S., Korczyński, M., Joosen, W.: Tranco: a research-oriented top sites ranking hardened against manipulation. In: Proceedings of the 26th Annual Network and Distributed System Security Symposium, NDSS 2019, February 2019
11. Mendoza, A., Chinprutthiwong, P., Gu, G.: Uncovering HTTP header inconsistencies and the impact on desktop/mobile websites. In: Proceedings of the 2018 World Wide Web Conference, WWW 2018, Republic and Canton of Geneva, CHE, pp. 247–256. April 2018
12. OWASP: OWASP Top Ten. https://owasp.org/www-project-top-ten/
13. OWASP: Secure Headers Project. https://owasp.org/www-project-secure-headers/
14. Petrov, I., et al.: Measuring the Rapid Growth of HSTS and HPKP Deployments p. 7
15. Scott Helme: Top 1 Million Analysis - March 2020. https://scotthelme.co.uk/top-1-million-analysis-march-2020/
16. Some, D.F., Bielova, N., Rezk, T.: On the Content Security Policy Violations due to the Same-Origin Policy. In: Proceedings of the 26th International Conference on World Wide Web, WWW 2017, Republic and Canton of Geneva, CHE, April 2017
17. Sood, A.K., Enbody, R.J.: The Conundrum of Declarative Security HTTP Response Headers: Lessons Learned, p. 6
18. Stock, B., Johns, M., Steffens, M., Backes, M.: How the Web Tangled Itself: Uncovering the History of Client-Side Web (In)Security, pp. 971–987 (2017)
19. Wang, C.C., Chen, S.Y.: Using header session messages to anti-spamming. Comput. Secur. **26**(5), 381–390 (2007). https://doi.org/10.1016/j.cose.2006.12.012
20. Weissbacher, M., Lauinger, T., Robertson, W.: Why Is CSP failing? Trends and challenges in CSP adoption. In: Stavrou, A., Bos, H., Portokalidis, G. (eds.) RAID 2014. LNCS, vol. 8688, pp. 212–233. Springer, Cham (2014). https://doi.org/10.1007/978-3-319-11379-1_11

Data Protection and Privacy Controls

Components and Architecture
for the Implementation
of Technology-Driven Employee
Data Protection

Florian Dehling[1], Denis Feth[2]([✉])[iD], Svenja Polst[2], Bianca Steffes[3],
and Jan Tolsdorf[1][iD]

[1] Bonn-Rhein-Sieg University of Applied Sciences, Sankt Augustin, Germany
{florian.dehling,jan.tolsdorf}@h-brs.de
[2] Fraunhofer IESE, Kaiserslautern, Germany
{denis.feth,svenja.polst}@iese.fraunhofer.de
[3] Saarland University, Saarbrücken, Germany
bianca.steffes@uni-saarland.de

Abstract. Many approaches, methods, and tools aim to support companies in the implementation of the European General Data Protection Regulation (GDPR). However, their focus is primarily on protecting the privacy of external data subjects (e.g., customers), whereas the privacy of employees tends to be disregarded. In order to provide employees with more transparency and stronger self-determination, we identified eighteen components that may be implemented depending on a company's needs and objectives. We present these components and discuss how they contribute to data protection and fulfill employers' legal obligations. In addition, we present an implementation concept that enables an incremental rollout of the components and a choice between different technical integration depths that best fit a company's business context.

Keywords: GDPR · Employee data protection · Privacy engineering

1 Introduction

The GDPR strengthens the right to privacy of all people living in the European Union by requiring controllers, processors, and data subjects to protect privacy collaboratively. To this end, the GDPR obliges controllers and processors to implement adequate organizational and technical measures to minimize the risk of potential privacy violations, as well as provide means to exercise the rights to transparency and intervention. As this is a non-trivial task, different approaches, methods, and tools have been proposed to help companies implement the GDPR in practice.

Previous work, however, mainly focuses on privacy frameworks and tools that aim at the customer sphere [3,7,8,13], but ignores the employee sphere. Yet this

© Springer Nature Switzerland AG 2021
S. Fischer-Hübner et al. (Eds.): TrustBus 2021, LNCS 12927, pp. 99–111, 2021.
https://doi.org/10.1007/978-3-030-86586-3_7

sphere is equally important, as the ongoing digitization also leads to significantly larger amounts of employee personal data being processed by employers. Whenever employers (i.e., data controllers, data processors) process personal data of their employees (i.e., data subjects), there is a debate about the possible consequences and challenges for the protection of employees' right to privacy [2,6,10]. In Germany, employees' privacy is protected by the right to informational self-determination, which warrants each individual transparency and personal control over the collection, use, and disclosure of personal data. The concept of informational self-determination was originally coined in the context of a German constitutional decision and is supposed to protect the fundamental values of human dignity and self-development [10]. Nowadays, the concept is very present in European and Canadian societies [6], and has also paved the way for our modern understanding of privacy, which is also reflected by the Privacy by Design (PbD) paradigm [4] in the development of contemporary information systems. With the advent of the GDPR, there are now also legally binding rules to provide tools that empower employees to exercise the right to informational self-determination at work. For employers, the GDPR resulted in new obligations and challenges for employee data protection. In practice, however, employers still lack tooling that support their employees in living up to their rights. To sum it up, the problem we address with this paper is that employees do not have the possibility to live up to their rights regarding transparency and self-determination with respect to their personal data.

We address this problem by developing eighteen components and a reference architecture that serve companies as a foundation to implement technology-driven employee data protection and enable employees to exercise the right to informational self-determination. The different components can be assessed, implemented, and deployed according to the companies' needs. Moreover, the reference architecture enables the efficient implementation of the various components and gives companies the flexibility of a gradual introduction of the components.

Companies benefit from implementing the proposed components, whether in their entirety or just selectively, by meeting legal obligations regarding employee data protection. The components also add significant value to employee privacy and increase mutual trust between employees and employers.

2   Components of Employee Data Protection

In this section we present the eighteen components grouped into six topics labeled A - F. We reference the corresponding component IDs in the following sections. To design the components and architecture we proceeded as follows: We conducted eleven workshops (cf. [9]) and an extensive interview study [11,12] with a heterogeneous sample of stakeholders (i.e., employees of different professions, works council, managers), as well as four interviews with experts in the field of introducing new technologies in organizations. In addition, we analyzed the GDPR and the German Federal Data Protection Act (BDSG) to extract the legal requirements regarding employee data protection rights. From these elicitation activities, we derived requirements regarding transparency, self-determination, usage (e.g. usability), data usage, and the introduction of privacy tools in organizations [5,9]. Based on the gathered requirements, we structured the different factors necessary to achieve the goals of informational self-determination in the workplace and finally designed the components. We discussed and fine-tuned them in several expert groups, comprising experts from the fields of law, requirements engineering, human-computer interaction, and usable privacy.

2.1   A – Information

The first thematic area concerns employees' right to transparency and deals with the various aspects of informing employees about personal data processing. It allows employees to become aware of whether and which personal data are processed, but also about how, when, and by whom the data are processed.

A.1 Knowledge Base. Legal and company regulations describe the details of employee personal data processing. Making the underlying processes transparent to employees is an important step toward informational self-determination. The *Knowledge Base* compiles all regulations and internal documents at a single place, and enriches the content with easy-to-understand summaries and notes.

A.2 Data Overview. Employees are rarely aware of the exact personal data processed by their employer. Component *A.1* provides such information, yet it is spread over many documents. To improve transparency, employees should be provided with a structured overview of the different categories of personal data being processed.

A.3 Usage Permissions. To further increase transparency, employees should be informed who has the permission to process which personal data for a specific purpose. In order to reduce the time required to manually extract this information from the documents provided by component *A.1*, *Usage Permission* presents the information in a structured way. This should also include links to the respective legal regulations.

A.4 Usage History. Components *A.1* and *A.3* only inform of potential data processing activities. *Usage History*, however, provides employees with an overview of actual data processing activities.

2.2   B – Self-determination

The previous thematic area *Information* solely aimed at increasing transparency. Transparency is the basis for this thematic area: *Self-determination* aims at enabling employees to express their individual data protection needs.

B.1 Privacy Settings. Privacy settings are already known from modern applications. Using them in a centralized manner, they can provide individual privacy policies which can be applied to corporate processes.

B.2 Consent Management. Data processors (e.g., HR department) have to ask for consent when using specific data. *Consent Management* provides data processors with templates to ensure that all legally mandatory information is included in consent requests. At the same time, the component lets employees manage consent requests they receive and reminds them to respond on time.

B.3 Objection to the Processing. Even if the right to object to data processing by the employer is restricted in most cases, there should be a low-threshold offer to do so in possible circumstances. Depending on the technical infrastructure, suspicious processing may also be automatically detected and reported to employees for their approval or objection.

B.4 Data Portability. If technically feasible and legally permissible, employees should receive a copy of their personal data in machine-readable form upon request, so that they can take them with them to another employer.

2.3   C – Enforcement

This thematic area concerns the enforcement of data protection policies as defined by corporate regulations, by consent requests, and in privacy settings.

C.1 Access and Usage Control. Access and usage control should be implemented in order to regulate data processing both before and after access to personal data has been granted. The policies for access and data usage control should reflect the permissions that employees expressed in their privacy settings and their consent. These policies could be enforced manually by a system administrator or automatically, provided a company is willing and able to provide the respective interfaces.

C.2 Anonymization. Anonymization is a typical mean to respect data subject rights. In corporate processes, anonymization of employee data could be reached by applying k-anonymity or differential privacy.

C.3 Data Correction and Deletion. In a corporate context, there are legally required minimum retention periods for certain data, which restricts the employees' rights. However, for some data, employees may request deletion or correction using a digital component instead of consulting an organizational unit (e.g., the HR department).

2.4   D – Data Query and Access

In contrast to the previous thematic areas, *Data Query and Access* deals with the view of employees responsible for the processing of personal data (e.g., HR department). These employees are in need of means to access and use personal data securely and in compliance with the laws and regulations. *Data Query and Access* allows them to collect the personal data required for a certain task, asking for consent if required, and keeping an overview over all requested data and their own permissions for using them.

2.5   E – Communication

This thematic area focuses on communication between employer and employee, which is crucial for building trust. Thereby, it addresses the socio-technical characteristics of corporate data protection.

E.1 Company-Wide News. To communicate data-privacy related news to all employees, corresponding senders (i.e., data protection officer, workers council) can use this component to inform about, e.g., threats or new regulations to be followed.

E.2 Individual Notifications. The components presented so far mostly trigger events that require actions of a certain person (e.g., consent) or group of persons (e.g., processing police) who should be informed by corresponding notifications.

E.3 Reporting of (Potential) Incidents. Employees may wish to draw attention to potential data protection incidents or problems in a simple manner. This component aims at reporting suspicious cases as conveniently as possible. Depending on the technical infrastructure, more advanced versions of this component may automatically inform employees about suspicious cases, which they then just need to confirm or dismiss.

2.6   F – Support

Even though data protection tools should be easy and intuitive to use and require little explanation, data protection is a complex subject. *Support* addresses this issue by supporting employees in privacy-related topics as well as topics related to the correct use of data protection tools.

F.1 Handbooks and Tutorials. The complexity of data protection (tools) requires appropriate documentation. Employees should be provided with manuals and tutorials that take their perspective and speak their language to support them in operating the tools.

F.2 Contact Persons. When it comes to data protection, unexpected issues arise time and again that are not covered by component F.1. Therefore, contact persons should be named for the various topics related to data protection (tools).

F.3 Search and Filter Functions. The combination of all the aforementioned components amounts to a considerable body of privacy-related information. Finding and extracting the relevant piece of information is not an easy task; therefore, employees should be supported by appropriate search and filter functions.

3   Legal Review of the Components

In this section, we discuss legal aspects of the components and show how they address the various employee data protection obligations under GDPR and BDSG. To this end, we divided the components into three groups to be discussed independently. Figure 1 provides an overview of our analysis. Unless otherwise indicated, all the following articles are taken from the GDPR.

3.1   Storage Limitation, Integrity, and Confidentiality

The first cluster of components focuses on fulfilling the principles of *storage limitation* and *integrity and confidentiality* (Art. 5(1)(e) and (f)) by means of the technical and organizational measures provided by Art. 25(1).

Component *C.2* is very specific in this regard, as the anonymization of personal data provides strong protection, even going beyond the minimum requirements for technical measures described in the GDPR. In particular, employers may use *C.2* to anonymize employee personal data for which no identification are required (anymore) (Art. 11) and thus strengthen the principle of storage limitation. This also reliefs employers of their obligations related to Art. 15–20.

Confidentiality on the other hand is ensured by the enforcement of the permission system using *C.1*, which provides monitoring and enforcement of a specific code of conduct as described in Art. 40 and 41.

In parts, this code of conduct can be enforced by the components in thematic area *D*. This thematic area helps processors accessing required employee personal data in accordance with the legal and company regulations and thus in accordance with the permission system provided by *C.1*. Therefore, those components can be seen as a technical measure in the sense of Art. 25(1) that assist employers in enforcing other components. Furthermore, these components uphold the principle of *data minimization* (Art. 5(1)(c)), since – depending on the implementation – they may only provide access to a distinct set of data types (e.g., photos, names) for specific purposes.

3.2   Transparency

The second group of components strives to aid in achieving the ideals of Art. 12 and thus focuses on the principle of *transparency* (Art. 5(1)(a)).

To a large extent, thematic area *A* corresponds to this principle. The detailed information provided by *A.3* aims to promote employees' understanding of the processing and satisfies parts of the obligations described in Art. 15(1)(c). The remaining components provide information about the categories of data being processed (Art. 15(1)(b)). Yet, these components help to meet other regulations: *A.1* and *A.4* represent a possible (partial) implementation of Art. 30 by providing records about all authorized data processing activities and a usage history, thus documenting all actually performed processing activities. Additionally, *A.1* contains the information to be provided when personal data are collected or obtained (Art. 13–14).

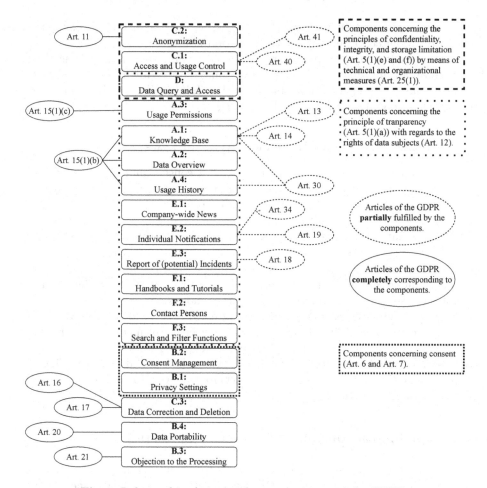

Fig. 1. Relationships between the components and the GDPR.

Similar to thematic area A, component D also promotes transparency by providing processors with a detailed overview of all relevant information regarding the rules that apply to the processing of the requested personal data. By offering only lawful processing steps and thus guiding processors in their actions, thematic area D effectively reduces unlawful processing due to human error and ignorance, complementing the principle of *lawfulness* (Art. 5(1)(a)).

Moreover, components $E.1$ and $E.2$ strive to enhance the communication between employer, processors, and employees. Processors may use individual notifications to inform others about the rectification or erasure of personal data or the restriction of processing (Art. 19). Moreover, these components provide an easy way for processors to communicate personal data breaches to employees, as demanded in Art. 34. Component $E.3$, in comparison, aides employees in exercising their right to restriction of processing (Art. 18), but also supports employers in detecting possible data protection flaws.

The components of thematic area F support employees in exercising their right to obtain information about their personal data. While these components focus on meeting user requirements rather than fulfilling legal obligations, they nevertheless contribute to Art. 12(1) and (2).

3.3 Consent and Direct Implementations of Laws

The remaining components concern the topic of consent and the direct fulfillment of specific regulations. Regarding the former, *B.2* focuses on giving or refusing consent in terms of Art. 6(1)(a) in everyday working life, whereas *B.1* lets employees decide in advance which (future) requests may be granted or denied automatically. We would like to point out that German legislation makes use of Art. 88 and provides more specific rules for consent in the employment context in § 26(2) BDSG. It puts strong emphasis on the imbalance of power between employees and their superiors. However, this aspect of the German law is not addressed by any component, since the whole set of subtleties of human interactions and relationships cannot be addressed in a technical manner.

Three components directly and comprehensively implement specific regulations: *B.3* strictly mirrors Art. 21 and implements the right to object to processing based on Art. 6(1)(e) or (f); *B.4* provides data portability according to Art. 20; and *C.3* implements the rights declared in Art. 16 (rectification) and Art. 17 (erasure) respectively.

4   Implementation and Integration Concept

The components presented in Sect. 2 comprise the essential functions for exercising the right to privacy at work, yet their specification is technology-agnostic. We designed a reference architecture to guide companies in assembling and implementing the various components in a comprehensive manner. It is designed to enable a gradual roll-out of the different components and to choose between different technical integration depths. In the following, we present the architecture and its integration concept.

4.1 Architecture

The chosen architecture results from breaking down the topics of employee data protection into functional domains. Within each domain, one or more services implement the domain's tasks and provide the functionality for implementing the different components. Overall, we differentiate between three core domains, whose functions are provided by seven services and a supplementary domain. An overview of the architecture is provided in Fig. 2.

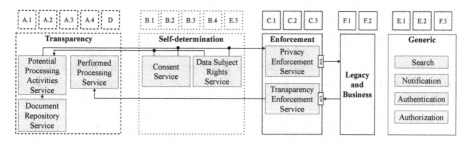

Fig. 2. Architecture for implementing components of employee data protection.

Transparency. The *transparency* domain focuses on the comprehensive documentation and preparation of information about personal data processing. It is characterized by a holistic underlying data model, which clearly describes the information related to employee data protection. Consequently, the *transparency* domain forms an important basis for all other privacy-specific domains, either for providing or consolidating information. The domain functions are provided by three services: The *Document Repository Service (DRS)* compiles all documents and regulations related to employee data protection. It provides the foundation for a knowledge base *(A.1)*. Furthermore, it forms the basis for the *Potential Processing Activities Service (PPAS)*, which transforms the unstructured "knowledge" held by the *DRS* into the structured data model of the transparency domain. The *PPAS* provides a repository of detailed records of potential processing activities that can be legitimately performed by employers and employees. To keep the repository up-to date, the service consumes and updates its records upon actions in the *self-determination* domain, but also forwards its information about rules for data processing to the *enforcement* domain. The *PPAS* can provide an overview on data and permissions *(A.2, A.3)*; it can also provide information about rules and obligations to processors *(D)*. Next to the *PPAS*, the *Performed Processing Service (PPS)* also supports the same holistic data model, yet the *PPS* keeps a log of performed processing activities only. To keep the log up-to-date, the *PPS* logs processing activities detected by the *enforcement* domain. Moreover, the *PPS* complements the implementation of component *D*, which also acts as a manual logging interface if employees use *D* in order to ask for consent and keep track of their processing activities. Consequently, *PPS* also enables a usage history *(A.4)*.

Self-determination. The *self-determination* domain aggregates functions that allow data subjects to obtain information about and intervene on the processing of their personal data. This is enabled by two services: The *Consent Service (CS)* acts as a gateway between *PPAS* and *PPS* by implementing explicit and implicit consent or refusal of data processing *(B.1, B.2)*. Additionally, the *Data Subject Rights Service (DSRS)* provides an interface for employees to exercise their rights regarding the current and future processing of personal data *(B.3,*

B.4, E.3). Both the *CS* and *DSRS* forward changes (e.g., new consent, data deletion requests) to the *PPAS* and the *enforcement* domain.

Enforcement. The *enforcement* domain is concerned with the technical integration of privacy-enhancing technologies into legacy systems that serve a company's core business. It provides the following services: The *Transparency Enforcement Service (TES)* technically enforces the logging of all personal data processing activities and forwards this information to the *PPS*. Thus, it complements the objectives of providing a usage history (*A.4*). The *Privacy Enforcement Service (PES)* technically enforces the application of data protection rules, including strict access and usage control as well as anonymization (*C.1–C.3*).

Generic. The *generic* domain contains services useful for implementing employee data protection, yet it is not characterized by any content strictly related to data protection. Its services implement internal (company-wide) communication and assistance (*E.1, E.2, F.3*).

4.2   Integration Concept

The full implementation and deployment of the proposed components and architecture requires significant efforts, which may deter organizations from adopting the proposed concept altogether. We address this concern with a gradual implementation approach that rewards employers for their efforts from the outset in terms of legally compliant implementation of employee data protection. More specifically, our approach divides the realization of the architecture into four stages of expansion, with lower stages designed to prepare organizations for more comprehensive implementation in later stages. Also, our approach takes particular account of the dependencies between the domains and services described in Sect. 4.1. The different stages are:

1. Static information – The first stage implements the *transparency* domain and satisfies employees' right to information. It lets employees learn about legal regulations and company-specific data processing rules. At this stage, the architecture fully supports all components of thematic area *A*, and it provides limited support for thematic areas *D*, *E*, and *F*. However, the first stage entails significant initial effort and constant manual work to keep the information up to date.
2. Digitized employee data protection – The second expansion stage provides for the integration of the *self-determination* domain and the components of thematic area *B*. As a result, all employee rights have been implemented. Stage 2 benefits from the data models already elaborated in stage 1 and reduces manual efforts for maintenance, since updates of information in the *transparency* domain can be triggered automatically.
3. Data usage – The third expansion stage contributes to the transparency of data processing and makes compliance with rules visible. Yet it requires partial technical integration into existing systems regarding read-permissions.

In return, the manual effort required for components $A.2$–$A.4$ and D is reduced significantly.

4. Technical enforcement – The fourth stage completes the expansion of both the *enforcement* domain and thematic area C. It requires a comprehensive role permissions system based on the *transparency* and *self-determination* domains as well as full technical integration of the *enforcement* domain into the existing infrastructure. In return, the architecture lets companies monitor data processing activities, providing evidence of legally compliant processing. It also enforces authorization and supports the use of privacy enhancing technologies to enforce the various data protection objectives.

The gradual implementation of the architecture according to the four stages gives companies the opportunity to also gradually adapt their internal processes and, if desired, to continue using the existing technical infrastructure. More specifically, the architecture minimizes dependencies on existing systems and creates technical dependencies only for the enforcement of rules. Here, the lower two stages can be operated completely independently of the existing corporate application environment, yet they offer the greatest added value for legally compliant implementation of employee data protection. Nevertheless, higher stages require a consolidation of the semantics of employee data protection and the semantics of legacy systems. In particular, the functionality provided by the enforcement domain establishes semantic dependencies that also require legacy systems to be adapted in stage 4. If legacy systems are retained, appropriate anti-corruption layers (ACLs) may bridge the semantic gap in order not to jeopardize the core business and to maintain the flexibility of the corporate application landscape. Since the actual data remains in the original applications, the effort is reduced to describing the metadata and rules.

5 Related Work

Since the introduction of the GDPR, the number of commercial privacy management tools has increased from 44 in 2017 to 343 in 2020, according to the 2020 Privacy Tech Vendor Report [1]. However, the focus of such tools is primarily on customer privacy and/or GDPR compliance in general, rather than on employee privacy. Existing solutions and research primarily strive to enable new or existing business models (e.g., based on Big Data) under the GDPR [3,7,8,13]. In particular, the *DEFeND* platform [8] and the *SPECIAL-K* reference architecture [3] present a similar scope, but with a different focus. The *DEFeND* platform constitutes a collection of multiple different state-of-the-art software tools, services, and frameworks, and divides them into five main components to assist controllers, processors, data subjects, and authorities in managing different use cases related to the GDPR. *SPECIAL-K*, on the other hand, provides privacy enhanced processing in the context of Big Data. The platform's focus is the use of semantic web technologies to enable compliance checking and verification of processing activities for data subjects. Our approach partially overlaps with existing work, but differs significantly in its focus on employee privacy. In particular, our framework extends the *DEFeND* platform with a concrete specification of components that take into account employees' extensive transparency but limited self-determination rights, as well as the corporate context. Moreover, our approach provides more comprehensive components and services beyond the use cases covered by *SPECIAL-K*. Nevertheless, our generic approach would allow the use of the *SPECIAL-K* architecture as an underlying layer for the *enforcement* domain, if desired.

6   Conclusion and Discussion

The implementation of employee data protection is not a trivial matter, but needs to consider several legal regulations as well as employee and employer requirements. We thus developed a flexible solution consisting of eighteen components based on a legal and stakeholder requirements. Our component-oriented approach acknowledges the fact that the deployment of technology-driven employee data protection must be tailored to each specific organization. The proposed architecture and gradual integration concept serves companies as recommendations for how to organize and implement the various components. Finally, our integration concept takes into account that employees' right for individual intervention in the processing of their personal data by employers is limited and that employees have limited knowledge of their data protection rights and a lack of awareness of data processing in the workplace [11,12].

In order to evaluate the feasibility and acceptance of our components and architecture, we developed a high-fidelity UI prototype that implements most of the presented components in the form of a privacy dashboard. We evaluated it with experts in the field of usable privacy, as well as with potential users. To further evaluate the components under real-world conditions, we have also integrated some of the components into the intranet of a small company in Germany. From the preliminary evaluation results, we are confident that the components and architecture add value to transparency and self-determination in the workplace, and that both employees and employers benefit from our solution. Nevertheless, we recognize that our current evaluations are few in number and cannot be generalized to organizations of other sizes and structures. We therefore plan to conduct further and more extensive evaluations in the future and intend to derive implementation guidelines from the feedback collected. Furthermore, we want to focus more on the integration into the existing corporate infrastructure (especially the connection to existing systems) and conduct studies on the development effort in order to better estimate the cost-benefit ratio.

Acknowledgements. This research is supported by the German Ministry of Education and Research in the context of the project "TrUSD" (grant no. 16KIS0898, 16KIS0899, and 16KIS0900). The responsibility for the content lies with the authors.

References

1. 2020 Privacy Tech Vendor Report. Report 4.2, iapp (2020)
2. Bhave, D.P., Teo, L.H., Dalal, R.S.: Privacy at work: a review and a research agenda for a contested terrain. J. Manag. **46**(1), 127–164 (2020)
3. Bonatti, P.A., Kirrane, S.: Big data and analytics in the age of the GDPR. In: 2019 IEEE International Congress on Big Data (BigDataCongress), pp. 7–16 (2019)
4. Domingo-Ferrer, J., et al.: European Union, European Network and Information Security Agency: Privacy and data protection by design - from policy to engineering. ENISA (2014)
5. Feth, D., Schmitt, H.: Requirement and quality models for privacy dashboards. In: 2020 IEEE 7th International Workshop on Evolving Security Privacy Requirements Engineering (ESPRE), pp. 1–6 (2020)
6. Krebs, D., Doctor, J.: "Privacy by design": nice-to-have or a necessary principle of data protection law? J. Intellect. Prop. Inf. Technol. E-Commer. Law (JIPITEC) **4**(1), 2–20 (2013)
7. Matzutt, R., et al.: myneData: towards a trusted and user-controlled ecosystem for sharing personal data. In: 47. Jahrestagung der Gesellschaft für Informatik (Informatik), pp. 1073–1084 (2017)
8. Piras, L., et al.: DEFeND architecture: a privacy by design platform for GDPR compliance. In: Gritzalis, S., Weippl, E.R., Katsikas, S.K., Anderst-Kotsis, G., Tjoa, A.M., Khalil, I. (eds.) TrustBus 2019. LNCS, vol. 11711, pp. 78–93. Springer, Cham (2019). https://doi.org/10.1007/978-3-030-27813-7_6
9. Polst, S., Kelbert, P., Feth, D.: Company privacy dashboards: employee needs and requirements. In: Moallem, A. (ed.) HCII 2019. LNCS, vol. 11594, pp. 429–440. Springer, Cham (2019). https://doi.org/10.1007/978-3-030-22351-9_29
10. Rouvroy, A., Poullet, Y.: The right to informational self-determination and the value of self-development: reassessing the importance of privacy for democracy. In: Gutwirth, S., Poullet, Y., De Hert,, P., de Terwangne, C., Nouwt, S. (eds.) Reinventing Data Protection?, pp. 45–76, Springer, Netherlands (2009). https://doi.org/10.1007/978-1-4020-9498-9_2
11. Tolsdorf, J., Dehling, F.: In our employer we trust: mental models of office workers' privacy perceptions. In: Bernhard, M., et al. (eds.) FC 2020. LNCS, vol. 12063, pp. 122–136. Springer, Cham (2020). https://doi.org/10.1007/978-3-030-54455-3_9
12. Tolsdorf, J., Dehling, F., Reinhardt, D., Lo Iacono, L.: Exploring mental models of informational self-determination of office workers in Germany. In: Proceedings on Privacy Enhancing Technologies (PoPETs) 2021, vol. 3, pp. 5–27 (2021)
13. Westphal, P., Fernandez, J.D., Kirrane, S., David, J., Lehmann, J.: SPIRIT: a semantic transparency and compliance stack. In: CEUR Workshop Proceedings, pp. 1–4 (2018)

Towards an Information Privacy and Personal Data Protection Competency Model for Citizens

Aggeliki Tsohou$^{(\boxtimes)}$

Ionian University, Corfu, Greece
atsohou@ionio.gr

Abstract. This paper aims to investigate the competencies that citizens should hold to protect own information privacy and personal data. Based on conceptual analysis, this study examines theoretical frameworks on competency models (e.g., the Iceberg Competency Model) and proposes a roadmap for developing the first information privacy competency model in the information systems literature. The study conducts a systematic analysis to reveal the lack of information privacy competency models in the literature and derive any reported information privacy competencies. In sequence, synthesizes the results into a preliminary information privacy competency model comprising attributes that citizens should hold to be competent to protect own information privacy and personal data, including knowledge, skills, attitudes, values, etc. The results of this work can be valuable for information privacy researchers, online service providers, policy makers and educators.

Keywords: Competencies · Information privacy · Competency model

1 Introduction

Citizens engage daily in the utilization of digital services, including browsing, e-shopping, social media interactions, etc. Technological advancements offer valuable services and increase citizens' options for entertainment, social interaction, and ways to implement personal and professional tasks. However, they also enable important privacy risks stemming from the processing of disclosed personal data. Researchers have raised several concerns on the capacity of citizens to manage this complex context, and particularly they notice the existence of information asymmetry between citizens and providers and the lack of citizens' privacy awareness. This is supported by the Special Eurobarometer survey according to which a significant percentage of citizens has not even heard of the GDPR (32% of respondents), while many others have heard of GDPR, but they do not know what it is (31% of respondents). Some citizens have heard about their personal data protection rights (31% of respondents), but only 10% of them has exercised any of those rights. Approximately 40% of the survey respondents are not concerned that they have partial or no control over the information they provide online. Finally, many citizens (34%) do not get informed about the conditions of processing for the data they provide online before they do so. Several works [2–7] have been dedicated in studying relevant topics, such as the factors influencing privacy awareness, personal data self-disclosure, privacy concerns, privacy protective intention, etc.

Overall, it is implied that citizens using online services are expected to exhibit protective behaviors over their privacy, by knowing the regulation, understanding the technical context of services, being active in reading privacy policies and changing privacy settings, and installing safeguards to be protected from privacy risks. Organization theories examine all these aspects as relevant to the concept of competencies. Although researchers have investigated the individual aspects of privacy behaviors separately, literature lacks studies in the information privacy competency domain, which can bind the multiple perspectives and findings and offer deeper insights on citizens privacy behaviors and how to motivate them. To bridge this gap, this paper investigates the following research question *"What are the competencies that a citizen should hold to protect own information privacy and personal data?"*. Following analysis of theoretical frameworks in the competency literature, a research roadmap for developing an information privacy competency model for citizens is proposed and a preliminary model is constructed based on conceptual analysis. This paper is the first, to the best of knowledge, to present an examination for an information privacy competency model for citizens. A competency model for information privacy can be valuable to policy makers, service providers and educators to implement interventions for preparing citizens who are competent to manage own privacy and personal data.

The paper is structured in five sections. Following this introduction, the theoretical background on competency models is presented. A roadmap of activities for developing a competency model is proposed in Sect. 3, and Sect. 4 presents the preliminary results of its application. Finally, Sect. 5 concludes the paper.

2   Theoretical Background

2.1   The Concept of Competency

The concept of competency has been studied in many disciplines, such as phychology, education, organizational management, human resources, and information systems (IS). Competency has been investigated mainly on the organization context and has been associated with the characteristics of an individual that lead to superior performance [9, 10]. Competency exceeds knowledge and commonly comprises three elements: knowledge, skills, and abilities/attitudes [11–14] that are necessary to solve a problem in a given context. Knowledge addresses content or technical information that is required to perform a task. It refers to a characteristic that activates the capacity to think. Skills refer to psychomotor processes manifested in behaviors, such as the selection of appropriate actions in a given situation. They refer to the characteristics related to the capacity to apply knowledge and fulfil a task. Abilities/attitudes refer to cognitive factors [10], that are not achieved through education, but instead are personality traits. Abilities/attitudes are related to the capacity of making knowledge and skills useful; to utilize knowledge and skill when needed.

Broader definitions of competency exist that comprise other characteristics, additionally to the three core ones. Lee [16] defines competency as knowledge, skills, abilities, behaviors and other characteristics that differentiate high from average performance. [9, 17] identify competencies as the knowledge, skills, traits, motives, and one's self-concept, which permit superior performance in a given domain.

2.2 Competency Models

A competency model is a descriptive tool that identifies the competencies needed to perform a role effectively in a given job [18]. In such models, competencies are often organized into a hierarchy or grouped into clusters. These models are commonly used in human resources management for employee hiring, training and performance evaluation. Although the different sectors develop own competency models, there are some generic ones that have been applied across many domains.

Boyatzis [9] provided a competency model for managers comprising six clusters of competencies: goal and action management, leadership, human resource management, directing subordinates, focusing on others and specialized knowledge. A competency is an underlying characteristic of the person which results in superior work performance, such as motives, traits, skills, self-image, social role or knowledge. [17] developed the Iceberg Model, based on which the elements of competency are represented as an iceberg which comprises a part that is visible on the top of the cold-water surface, and a part that is hidden underneath the water surface. Knowledge and skills tend to be visible and relatively surface characteristics of individuals, whereas traits and motives are deeper and more central to personality. Self-concept characteristics fall somewhere in between. Hidden and visible competencies play different roles in a given job. Hidden competencies are the behavioral competencies that drive an individual's performance in a job, whereas visible competencies tend to be the technical competencies required by employers. Another example is the Hudson 5 + 1 Competency Model, which was developed by a private organization, comprising five generic competency clusters and a technical or organization-specific cluster. The clusters of generic competencies are information management, task management, people management, interpersonal management, and personal management. The sixth cluster refers to the domain and organization-specific technical competencies.

2.3 Competency Models in Information Systems Literature

Limited competency models exist in the IS literature; most developed for IS professionals, such as software requirements' analysts or software developers. Few competency models have been developed for IS end-users. Even less models exist for citizens who use online services as part of their daily activities.

Starting with the competency models for IS professionals, Klendauer et al. [21] have developed a competency model for software requirements analysts. Their model comprises sixteen competencies that are critical for the role of software requirement analysts, including leading competencies, cooperation ones, competencies for persuading and influencing others, planning and organizing work and tasks, writing and reporting, as well as applying technical expertise. Additionally, they have examined the work situations and challenges that requirements analysts are frequently confronted with (e.g., software product scope being too broad, customers disagreeing among themselves about the system requirements), and elaborated further on competencies relevant to those situations and challenges. [13, 14] have developed a competency model for software developers who work in global settings. They have explored and revealed the soft competencies that are required, such as adaptability and cultural awareness, communication and collaboration competencies. Similarly, [22] have proposed a competency model for software developers comprising three main clusters of competencies, i.e., professional ones (e.g., software design skills), innovation ones (e.g., creativity, managing change) and social ones (e.g., affective characteristics).

Regarding competency models that have been developed for IS end-users, [23] have developed the Competency Model for "Industrie 4.0" Employees, emphasizing the competencies that employees should hold in the modern digitally transformed work environments which imply that job profiles should be outfitted with a wide range of competencies much broader than in previous eras. [19] have also developed a model for IS end-users titled "Competency Model for the Information Technology workers". They have adapted the Iceberg model and identified five clusters of competencies for IT architects, including skills (e.g., critical analysis and problem solving), knowledge (e.g., technical, contextual), self-concept (e.g., being visionary), traits (e.g., being open-minded) and motives (e.g., being passionate). Similarly, [24] have developed a competency model for IS endusers, comprising three main clusters of competencies: 1) cognitive and personal factors (e.g., understanding IS components and representations), 2) learning from IS environments (e.g., learning from training), and 3) behaviors (e.g., experimenting with IS). In the same scope, [25] have developed a competency model for information technology workers, with emphasis on the development for an IS curriculum. They have identified essential competency areas (e.g., cybersecurity, networks, system administration) and applied competency areas (e.g., applied networks, Internet of Things, data scalability), with a focus on how these can match an IS curriculum for higher education. Further, the European Union has developed a digital competency framework for citizens as future employees (i.e., DigComp 2.1). The model includes five areas of digital competencies: 1) information and data literacy (e.g., browsing, searching and filtering data, information and digital content), 2) communication and collaboration (e.g., managing digital identity), 3) digital content creation (e.g., copyright and licenses), 4) safety (e.g., protecting personal data), and 5) problem solving (e.g., solving technical problems).

Few competency models have been articulated for information security. [26] analyzed industrial challenges and priorities for cybersecurity professionals to reveal relevant competencies, such as personal effectiveness competencies (e.g., integrity, interpersonal skills), academic competencies (e.g., writing, critical and analytic thinking), workplace competencies (e.g., teamwork, creative thinking), and technical competencies (e.g., incident detection, risk management), functional competencies (e.g., threat investigation, operation and maintenance of security). [27] have analyzed the factors that influence end-users' information security policy compliance behavior and identified associated competencies for IS end-users to comply with such policies.

3   A RoadMap for Developing the Competency Model

3.1   Activities Involved in the Development of Competency Models

This section presents a methodology for developing an information privacy competency model for citizens, based on previous relevant works and the Iceberg Model as theoretical foundation. Given that for citizens the notion of performance is not as relevant as in a work context, the Iceberg Model was selected as it offers a broader and behavior-oriented (rather than performance-oriented) perspective. Next, we analyze the processes that relevant works have followed to develop competency models.

To develop the Competency Model for the information technology workers, [19] have conducted an exploratory analysis on the relevant work tasks. Sequentially, they collected qualitative data from workers and identified competencies that could be derived. They classified the derived competencies based on the Iceberg Model into skills and knowledge and into competencies relevant to self-concept, traits, and motives and they proposed interventions for attaining them. [22] followed a similar strategy to develop a competency model for software engineers. They proposed a competency model after attaining an understanding of the tasks that software engineers perform. Further, they empirically assessed the validity of the competency model with data from software development companies. [13, 14] explored the work processes that exist in global software development and also examined common situations and challenges that global software developers face. They map those situations and challenges in software development processes with proposed competencies. In following work, they offer suggestions for improving IS curriculums for cultivating global software development competences [15]. A similar approach was followed by [21] who developed a competency model for software requirements analysts. First, they identified the expertise that is required for software requirements' analysis and in sequence they performed an empirical investigation with interviews to gain deeper insights into the work situations that requirements analysts can be found. Using the results of both steps, they developed a proposed competency model. [10] studied an existing competency model for cybersecurity experts (i.e., the Department of Labor's Cybersecurity Industry Model) and indicate which competencies are top priority for cybersecurity professionals. [27] studied existing information security policy compliance theories to reveal the factors that affect such behavior. They conceptually derived competencies inductively from those factors and in sequence they examine professional competency models in various sectors to highlight that there is a gap between hiring processes and expectations from end-users. [24] developed their competency model based on the theoretical foundations of social cognitive theory and by applying the relevant theoretical constructs into the IS work tasks.

3.2   The Proposed RoadMap

Based on the relevant works, in the IS field, but also in other fields in which competency models are developed, the following roadmap of activities is proposed to articulate an information privacy and personal data competency model (Table 1).

Table 1. Activities for developing the competency model.

Activity	Description
Step 1: Identification of information privacy competency models	In this step a systematic literature review will be conducted with the purpose to identify existing information privacy competency models for either professionals or users/citizens. It includes searching in the scientific databases of Scopus, Science Direct, Google Scholar, and the digital libraries of Emerald, Springer Link, ACM Digital Library. Also, investigation in IS journals and conferences (i.e., basket of eight journals and AIS conferences), and domain specific journals and conferences, including Computers and Security, Journal of Information Privacy and Security, and IEEE Security & Privacy
Step 2: Specification of implied privacy competencies	This step will include broader analysis of literature to identify elements of competency (e.g., knowledge) that have been studied by researchers, without being identified as part of a competency model
Step 3: Synthesis of initial set of competencies	This step will result in the collection of competencies that are identified as scattered findings in the literature, thus finding that are not identified as part of a competency model
Step 4: Realization of an exploratory analysis of information privacy challenges and processes for citizens	This step will include reviewing of literature for the identification of the situations that citizens face while managing their personal data and the challenges and barriers that they face during their decisions and actions. Those challenges and barriers will be examined later with respect to potential lack of competences or the necessity for strengthening relevant competences
Step 5: Implementation of empirical investigation	An empirical analysis using qualitative research techniques will offer deeper insights on the personal data handling situations and challenges that citizens face (e.g., via interviews with citizens to understand the various situations and processes they follow, but also the obstacles that they are confronted with)

(*continued*)

Table 1. (*continued*)

Activity	Description
Step 6: Analysis of empirical data and synthesis of a competency model	The collected empirical data will be analyzed using qualitative coding techniques (e.g., grounded theory coding processes) and potentially using as theoretical foundation an existing competency model framework (e.g., the Iceberg model)
Step 7: Validation of the proposed competency model	Once the competency model is developed an empirical validation process will follow using quantitative methods (e.g., survey)

In this paper we present the results of the first three steps, thus, the analysis of literature on information privacy competency models and competences for citizens and the suggestion of a preliminary competency model.

4 Preliminary Results

4.1 Existing Information Privacy Competency Models for Citizens

A systematic literature review was conducted to identify existing information privacy competency models using the keywords "information privacy competency model", "information privacy competencies", "personal data protection competency model". Search was conducted in scientific databases and digital libraries (i.e., Scopus, Science Direct, Google Scholar, and the digital libraries of Emerald, Springer Link, ACM Digital Library), IS journals and conferences (i.e., basket of eight journals and AIS conferences), and domain specific journals and conferences (e.g., Computers and Security, Journal of Information Privacy and Security). This search has not produced any results, indicating that this is a highly under investigated domain for both citizens and IS professionals. In sequence, the scope of the literature sampling was broadened by including the keywords "competency model" AND "information privacy", "privacy" AND "competencies". Results referring to competencies of IS professionals were excluded and only articles referring to users/citizens were included. The results were limited, four papers match the search criteria, which are analyzed below. Finally, the search was further broadened to include any official reports from international organizations which resulted in the identification of one competency model.

[29] investigate citizens' competency regarding information self-disclosure, focusing on social media usage. They identify two competencies, namely knowledge about one's self-disclosure and metacognitive accuracy (i.e., if users can accurately judge the extent of their own disclosure-related knowledge). [30] specify five core competencies necessary for the use of mobile health care applications, the application of safeguards related to the use of those mobile applications. They also mention that citizens should hold competencies associated with reviewing privacy policies. [31] explore education that should be provided at the early childhood to prepare future digital citizens and

propose six clusters of competencies. Privacy and safety is one cluster, which includes how to protect online data, understand online tracking and be careful of online scams. [32] explore privacy training as a strategy for promoting good practices regarding online disclosure intention, emphasizing on the element of knowledge of privacy risks and the creation of privacy concerns. Finally, the International Digital Education Working Group [33] has published a personal data protection competency model for citizens, structured upon nine foundational principles. The nine foundational principles are: 1) understanding the concept of personal data is essential, 2) understanding own rights, 3) understanding the digital environment (technical aspect), 4) understanding the digital environment (financial aspect), 5) understanding personal data regulations and legislation, 6) understanding the controlled use of own personal data, 7) learning to exercise own rights, 8) learning safeguards to protect oneself online, and 9) having confidence and responsibility as a digital citizen.

4.2 Information Privacy Competencies Implied in the Literature

Even if researchers do not directly refer to competency models, there is significant body of studies addressing relevant topics, such as users' information privacy awareness, concerns, attitudes, etc. These words are analyzed below to offer insights for the information privacy competency model.

Several works explore the factors that affect information self-disclosure intention, including privacy concerns [2, 3], privacy value [3], self-presentation and enjoyment as motives [8], personality factors (e.g., extraversion, openness, self-esteem) and psychological states (e.g., loneliness) [2]. Further, several works identify determinant factors for information privacy protective behaviors, including privacy risk perception [4–7, 34, 35] and privacy awareness [3, 6, 7, 35, 36]. Additionally, as [42] reveal the intention to adopt privacy protective tools is influenced by users' values, such as freedom, self-control, personal dignity and fear-free living. Further, besides having privacy concerns and understanding the value of privacy which motivate privacy protective behaviors, research highlights that it is also important for users to have the capacity to act towards the protection of their privacy protection. This refers to their capacity to customize the privacy settings and to be familiar with privacy enhancing technologies [38, 39]. Research also indicates as a typical problem that the users do not read privacy policies, due to their length, complexity and technical language [40], thus indicating that citizens should be patient and passionate about their privacy to insist and overcome such obstacles.

Additionally, examining the personal data protection regulations, which are the backbone of the personal data protection context, one can identify several implied information privacy competences. For example, when citizen's consent is the legal basis for personal data processing, the citizen is requested to read and understand the terms that apply to the processing to provide informed consent (GDPR, Article 7). The citizen should also have knowledge of the right to withdraw consent at any time and should have the skills to exercise this right by using the means that the provider offers for this purpose. Further, Sect. 3 of the GDPR presents citizens' rights regarding personal data processing (e.g., the right for data portability) and the citizen should not only be knowledgeable about those rights, but should also have the skills to follow the processes that the providers offer for this purpose, such as to find the related online forms for requesting to exercise the relevant right. Completing such forms is not always straightforward and might require further reading from the part of the citizen. This indicates a personality trait of being persistent and active.

4.3   Information Privacy Competencies for Citizens: Initial Results

Using the above conceptual analysis, a preliminary competency model is developed using the scattered competencies that have been mentioned throughout the literature. Thus, the competencies identified as scattered elements in the literature are synthesized into a competency model presented in Table 2, organized following the Iceberg Model. Competencies that are visible are highlighted with light grey color, while competencies that are hidden are highlighted with darker grey color.

Table 2. A preliminary information privacy competency model for citizens

Element of the iceberg model	Element of the information privacy competency model	References
Knowledge	Knowledge about own self-disclosure (i.e., if citizens know which contents they disclose and to which audiences their contents are accessible)	[29]
	Knowledge of safeguards (i.e., knowing technical protection solutions and settings in online services and applications)	[30, 33]
	Knowledge of privacy risks (i.e., knowing various privacy risks including commercial exploitation of personal data, online tracking, etc.)	[32]
	Knowing own personal data rights (i.e., knowing what rights the individual holds as data subject)	[33]
	Knowing regulation and legislation (i.e., knowing the applicable regulation and legislation)	
Skills	Metacognitive accuracy (i.e., knowing and accurately judging the extent of their own self-disclosure)	[29]

(*continued*)

Table 2. (*continued*)

Element of the iceberg model	Element of the information privacy competency model	References
	Ability to install and customize safeguards (i.e., being able to apply solutions, such as password protection)	[30]
	Ability to read and understand privacy policies (i.e., being able to read and evaluate terms of service agreements and privacy policies)	[30]
	Ability to understand online tracking (i.e., understanding how individuals are tracked online)	[31]
	Ability to understand technological environments (i.e., understanding the hardware and technical infrastructure of information systems)	[33]
	Ability to exercise own rights (i.e., being able to exercise own rights by contacting the service in question and filing a complaint to a supervisory authority)	
	Ability to perceive risks (i.e., being able to identify different levels of risk)	[5, 4, 7, 34, 6, 35]
Social Role (Attitudes and Values)	Privacy concerns (i.e., having concerns about the ways that companies collect and use personal information)	[32, 3, 2]
	Privacy (i.e., believing that privacy is very important)	[3]
	Self-control on disclosure of personal data (i.e., managing own digital identity)	[33]
	Confidence (i.e., adopting a critical and ethical approach to navigate the digital environment with confidence and clarity and act accordingly	

(*continued*)

Table 2. (*continued*)

Element of the iceberg model	Element of the information privacy competency model	References
	Freedom (i.e., navigating freely on the Internet)	[42]
	Anonymity (i.e., navigating anonymously on the Internet)	
	Self-control (i.e., having control over personal information)	
	Personal dignity (i.e., having control on personal life)	
	Fear-free living (i.e., not to fear to browse on the Internet)	
Traits	Extraversion vs. introversion	[2]
	Openness vs. secretiveness	
Self-Image	Self-esteem (i.e., the evaluation of oneself)	[8]
Motives	Self-presentation (i.e., the way one presents oneself online)	[8]
	Responsibility (i.e., act responsible towards the privacy of others)	[33]

The proposed preliminary competency model can become the basis for future research that will include empirical investigation of the personal data protection situations and challenges, refinement of the model and finally, empirical validation by citizens.

5 Conclusions

This paper presents the first attempt in the IS literature, to the best of knowledge, on the information privacy and personal data competencies for citizens. The study was conducted conceptually by examining competency theories and frameworks from other disciplines and by identifying existing works in the IS literature which directly or indirectly relate to this topic. Based on this exploratory analysis, the paper presents a roadmap of activities to develop a competency model and demonstrates the results from the application of the initial steps towards the development of the model.

The contribution of the paper is both theoretical and practical. First, the systematic literature review reveals that information privacy and personal data competency models are missing from the IS body of knowledge, both for professionals and citizens. Such competency models are expected to benefit information privacy researchers who can find potential research avenues, online service providers who address citizens as users of their services, as well as policy makers and educators who conduct educational interventions for citizens.

Acknowledgements. This paper has received funding from the GSRT for the European Union's Horizon 2020 research and innovation programme under grant agreement No 787068.

References

1. Special Eurobarometer 487a, The General Data Protection Regulation. https://ec.europa.eu/commfrontoffice/publicopinionmobile/index.cfm/Survey/getSurveyDetail/surveyKy/2222
2. Abramova, O., Wagner, A., Krasnova, H., Buxmann P.: Understanding Self-Disclosure on Social Networking Sites - A Literature Review. AMCIS, Boston (2017)
3. Zlatolas, L., Welzer, T., Heričko, M., Hölbl, M.: Privacy antecedents for SNS self-disclosure: the case of Facebook. Comput. Hum. Behav. **45**, 158–167 (2015)
4. Ginosar, A., Ariel, Y.: An analytical framework for online privacy research: what is missing? Inf. Manag. **54**(2017), 948–957 (2017)
5. Chou, H., Liu, Y., Chou, C.: Privacy behavior profiles of underage Facebook users. Comput. Educ. **128**, 473–485 (2019)
6. Jozani, M., Ayaburi, E., Ko, M., Choo, K.: Privacy concerns and benefits of engagement with social media-enabled apps: a privacy calculus perspective. Comput. Hum. Behav. **107**, 106260 (2020)
7. Gerber, N., Gerber, P., Volkamer, M.: Explaining the privacy paradox: a systematic review of literature investigating privacy attitude and behavior. Comput. Secur. **77**, 226–261 (2018)
8. Chen, J.V., Widjaja, A.E., Yen, D.C.: Need for affiliation, need for popularity, self-esteem, and the moderating effect of big five personality traits affecting individuals' self-disclosure on Facebook. Int. J. Hum.-Comput. Interact. **31**(11), 815–831 (2015)
9. Boyatzis, R.E.: The Competent Manager: A Model for Effective Performance. Wiley, New York (1982)
10. Winterton, J.: Competences across Europe: highest common factor or lowest common denominator. J. Eur. Ind. Train. **33**(8/9), 618–670 (2009)
11. Tobias, L., Dietrich, A.: Identifying employee competencies in dynamic work domains: methodological considerations and a case study. J. Univ. Comput. Sci. **9**(12), 1500–1518 (2003)
12. Levy, P.E.: Industrial/Organizational Psychology, 2nd edn. Houghton Mifflin Company, Boston (2006)
13. Holtkamp, P., Jokinen, J.P., Pawlowski, M.Y.: Soft competency requirements in requirements engineering, software design, implementation, and testing. J. Syst. Softw. **101**, 136–146 (2015)
14. Holtkamp, P.: Competency requirements of global software development conceptualization, contextualization, and consequences. Ph.D. thesis, University of Jyvaskyla (2015)
15. Holtkamp, P., Lau, I., Pawlowski, J.M.: How software development competences change in global settings—an explorative study. J. Softw. Evol. Process. **27**, 50–72 (2015)
16. Lee, Y.-T.: Exploring high-performers' required competencies. Expert Syst. Appl. **37**(1), 434–439 (2010)
17. Spencer, L.M., Spencer, P.S.M.: Competence at Work: Models for Superior Performance. Wiley, Hoboken (1993)
18. Sampson, D., Fytros, D.: Competence models in technology-enhanced competence-based learning. In: Adelsberger, H.H., Kinshuk, J.M., Pawlowski, D.G., Sampson, (eds.) Handbook on Information Technologies for Education and Training, pp. 155–177. Springer, Heidelberg (2008). https://doi.org/10.1007/978-3-540-74155-8_9

19. Ho, S., Frampton, K.: A competency model for the information technology workforce: implications for training and selection. Commun. Assoc. Inf. Syst. **27**(5), 63–80 (2010)
20. Sydänmaanlakka, P.: Intelligent leadership and leadership competencies - developing a leadership framework for intelligent organizations. Ph.d. thesis (2003)
21. Klendauer, R., Berkovich, M., Gelvin, R., Leimeister, J., Krcmar, H.: Towards a competency model for requirements analysts. Inf. Syst. J. **22**(6), 475–503 (2012)
22. Moustroufas, E., Stamelos, I., Angelis, L.: Competency profiling for software engineers: literature review and a new model. In: PCI 2015: Proceedings of the 19th Panhellenic Conference on Informatics, pp. 235–240, October 2015
23. Prifti, L., Knigge, M., Kienegger, H., Krcmar, H.: A competency model for "industrie 4.0" employees. In: Leimeister, J.M., Brenner, W. (eds.) Proceedings der 13. Internationalen Tagung Wirtschaftsinformatik (WI 2017), St. Gallen, pp. 46–60 (2017)
24. Eschenbrenner, B., Nah, F.: Information systems user competency: a conceptual foundation. Commun. Assoc. Inf. Syst. **34**, 80 (2014)
25. Impagliazzo, J., Sabin, M., Alrumaih, H., Viola, B.: An information technology competency model and curriculum. In: 2016 IEEE Global Engineering Education Conference, Abu Dhabi, United Arab Emirates, pp. 892–895 (2016)
26. Whitman, M.: Industry priorities for cybersecurity competencies. In: Journal of the Colloquium for Information System Security Education (CISSE), 6th edn, no. 1 (2018)
27. Tsohou, A., Holtkamp, P.: Are users competent to comply with information security policies? An analysis of professional competence models. Inf. Technol. People **31**(5), 1047–1068 (2018)
28. Holtkamp, P., Pawlowski, J.M.: A competence-based view on the global software development process. J. Univ. Comput. Sci. **21**(11), 1385–1404 (2015)
29. Moll, R., Pieschl, S., Bromme, R.: Competent or clueless? Users' knowledge and misconceptions about their online privacy management. Comput. Hum. Behav. **41**, 212–219 (2014)
30. Schueller, S., Armstrong, C., Neary, M., Ciulla, R.: An Introduction to Core Competencies for the Use of Mobile Apps in Cognitive and Behavioral Practice. Cogn. Behav. Pract. (2021, forthcoming)
31. Lauricella, A., Herdzina, J., Robb, M.: Early childhood educators' teaching of digital citizenship competencies. Comput. Educ. **158**, 103989 (2020)
32. Desimpelaere, L., Huddersa, L., Van de Sompela, D.: Knowledge as a strategy for privacy protection: how a privacy literacy training affects children's online disclosure behaviour. Comput. Hum. Behav. **110**, 106382 (2020)
33. International Digital Education Working Group: Personal data protection competency framework for school students: intended to help educators. In: International Conference of Privacy and Data Protection Commissioners (2016). https://edps.europa.eu/sites/edp/files/pub lication/16-10-18_resolution-competency-framework_en.pdf
34. Hatamian, M., Serna, J., Rannenberg, K.: Revealing the unrevealed: mining smartphone users privacy perception on app markets. Comput. Secur. **83**, 332–353 (2019)
35. Lankton, N., McKnight, D., Tripp, J.: Facebook privacy management strategies: a cluster analysis of user privacy behaviors. Comput. Hum. Behav. **76**, 149–163 (2017)
36. Li, P., Cho, H., Goh, Z.: Unpacking the process of privacy management and self-disclosure from the perspectives of regulatory focus and privacy calculus. Telematics Inform. **41**, 114–125 (2019)
37. Hallam, C., Zanella, G.: Online self-disclosure: the privacy paradox explained as a temporally discounted balance between concerns and rewards. Comput. Hum. Behav. **68**, 217–227 (2017)
38. Soumelidou, A., Tsohou, A.: Towards the creation of a profile of the information privacy aware user through a systematic literature review of information privacy awareness. Telemat. Inform. **61**, 101592 (2021)

39. Harborth, D., Pape, S.: How privacy concerns, trust and risk beliefs, and privacy literacy influence users' intentions to use privacy-enhancing technologies: the case of tor. In: Proceedings of the 52nd Hawaii International Conference on System Sciences, pp. 4851–4860 (2019)
40. Capistrano, P.E., Chena, V.J.: Information privacy policies: the effects of policy characteristics and online experience. Comput. Stand. Interfaces **42**, 24–31 (2015)
41. General Data Protection Regulation, Regulation (EU) 2016/679 of the European Parliament and of the Council of 27 April 2016 on the protection of natural persons with regard to the processing of personal data and on the free movement of such data
42. Skalkos, A., Tsohou, A., Karyda, M., Kokolakis, S.: Identifying the values associated with users' behavior towards anonymity tools through means-end analysis. Comput. Hum. Behav. Rep. **2**, 100034 (2020)

A Category-Based Framework for Privacy-Aware Collaborative Access Control

Denis Obrezkov$^{(\boxtimes)}$, Karsten Sohr$^{(\boxtimes)}$, and Rainer Malaka$^{(\boxtimes)}$

University of Bremen, 28359 Bremen, Germany
{obrezkov,sohr,malaka}@uni-bremen.de

Abstract. The increased availability of portable devices with high computational power gave birth to such phenomenon as Bring Your Own Device (BYOD)—a situation when an employee uses his own device for accessing enterprise sensitive resources. This situation in turn created a new conflict—an employee wants to keep his data private, and an employer want to preserve the confidentiality of their sensitive resources. Since in case of BYOD both employees' and employers' data are stored on the employee's device, a problem of distributed and collaborative access control appears.

In this paper we propose a novel framework for distributed systems with multiparty data ownership. The underlying formal model is based on the notion of Category-Based Access Control (CBAC). It is expanded with a concept of categories, representing a remote third-party policy decision point. The model is designed and evaluated against requirements for collaborative systems.

Keywords: Usable security · Privacy · BYOD · Access control · CBAC

1 Introduction

Naturally, modern technologies create new requirements for access control systems. The high prevalence of mobile devices with high computing and communicative capabilities create new challenges in the area of access control.

Bring Your Own Device phenomenon. Bring Your Own Device (BYOD) is a situation when an employee can access company-sensitive resources from a device which is not controlled by an employer. To keep his data confidential the employer uses several techniques. One of them is allowing access to the data only via trusted apps installed on the employee's smartphone or laptop. Another technique is usage of corporate-owned personal-enabled mobile devices. In this case an employee is provided with a device controlled by an employer [6].

Garba et al. note that "BYOD has reorganized ownership and control of electronic devices in the present day. It is a new model that replaces the long-standing use what you are told (UWYT) model at work, in which employers

© Springer Nature Switzerland AG 2021
S. Fischer-Hübner et al. (Eds.): TrustBus 2021, LNCS 12927, pp. 126–139, 2021.
https://doi.org/10.1007/978-3-030-86586-3_9

define and have full control over the devices used for work-related tasks by their employees. BYOD is a simple strategy that permits staff in an organization to use the device of their choice to access and execute organizational applications and other information resources" [4]. In other words, in the BYOD situation employers lost their ability to fully control their employees' work devices. The authors list several approaches to protecting the data: network approach, mobile device management, virtualization, and phone-centric approaches. Nevertheless, the employees' privacy issues are out of scope of the paper.

The BYOD phenomenon can be faced in many different fields, e.g. in medical and educational sectors [10,12,23]. Wani et al. enumerate BYOD issues in hospitals [23]. Among others, access control issues are identified. Kurniawan et al. also face access control issues while utilizing a BYOD-oriented technology for conducting exams [10]. At the same time little research has been done on the topic of privacy for employees.

Table 1. Requirements for access control models

Req	Type	Description
R1	Policy specification	Access control models should be able to manage the increased complexity that multiparty data ownership introduces
R2	Policy specification	Access control models should be able to capture the dynamics and context of relationships of multiple data owners on one system
R3	Governance	Access control models should allow the collaborative administration of shared resources
R4	Governance	Access control models should support conflict resolution methods
R5	Usability	Access control systems should be unobtrusive and should not impose extra overhead on users
R6	Usability	Access control systems should support users in the inspection and configuration of their access preferences
R7	Transparency	Access control systems should be transparent to users and should allow users to understand collaborative decisions and their effect

Since the BYOD phenomenon involves interactions between two or more actors, we consider it to be of a collaborative nature. Paci et al. formulate requirements for a collaborative and community-centered system [17]. On Table 1 we list them slightly modified to better reflect the specifics of the described problem. There are four types of the requirements:

- **Policy Specification.** Given that a new access control framework should address the BYOD problem, where the employer and the employee store their confidential data on the same device, the new access control model should be able to provide data protection for each data owner.
- **Governance.** Several parties have different and sometimes competing access control policies. The employer is interested in the protection of his confidential data and in allowing access for the employee only to the data required

to perform the latter's duties. The employee, in turn, is interested in protecting his privacy. Since both sides require data protection all the time (not only during working hours), it is highly possible that conflicts are inevitable. Thereby, an access control system should be capable of conflicts resolution.

– **Usability and transparency.** In order to efficiently protect data, a user should be able to identify the system's security state, understand possible actions and their consequences, perform the required operations. The efficiency of each step depends on the transparency and usability of the access control system.

In this paper we propose an access control framework which aims to address all the listed requirements in Table 1. We introduce a Shared-CBAC access control policy which is based on the traditional CBAC model [1]. Using a BYOD use case, we demonstrate how to incorporate third-party access control policies into the decision making process by using specific mechanics of our framework and CBAC. Lastly, we evaluate our model against the usability requirement and formulate future work directions.

2   Background

2.1   Classical Access Control Models

One of the widely known access control models is Mandatory Access Control (MAC). It was defined in The Trusted Computer System Evaluation Criteria (TCSEC) as "a means of restricting access to objects based on the sensitivity (as represented by a label) of the information contained in the objects and the formal authorization (i.e., clearance) of subjects to access information of such sensitivity" [11]. Though MAC can be used in distributed systems, usually a user cannot change or create labels and cannot protect his own information in the computer system.

Another popular model is based on Role Based Access Control, or RBAC [19]. RBAC was created to better represent the organizational structure in access control systems. It assigns roles with corresponding privileges to employees and makes security decisions based on these roles. RBAC policies are usually very flexible, for example, it is often possible to create specific roles in the BYOD use case. Nevertheless, it is hardly possible to protect an employee's data on his device—each employee has his own security preferences, thus, a new role is required for protecting each employee's privacy.

In order to address the dynamic nature of computer system environments, Attribute Based Access Control (ABAC) models were created. There are several different varieties of ABAC systems [8,9,25]. Their common trait is the ability to change access control decisions based on environmental changes, e.g. owner's age or time of day. Those systems are capable of solving most of the problems in collaborative and distributed access control. At the same time, ABAC-based models do not usually assume the possibility of several security administrators with different needs in data protection. Moreover, it is usually assumed that there is only one security administrator (or a common ancestor node in a security hierarchy), and special steps are needed to allow collaborations [8,20].

Category-Based Access Control model, or CBAC, is a generalization of ABAC models proposed by Barker [1]. It introduces the notion of category and defines a simple metamodel that can be changed to meet the requirements of a specific area. In CBAC, a category is considered to be a generalization of other access control concepts, like roles, clearance and attributes. In our work we present Shared-CBAC model that is aimed to fulfill the privacy requirements in collaborative environments.

2.2 Collaborative and Concurrent Access Models

In order to address the issue of collaborative access control, several models and supporting access control specification languages were proposed.

The XACML language was one of the first attempts to standardize the access control for collaborative environments [24]. The most recent version, XACMLv3, recognizes that some actions require more than one subject. XACML utilizes unique attribute categories to distinguish between subjects with different capacities. At the same time, though being flexible, XACML is far from being transparent or usable for lay users. Stepien et al. enumerate the following factors for its complexity: the length of XML categories, long domain names, a vast collection of operators and structural components [21].

Mahmudlu et al. proposed a data governance model for collaborative environments. The authors classify users into different levels based on their archetypes [13]. One of the major restrictions of this work is the assumption of the existence of one collaboration platform that controls each access request. Although this is a common feature in modern social platforms, this might be not desirable for people who aim to keep their privacy.

Another collaborative access control model, CollAC, also utilizes the archetype concept [3]. It introduces a notion of mismatch—a situation when a user's access control decision differs from a collaborative policy inference. The work also assumes the existence of one central access control platform. Another possible weakness of CollAC is the fact that those mismatches can potentially create big usability issues (Will a user work with the mechanism that sometimes ignores his decisions?).

It should be noted that all previously mentioned works fail to fulfill one or more requirements from Table 1. Some systems, e.g. frameworks based on XACML, are too complex to be transparent and usable for a lay user, others, e.g. based on traditional models, are not capable of allowing efficient collaborative governance. In our work we attempt to build an access control framework that meets all the listed requirements.

3 Our Solution for Privacy-Aware Access Control

In our work we assume that a framework based on the category-based approach will be more usable for lay users. The reason to choose the category-based approach lies in the area of human cognition. It was previously shown that categorization is one of the basic cognition features [5]. Since one of the main heuristics of usable systems is low memory load and high learnability [16], we choose the notion of categories as the basis for our framework. The evaluation of this design decision is the future work.

3.1   Framework Architecture

The architecture of our framework is shown in Fig. 1. The figure presents a typical collaboration scenario. There is a user and a third-party. The latter usually wants to keep confidentiality of his data, while the user is more interested in his privacy.

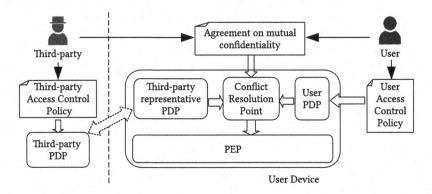

Fig. 1. Framework architecture for systems with multiple data-owners

The third-party usually represents a company with its own access control policy (it might be MAC, RBAC, etc.). There is also a Third-party Representative Policy Decision Point (PDP). As the name implies, it serves to represent the third-party in a collaborative decision making. Thus, some user action requests are evaluated on the third-party side. The examples of how Shared-CBAC complements our framework can be found in Sect. 4.

The access request is performed as follows. A subject requests access for an object. The request is evaluated in the Conflict Resolution Point (CRP). If conflicts are not possible, for example, when the resource is exclusively owned and requested by the user, then only a decision from User PDP is taken into consideration. Otherwise, the request is also sent to all relevant Third-party PDPs and evaluated based on Third-Party Access Control Policies. In the latter case the decisions of Third-party PDPs and the User PDP are evaluated in CRP according to the "Agreements on mutual confidentiality". The final decision is then evaluated in system-wide PDP and passed to the Policy Enforcement Point (PEP).

In order to resolve conflicts, we use a predefined set of rules for conflict resolution. As an employment contract or any other agreement, "Agreement on mutual confidentiality" is made before the collaboration. This design solution allows one to adequately capture the dynamics of some relations (BYOD), thus meeting the requirements **R2–R4** from Table 1.

To fulfill **R6**, **R7** requirements, we are not considering conflict resolution based on dynamic rules. Firstly, though, some works on collaborative access control might infer decisions opposite to the ones of the user, we believe that a user should clearly understand the consequences of his decision (**R7**). Secondly, a dynamic collaborative decision making might be opaque for a lay user. There is a possibility that a malicious company might utilize weaknesses of the conflict resolution policy, for example, by adding an additional party into a voting process, and get access to the user's data. Thus, we believe that a conflict resolution policy should be static, observable and possible to inspect at any given moment (**R6**).

Considering the aforementioned premises, we propose the following conflict resolution scheme. For each category of interest, several properties are specified in "Agreement on mutual confidentiality": `activation_event`, `release_event`, `on_conflict`. `Activation_event` and `release_event` correspond to arriving into/leaving a working environment, they can have values like *VPN.enabled/ VPN.disabled* or *8:00/17:00*. Thus, `activation_event`:*VPN.enabled* for category "Cat1" means that access requests involving category "Cat1" are processed by the "Third-party representative PDP" after the VPN is enabled. Otherwise, a conflict arises.

The property `on_conflict` specifies possible actions in case of conflict. Possible values are: *deny* and *make_request*. Thus, `on_conflict`:*deny* denies access request in case of a conflict, and `on_conflict`:*make_request* makes request via the "Third-party representative PDP" to the "Third-party PDP" (or it makes request to the "User PDP", since the third-party apps can also try to access user's data).

The weak point of the proposed conflict resolution approach is the inflexibility in big collaborative environments. In situations with multiple conflict resolution agreements, complicated conflicts might arise. The reason for this is a pairwise nature of such contracts, which is inevitable in many situations. For example, in the BYOD use case an employee might have two employers which might require the same camera access time on a user device. It is evident that it is not always possible to make the employers make their own agreement. At the same time, dynamic conflict resolution schemes might also be unsuitable in this situation— two concurring companies generally want a static 'deny' for the other party. In order to satisfy the requirement **R1**, we propose to use static pairwise contracts with priorities.

3.2 Shared-CBAC Model

Shared-CBAC is based on the Category Based Access model [1]. It operates with the following entities: a countable set of principals P, a countable set of resources R, a countable set of categories C and a countable set of actions A. The metamodel itself is defined with the following relationships:

- *Principal-Category Assignment, $PCA \subseteq P \times C$*, which assigns categories to principals: $(p, c) \in PCA$ iff the principal $p \in P$ is assigned to the category $c \in C$.
- *Resource-Category Assignment, $RCA \subseteq R \times C$*, which assigns categories to the resources in the system: $(r, c) \in RCA$ iff the resource $r \in R$ is in the category $c \in C$.
- *Permitted actions for principals with categories, $PAPC \subseteq A \times C \times P$*, which assigns permitted actions to categories of principals; such that $(a, c, p) \in PAPC$ iff the action $a \in A$ is permitted for the principal with the category $c_p \in C$.
- *Permitted actions for resources with categories, $PARC \subseteq A \times C \times R$*, which assigns permitted actions to categories of resources; such that $(a, c, r) \in PARC$ iff the action $a \in A$ is permitted on the resource with the category $c_p \in C$.
- *Authorizations, $PAR \subseteq P \times A \times R$*, such that $(p, a, r) \in PAR$ iff the principal $p \in P$ is allowed to perform the action $a \in A$ on the resource $r \in R$.

The distinctive feature of our model comparing to classical CBAC is the addition of new relationships: permitted actions for principals with categories ($PAPC$) and permitted actions for resources with categories ($PARC$). This makes our model capable of handling decisions from integrated third-party models in a straightforward manner.

The main idea behind the mapping of principals/resources, categories and actions can be described as follows. Firstly, a category can represent another access control policy. For example, a user can have a category "work_abac" where all decisions are made in accordance with some third-party ABAC policy. Secondly, in order to enable those third-party decisions, we allow assignment of possible actions to pairs of principles/resources and categories. Thus, our model allows us to incorporate other models into decision-making by providing high-grained control on resources via attached actions.

In order to deduce *Authorizations*, we should formulate our core axiom:

$$\forall a \in A, \forall p \in P, \forall r \in R$$
$$(\exists a_r, \forall c_r, \exists c_p,$$
$$(p, c_p) \in PCA \land (r, c_r) \in RCA \land$$
$$(a_r, c_r, r) \in PARC \land (a, c_p, p) \in PAPC \land$$
$$a = a_r \land c_r = c_p) \iff (p, a, r) \in PAR$$

This set of relationships and the core axiom form our metamodel. In simple words, we allow a security administrator of a device to categorize principals, or subjects (e.g. programs), to categorize resources or objects (e.g. files) and to assign specific actions allowed for each category assigned to a resource or to a principal. The security decision is then made based on the following rule: if a set of a resource's categories is a subset of a principal's categories, then the intersection between actions assigned to the resource categories and to the principal categories defines the allowed actions. In Sect. 4, the role of a security administrator is distributed among a user and third-parties in accordance with agreements on mutual confidentiality (see Fig. 1).

Since our model can be transformed into a finite CBAC model by introducing mapping categories for the introduced relationships, the same reasoning can be applied to our model to show its decidability as done by Bertolissi et al. [2].

4   BYOD Use Case

Our goal is to show how our framework functions in BYOD scenario and how the Shared-CBAC policy in the system architecture is located.

In Fig. 2 you can see a scheme for a BYOD use case. In this scenario we have an employee (or a user), Company 1, Company 2 and the user's family. Company 1 and Company 2 are the user's employers. A User Device is a device that is used by the user for performing his duties for Company 1 and Company 2.

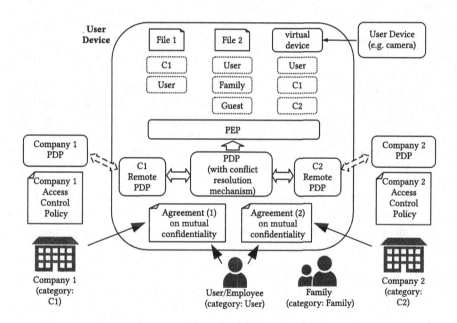

Fig. 2. Access control scheme for BYOD use case

There are several desirable properties in this scenario:

1. the User does not want to share his private information with other entities: Company 1, Company 2 and sometimes with the family
2. Company 1 and Company 2 want to keep confidentiality of their data.

Let us investigate the example. The User has three files: File 1, File 2 and a file, representing a virtual device, a camera in our case. File 1 has the security categories $C1, User$. This means that only applications that have both categories $C1$ and $User$ can have access to the file. A more fine-grained control is possible if actions are specified: $C1(rw), User(rw)$. In this case an app requesting access should have the same category and the required set of actions for each category (r and/or w). For example, if an app has the following security context: $C1(r), User(rw)$ then it can read from the file. At the same time, if the user wants to write to a file with the category $C1(r)$, the conflict arises. The resulting decision is based on a combination of a company response and user categories.

A similar situation occurs when a company application tries to access user files having no appropriate permissions. Let's say that a company app has the categories $C1, User$ and tries to access File 2 with the context $User, Family, Guest$. In that case a conflict arises and the access is either denied, or the user is asked to grant the permission to the app (it depends on the specified conflict resolution strategy). Eventually, the user has a privacy-oriented system that allows him to efficiently separate programs and files between security domains of different nature (family, work, personal).

It is worth noting that category $C1$ is just a representation of the fact that the security context is evaluated by a third-party PDP. Let us show how the access control request is processed in general. Firstly, the access control request is processed by the conflict resolution mechanism. At this step, it is decided what policies should be evaluated. Since the requested resource has both a common $User$ and a third-party representing $C1$ category, a default PDP, a remote PDP of C1 called "C1 Remote PDP" and a conflict resolution should be used. The remote PDP can evaluate the access decision on the device or send a request to the remote company server. The final decision is made according to the results of both PDPs and the conflicts resolution policy. This decision is enforced by PEP.

An interesting situation occurs with the creation of new resources. In Fig. 2 there is a virtual device, representing, for example, a camera. Since the device has categories $User, C1$ and $C2$, the decision is made based on the default PDP, "$C1\ Remote\ PDP$" and "$C2\ Remote\ PDP$". Since companies C1 and C2 can be competitors, the conflict resolution policies should be prepared carefully to define a dominance order for shared resources, for example, when one policy has exclusive rights for a speaker device. Generally, it is not a problem for BYOD— typically, employees are constrained temporarily (e.g., the policy $C1$ is dominant from 8 a.m. till 1 p.m. for Company 1 and the policy $C2$ from 2 p.m. till 6 p.m. for Company 2) or spatially (e.g., the policy C1 is active when NFC signal 'C1-on' was received, the policy C2 is active when NFC signal 'C2-on'; those signals represent entrance checkpoints of the companies).

Secondly, it is worth noting that a company policy can be of any nature, e.g. MAC, RBAC and ABAC. For example, a company policy can be ABAC, and the decision can be made based on user id, file id, user age, etc. In this case a security context can only represent a security decision (r, w, a, e) and additional information should be stored on a company side.

5 Evaluation

It is shown that one of the most significant factors of user satisfaction is a
response time [18]. Hoxmeier et al. show a significant positive relation between
"ease-of-use" and user satisfaction [7]. Thus, in order to evaluate the feasibility
of model implementation in terms of cognitive unobtrusiveness (**R5** requirement
from Table 1), we assess how fast a user can get a response with an access control
decision from a remote server. At the same time we evaluate the performance of
the proposed framework.

5.1 Model Design

For evaluation we use an $M/D/1$ queuing model. The "$M/D/1$" notion means
that the arrival rate is modeled on exponential pdf with the parameter λ, and
the service rate is deterministic and defined by the constant μ, and $\lambda < \mu$. We
use the constant rate as a worst-case scenario. The model is shown on Fig. 3a.

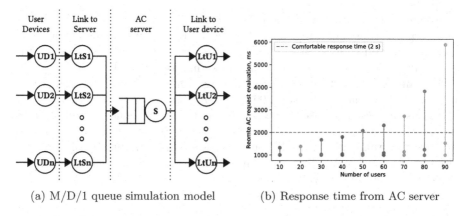

(a) M/D/1 queue simulation model   (b) Response time from AC server

Fig. 3. Simulation model of a distributed access control environment and the results
of response time analysis

There are three types of objects in the model: User Devices ($UD1...UDn$)
that generate access control requests, links to and from the Access Control server
($LtS1...LtS2$ and $LtU1...LtU2$) and the Access Control server itself (S) with an
infinite queue. In our model we use the following assumptions. Firstly, a user
makes policy evaluation on its own device and then sends the access request
to the Access Control server. We assume that the policy evaluation takes less
than 125 ms. We base this assumption on the work of Turkmen et al., where the
authors report this number as an upper bound for policy evaluation for XACML
Enterprise [22]. Secondly, we assume that the communication link to/from the
Access Control server has a speed of 32 kbit/s. The package size is assumed to
be of the standard length—1500 bytes. Thirdly, the Access Control server has

the constant service rate. It also performs policy evaluation in 125 ms. Given that constant rate we assume that for 100 users the maximum mean arrival time should be 12500 ms (then the system is stationary). That means that in a company with 100 people each user makes one access request each 12.5 s. Lastly, we assume that the arrival rate is exponential. Its parameter is 12500.

5.2   Analysis

We ran our simulation for a period of a typical working day of 8 h. The results for different number of users are shown on Fig. 3b (markers are for minimum, average and maximum response time).

Hoxmeier et al. show that acceptable response time in a computer system lies between 0 and 12 s [7]. A two-seconds interval is shown to be acceptable as a response interval for many applications [14]. We use this value as the upper bound of a comfortable response time. Other limiting values could be used as well, but since we aim to measure a feasibility of model implementation in terms of cognitive unobtrusiveness, a perception related boundary seems to be more acceptable.

Figure 3b illustrates how the response time is affected by the number of users. Each response time line is represented by three markers: minimum, average and maximum response times. It is interesting to note that even 50% load on the server gives a maximum response time worse than two seconds.

We can further examine our system in three different modes: low load (10%), high load (90%), maximum load (100%) (see Fig. 4). It can be seen that the low load gives the best response time and all access control requests are processed under two seconds. In the high load mode the majority of requests are also processed less than in two seconds, but there is a significant number of responses with higher latencies. And during the maximum load the system has the majority of response times out of two seconds.

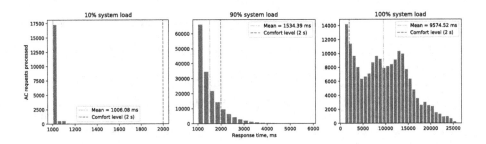

Fig. 4. Response time for different loads

The minimum response time is around 1 s. This response time can be calculated as: $UserDevicePolicyEvaluation + CommunicationLineDelays + ServerPolicyEvaluation$. Given this formula, we can see that there are several possibilities for decreasing the response time: to lower policy evaluation time (via utilizing better hardware or more efficient policy evaluation software); to use faster communication lines; to change the AC request rate.

In real-life scenarios users/employees have different behavior patterns. Some of them generate several access requests in a small amount of time occasionally, others make requests moderately all through the working day. This leads us to the conclusion that a privacy-oriented system design cannot be a "one-fits-all" solution. At the same time, we have shown that our framework can demonstrate an acceptable response rate, thus addressing the major factor of the usability requirement. A deeper evaluation of our model is a topic of future work.

6   Conclusion

In this paper we have discussed problems of modern access control systems in collaborative environments with multiple data owners. We have proposed our framework and model, *Shared-CBAC*, as a solution for the revealed security challenge. We have introduced a notion of third-party decision points, which are represented as usual categories in the model. We have also proposed a static conflict resolution scheme that reflects real-life relationships (e.g. work contracts). Lastly, we have evaluated the usability of our model by measuring response times for access control decisions in a queue-based simulation.

Future work includes several directions to address the aforementioned usability requirements (see Table 1):

Development of the Prototype. To assess the designed access control framework, a prototype should be developed. It should incorporate PDPs, PEPs and CRPs implementations. Since these modules are located on a user device, special attention should be paid to security. For example, in order to establish trust in the system, special technologies of isolated execution environments, e.g. ARM Trust-Zone [15], should be utilized. Also, the questions on authorizations and lifecycles of user agreements and categories should be addressed in a secure manner.

Usability and Transparency Evaluation. In our work we assumed that a category-based approach fits better human cognition. A special comparative study is required to assess this preposition. Other associated directions include assessment of means for representing a current access control state of the system and evaluation of supporting security decision mechanisms.

Evaluation of Conflict Resolution Strategies. As mentioned before, there are static and dynamic strategies for conflict resolution. In our work we assumed that a static conflict resolution scheme is a better choice for privacy-aware access control systems. It might, however, not be true for all collaborative environments.

Acknowledgments. This work was partially supported by Klaus Tschira Foundation (Empowering Digital Media project) and the German Federal Ministry of Education and Research (BMBF) under the grant 16SV8503 (UsableSec@Home project).

References

1. Barker, S.: The next 700 access control models or a unifying meta-model? In: Proceedings of the 14th ACM Symposium on Access Control Models and Technologies, SACMAT 2009, pp. 187–196. Association for Computing Machinery, New York (2009). https://doi.org/10.1145/1542207.1542238
2. Bertolissi, C., Fernández, M., Thuraisingham, B.: Admin-CBAC: an administration model for category-based access control. In: Proceedings of the Tenth ACM Conference on Data and Application Security and Privacy, CODASPY 2020, pp. 73–84. Association for Computing Machinery, New York (2020). https://doi.org/10.1145/3374664.3375725
3. Damen, S., Hartog, J., Zannone, N.: CollAC: collaborative access control, pp. 142–149 (May 2014). https://doi.org/10.1109/CTS.2014.6867557
4. Garba, A.B., Armarego, J., Murray, D., Kenworthy, W.: Review of the information security and privacy challenges in bring your own device (BYOD) environments. J. Inf. Priv. Secur. **11**(1), 38–54 (2015). https://doi.org/10.1080/15536548.2015.1010985
5. George, L.: Women, Fire, and Dangerous Things: What Categories Reveal about the Mind. University of Chicago, Chicago (1987)
6. Howell, G.E., et al.: Mobile device security: corporate-owned personally-enabled (COPE) (2020)
7. Hoxmeier, J.A., DiCesare, C.: System response time and user satisfaction: an experimental study of browser-based applications. In: AMCIS 2000 Proceedings, p. 347 (2000)
8. Hu, V., et al.: Guide to attribute based access control (ABAC) definition and considerations. National Institute of Standards and Technology Special Publication, pp. 162–800 (January 2014)
9. Jin, X., Krishnan, R., Sandhu, R.: A unified attribute-based access control model covering DAC, MAC and RBAC. In: Cuppens-Boulahia, N., Cuppens, F., Garcia-Alfaro, J. (eds.) DBSec 2012. LNCS, vol. 7371, pp. 41–55. Springer, Heidelberg (2012). https://doi.org/10.1007/978-3-642-31540-4_4
10. Kurniawan, O., Lee, N.T.S., Poskitt, C.M.: Securing bring-your-own-device (BYOD) programming exams. In: Proceedings of the 51st ACM Technical Symposium on Computer Science Education, SIGCSE 2020, pp. 880–886. Association for Computing Machinery, New York (2020). https://doi.org/10.1145/3328778.3366907
11. Latham, D.C.: Department of defense trusted computer system evaluation criteria. Department of Defense (1986)
12. Lennon, R.G.: Bring your own device (BYOD) with cloud 4 education. In: Proceedings of the 3rd Annual Conference on Systems, Programming, and Applications: Software for Humanity, SPLASH 2012, pp. 171–180. Association for Computing Machinery, New York (2012). https://doi.org/10.1145/2384716.2384771
13. Mahmudlu, R., den Hartog, J., Zannone, N.: Data governance and transparency for collaborative systems. In: Ranise, S., Swarup, V. (eds.) DBSec 2016. LNCS, vol. 9766, pp. 199–216. Springer, Cham (2016). https://doi.org/10.1007/978-3-319-41483-6_15
14. Nah, F.F.H.: A study on tolerable waiting time: how long are web users willing to wait? Behav. Inf. Technol. **23**(3), 153–163 (2004). https://doi.org/10.1080/01449290410001669914

15. Ngabonziza, B., Martin, D., Bailey, A., Cho, H., Martin, S.: Trustzone explained: architectural features and use cases. In: 2016 IEEE 2nd International Conference on Collaboration and Internet Computing (CIC), pp. 445–451. IEEE (2016)
16. Nielsen, J.: Usability Engineering. Morgan Kaufmann, Burlington (1994)
17. Paci, F., Squicciarini, A., Zannone, N.: Survey on access control for community-centered collaborative systems. ACM Comput. Surv. **51**(1), 1–38 (2018). https://doi.org/10.1145/3146025
18. Rushinek, A., Rushinek, S.F.: What makes users happy? Commun. ACM **29**(7), 594–598 (1986)
19. Sandhu, R.S., Coyne, E.J., Feinstein, H.L., Youman, C.E.: Role-based access control models. Computer **29**(2), 38–47 (1996)
20. Servos, D., Osborn, S.L.: HGABAC: towards a formal model of hierarchical attribute-based access control. In: Cuppens, F., Garcia-Alfaro, J., Zincir Heywood, N., Fong, P.W.L. (eds.) FPS 2014. LNCS, vol. 8930, pp. 187–204. Springer, Cham (2015). https://doi.org/10.1007/978-3-319-17040-4_12
21. Stepien, B., Felty, A., Matwin, S.: A non-technical XACML target editor for dynamic access control systems. In: 2014 International Conference on Collaboration Technologies and Systems (CTS), pp. 150–157 (2014)
22. Turkmen, F., Crispo, B.: Performance evaluation of XACML PDP implementations. In: Proceedings of the 2008 ACM Workshop on Secure Web Services, pp. 37–44 (2008)
23. Wani, T.A., Mendoza, A., Gray, K.: BYOD in hospitals-security issues and mitigation strategies. In: Proceedings of the Australasian Computer Science Week Multiconference, ACSW 2019. Association for Computing Machinery, New York (2019). https://doi.org/10.1145/3290688.3290729
24. XAMCL, Committee, O., et al.: eXtensible access control markup language (XACML) committee specification 1.0 (2003)
25. Yuan, E., Tong, J.: Attributed based access control (ABAC) for web services. In: IEEE International Conference on Web Services (ICWS 2005), p. 569 (2005)

Privacy and Users

Car Drivers' Privacy Concerns and Trust Perceptions

Giampaolo Bella, Pietro Biondi[✉], and Giuseppe Tudisco

Dipartimento di Matematica e Informatica, Università degli Studi di Catania,
Catania, Italy
giamp@dmi.unict.it, pietro.biondi@phd.unict.it,
giuseppe.tudisco@studium.unict.it

Abstract. Modern cars are evolving in many ways. Technologies such as infotainment systems and companion mobile applications collect a variety of personal data from drivers to enhance the user experience. This paper investigates the extent to which car drivers understand the implications for their privacy, including that car manufacturers must treat that data in compliance with the relevant regulations. It does so by distilling out drivers' concerns on privacy and relating them to their perceptions of trust on car cyber-security. A questionnaire is designed for such purposes to collect answers from a set of 1101 participants, so that the results are statistically relevant. In short, privacy concerns are modest, perhaps because there still is insufficient general awareness on the personal data that are involved, both for in-vehicle treatment and for transmission over the Internet. Trust perceptions on cyber-security are modest too (lower than those on car safety), a surprising contradiction to our research hypothesis that privacy concerns and trust perceptions on car cyber-security are opponent. We interpret this as a clear demand for information and awareness-building campaigns for car drivers, as well as for technical cyber-security and privacy measures that are truly considerate of the human factor.

Keywords: Automotive · Cyber physical systems · Crowdsourcing · Personal data

1 Introduction

The cars people are driving at present are complicated cyber-physical systems involving tight interaction between rapidly evolving car technologies and their human users, the drivers. To meet the needs and preferences of (at least) drivers, the infotainment system is more and more integrated with the setups for passengers' physical preferences, such as seating configuration, driving style and air conditioning, as well as for non-physical preferences, such as music to play, preferred numbers to call and on-line payment details.

A plethora of data originates, whose processing enhances the driving experience and exceeds that towards increased support for autonomous driving, a goal

© Springer Nature Switzerland AG 2021
S. Fischer-Hübner et al. (Eds.): TrustBus 2021, LNCS 12927, pp. 143–154, 2021.
https://doi.org/10.1007/978-3-030-86586-3_10

of large interest at present. Modern cars also come with Internet connectivity ensuring, at least, that car software always gets over-the-air updates from the manufacturer. Cars expose services remotely via dedicated apps that the driver installs on their smartphone to remotely operate functions such as electric doors, air conditioning, headlights, horn and even start/stop the engine. Therefore, car and driver's smartphone apps form a combined system that exposes innovative services, including locating the car remotely via GPS or even geo-fencing it, so that the app user would be notified if their car ever exceeds a predefined geographical area [1]. Because cars are progressively resembling computers, offering services while treating personal data, they also attract various malicious aims.

The field of car cyber-security shows that software vulnerabilities can be exploited on a Jeep [10], on a General Motors [6] as well as on a Tesla Model S [2]. Such vulnerabilities may, in particular, impact data protection, and the sequel of this manuscript will discuss the variety of personal data treated through cars, thus calling for compliance, at least in the EU, with the General Data Protection Regulation (GDPR) [5]. Car cyber-security ("security", in brief) is certain to be more modern than car safety, hence our overarching research goal is to understand whether the former is understood as well as the former is. We formulate the hypothesis that privacy concerns decrease when trust perceptions on the underlying security and data protection measures are correspondingly high. For example, it means that if a driver feels that their personal data is protected, then that is because the driver trusts that the car is secure. To assess such hypothesis, this paper does not take a common attack-then-fix approach but, rather, addresses the following research questions pivoted on drivers' perceptions.

RQ1. Are drivers adequately concerned about the privacy risks associated with how that their car and its manufacturer treat their personal data?

RQ2. Do drivers adequately perceive the trustworthiness of their car, in terms of security especially?

We are aware that these research questions are not conclusive, and we have gathered data to specialise the answers by categories of drivers, e.g. by age or education. To the best of our knowledge, this is the first large-scale study targeting and relating privacy concerns and trust perception of car drivers. We took the approach of questionnaire development and survey execution through a crowdsourcing platform. Our goal was to get at least 1037 sets of responses in order for the findings to be statistically relevant, as explained below. We first piloted the questionnaire with 88 friends and colleagues with the aim of getting feedback but no significant tuning was required. After crowdsourcing, a total number of 1101 worldwide participants was reached.

We analysed the results obtained from the questionnaire through standard statistical analysis by Pearson's correlation coefficient, Spearman's rank correlation coefficient and Coefficient Phi. In a nutshell, most drivers believe that it is unnecessary for their car to collect their personal data because they find the collection unnecessary to the full functioning of modern cars; this indicates that privacy concerns are low, which in turn may be due to wrong preconceptions, given that cars do collect personal data. Also, it appears that most drivers do not fully agree that their data is protected using appropriate security measures; this may be interpreted as a somewhat low trust on security. To our surprise, pairing these two abstracted findings clearly disproves our hypothesis.

Section 2 comments on the related work, Sect. 3 outlines our research method, particularly the questionnaire design, the crowdsourcing task and the statistical approach, Sect. 4 discusses our results and Sect. 5 concludes.

2   Related Work

In 2014, Schoettle and Sivak [9] surveyed public opinions in Australia, the United States and the United Kingdom regarding connected vehicles. Their research noted that people (drivers as well as non-drivers) expressed a high level of concern about the safety of connected cars, which does not seem surprising on the basis of the novelty of the concept at the time. However, participants demonstrated an overall positive attitude towards connected car technology, with particular interest in device integration and in-vehicle Internet connectivity. In 2016, Derikx et al. [4] investigated whether drivers' privacy concerns can be compensated by offering monetary benefits. They analysed the case of usage-based auto insurance services where the rate is tailored to driving behaviour and measured mileage and found out that drivers were willing to give up their privacy when offered a small financial compensation. Therefore, what appears to be missing is a study on drivers' understanding on the amount and type of personal data that modern cars process, which is the core of this paper.

There are relevant publications on drivers' trust on car safety but are limited to self-driving cars. Notably, Du et al. [7] conducted an experiment to better understand whether explaining the actions of automated vehicles promote general acceptance by the drivers. They found out that the specific point in time when explanations were given was crucial for their effectiveness—explanations provided before the vehicle started were associated with higher trust by the subjects. Similar results were obtained by Petersen et al. [8] in another study in 2019. They manipulated drivers' situational awareness by providing them with different types and details of information. Their analysis showed that situational awareness influenced the level of trust in automated driving systems, allowing drivers to immerse themselves in non-driving activities. Clearly, the more people are aware of something, the more trust they manage to place in it.

It is clear that modern cars technologies are not limited to self-driving features. Modern cars include innumerable digital components, often integrated in the infotainment system, which interact with drivers and collect their data. It follows that modern cars process personal data to some extent, as detailed in the next Section, hence car manufacturers must meet specific sets of requirements to comply with the relevant regulations. Therefore, it becomes important to assess drivers' concerns on their privacy through their use of a car and drivers' trust on the security (also in relation to their trust on the safety) of the car.

3 Research Method

We took the approach of questionnaire development and survey execution to assess car drivers' privacy concerns and trust perceptions. Specifically, we built questionnaire with 10 questions, administered it through a crowdsourcing plat-form and carried out a statistical analysis of the answers. Opinions were mea-sured using a standard 7-point Likert scale. With a very low margin of error, of just 4%, and a very high confidence level, of 99%, the necessary sample size to represent the worldwide population is 1037. Our total respondents were 1101, including piloting over 88, so our findings are statistically relevant of the entire world—a limitation is that, while Prolific ensures that respondents are some-how geographically dispersed, it cannot guarantee that they are truly randomly sampled from the entire world.

4 Results

The answers are catalogued and statistically studied by analysing indexes of central tendency and correlation coefficients. The indexes of central tendency (mean and median) synthesise with a single numerical value the values assumed by the data. The mean value is coupled with the standard deviation in order to measure the amount of variation of the values. There is no room to present the demographic and its correlations with other answers here; we recall that driving at least 3 h a week was a prerequisite to enter the study, along with being over 18.

To simplify the analysis of the answers to the core questions, we follow the standard practice of grouping the 7 levels of agreement into three categories. Specifically, if the participants reply with "Strongly agree", "Agree" or "Some-what agree", then we consider their value as "Agreeing"; if instead they select "Neither agree nor disagree", then we consider them in the category "Unde-cided"; and finally, if the participants select "Somewhat disagree", "Disagree" or "Strongly disagree", then we consider those answers as "Disagreeing".

Knowledge on Modern Cars. Question Q1 evaluates the driver's knowledge on modern cars. Considering the values of the mean and the median, shown in Table 1, it can be stated that the interviewed sample considers itself knowl-edgeable about modern cars. The data show that 55% of participants are quite confident about their knowledge, while a minority of the participants (about 29%) think they are not. Finally, 16% of participants think they have average knowledge about modern cars. Thus, considering the answers of the preliminary question, there does not seem to be a substantial difference between those who drive a few hours a week and those who drive more with regard to the level of knowledge they claim to have on modern cars.

Then, question Q2 asks respondents whether or not they agree that modern cars are similar to modern computers. Also this question receives a high rate of agreement. We note that 72% of participants agree that a modern car is similar to a modern computer. Furthermore, it turns out that 14% of them are undecided while 14% of them disagree with the statement. The mean and the median are shown in Table 1.

Table 1. Q1, Q2 answers and their statistics

Knowledge level	[%]	Agreement level	[%]
Knowledgeable about modern cars	55	Agreeing	72
Average knowledge	16	Disagreeing	14
Not knowledgeable about modern cars	29	Undecided	14
Mean	4.37	Mean	5
Median	5	Median	5
Standard deviation	1.55	Standard deviation	1.35

Concerns on Data Privacy. The first of these questions (Q3) asks participants to select all the categories of data they think a car collects. It must be remarked that this answer allows for multiple choice, so a respondents can choose from multiple categories of data. Table 2 shows the answers selected by the respondents. The predominant categories according to the interviewed sample are: "personal data about the driver" (selected by 56% of the sample); "public data about the driver" (selected by 54% of the sample); "public data not about the driver" (selected by 47% of the sample). A few participants think that their vehicle collects more sensitive data belonging to the special categories of personal (13%) and financial data (11%). Finally, we note that just 8% of the participants think that modern cars do not collect any data at all.

Overall, these findings confirm a modest level of awareness in terms of what data a car collects. In particular, while it is positive that the majority (56%) understands that driver's personal data are involved, it is concerning that a similar subset (54%) deem such data about the driver to have been made public. It would be surprising if any car manufacturer's privacy policy stated that the driver's collected data would be made public (and such policies are well worthy of a dedicated comparative study). This potential confusion calls for awareness campaigns, more readability of official documents and innovative technologies to ensure policies are understood. By contrast, a positive sign that a small kernel of participants is highly informed is the appreciable understanding that special categories of personal data (13%) or financial data (11%) may be gathered.

Question Q4 asks participants whether they think it is necessary to collect personal data to achieve full vehicle functionality. The indexes and a summary of the answers are shown in Table 3. It shows that 27% of the participants agree with the statement above, moreover, 19% of them are undecided and 54% of them disagree with the statement. Thus, we could argue that the participants disagree with the statement proposed in the question.

Table 2. Q3 answers

Collected data	[%]
Personal data about the driver	56
Public data about the driver	54
Public data not about the driver	47
Special categories of personal data about the driver	13
Financial data about the driver	11
No data at all	8

This finding can be interpreted in various ways. On one hand, it denounces a false preconception because that the customised, driver-tailored experience that is getting more and more common at present is certain to stand on a trail of data collected about the driver's. It clearly also signifies that drivers are neither adequately informed on what data is being collected and for what purposes, contradicting art. 5 of GDPR, nor have they been able to grant an informed consent, contradicting art. 7 of GDPR.

Table 3. Q4, Q5 answers and their statistics

Agreement level	[%]	Agreement level	[%]
Agreeing	27	Agreeing	21
Disagreeing	54	Disagreeing	65
Undecided	19	Undecided	14
Mean	3.35	Mean	2.97
Median	3	Median	3
Standard deviation	1.58	Standard deviation	1.67

Moving on to the answers of question Q5, it can be noticed that just 21% of the sample agrees to the transmission of data over the Internet, only 14% of participants are undecided moreover 65% of them disagree with the statement. This means that the sample is not very convinced to send personal data over the Internet. Table 3 shows agreement levels and indexes of Q5's answers.

This may again be interpreted as a wrong preconception because it is clear that remote services, including eCall, location-tailored weather forecasts, music streaming and many others, must generate Internet traffic.

Perceptions of Trust on Safety. Question Q6 asks whether participants agree that a modern vehicle safeguards the life of its driver. The agreement levels and the indexes of central tendency are shown in Table 4. It turns out that 77% of participants agree with the statement above, then just 8% disagree with the statement, and 15% of them are undecided.

Question Q7 asks participants whether a modern car protects its driver's personal data better than its driver's life. It appears that a part of the sample is undecided with this statement (26%), just 18% of participants agree with the statement moreover 56% of them disagree. Table 4 shows also that the indexes of central tendency are not as high when compared to the previous question.

There is considerable uncertainty in front of this question, if not for the majority's expression of disagreement (56%). It signifies that trust on security still has a great lot to grow in comparison to trust on safety, perhaps due to the much longer establishment of the latter. It is well known that trust may take a long time to root, and car security is certain to be a somewhat recent problem.

Table 4. Q6, Q7 answers and their statistics

Agreement level	[%]	Agreement level	[%]
Agreeing	77	Agreeing	18
Disagreeing	8	Disagreeing	56
Undecided	15	Undecided	26
Mean	5.26	Mean	3.26
Median	5	Median	4
Standard deviation	1.20	Standard deviation	1.46

Perceptions of Trust on Security. Question Q8 asks whether the data collected from the vehicle is legitimately processed according to the relevant regulations. Table 5 shows that 44% of the participants agree with this statement moreover 25% disagree and the rest of them (31%) are undecided.

Trust one the legitimacy of the data processing is not higher than 44%. This indicates, once more, that car drivers need to be better informed, first of all. Conversely, this means that the majority, 56%, are not sure about the legitimacy of the processing of their personal data. Being informed correctly is essential for raising awareness, which in turn is essential for trust building.

Question Q9 asks if participants believe that the personal data collected is systematically analysed and evaluated using automated processes (including profiling). From Table 5, around 42% of participants agree with this statement, moreover 32% of them disagree and 26% are undecided with the statement.

This question is designed to be self-contained and understandable by everyone. A notable 42% show concern that profiling takes place, which may be taken to signify a correspondingly low trust on the security of the treatment. There is no official public information on whether car manufacturers really carry out profiling but, if this were the case, then a Data Protection Impact Assessment, pursuant art. 35 of GDPR, would have been necessary.

The last question (Q10) asks whether the participants feel that the data transmitted over the Internet are protected by adequate technologies. Table 5 confirms the representation that agrees with the question (46%) to be considerable. The fact that those who agree do not exceed the majority of the sample clearly indicate, also in this case, room for improving drivers' trust on security.

Table 5. Q8, Q9, Q10 answers and their statistics

Agreement level	[%]	Agreement level	[%]	Agreement level	[%]
Agreeing	44	Agreeing	42	Agreeing	46
Disagreeing	25	Disagreeing	32	Disagreeing	32
Undecided	31	Undecided	26	Undecided	22
Mean	4.28	Mean	4.07	Mean	4.19
Median	4	Median	4	Median	4
Standard deviation	1.31	Standard deviation	1.43	Standard deviation	1.49

4.1 Correlations

There are statistically significant correlations that arise by analysing the relevant coefficients over the data obtained from the sample. In brief, Pearson's linear correlation coefficient, denoted by the letter r, allows us to evaluate a possible linearity relationship between two sets of data. Spearman's rank correlation coefficient, denoted by the Greek letter ρ, measures the correlation between two numerical variables; these must be sortable because Spearman's correlation coefficient is defined as Pearson's correlation coefficient applied to the ranks. The Phi coefficient (or mean square contingency coefficient), denoted with the Greek letter ϕ, is a measure of association for two binary variables and is calculated from the frequency distributions of the pairs. Correlation coefficient values are accompanied by a significance level (the *p-value*) to establish the reliability of the calculated value. The p-value is a number between 0 and 1 representing the probability that the result would have been obtained if the data had not been correlated. If the p-value is less than 0.01 then the relationship found is statistically significant.

The analysis looks at the core questions, those from Q1 to Q10, to focus on general correlations between knowledge on the subject matter, privacy concerns, trust perceptions of safety and on security.

Core Question Analysis. We noted a significant correlation between question Q1 and question Q2 ($\rho = 0.48$, $p < 0.001$). Therefore, it seems that participants who are knowledgeable about modern cars also think that modern cars are similar to modern computers, reinforcing the conclusion. Moreover, thanks to the correlation between question Q1 and question Q4 ($\rho = 0.35$, $p < 0.001$) we can state that those who consider themselves informed about modern cars also believe that the data collected by the car is necessary for the full functioning of the car. This aligned with our own, specialist view. There is also a significant correlation between question Q1 and question Q6 ($\rho = 0.40$, $p < 0.01$), that is, those who are knowledgeable about modern cars think that a modern car safeguards its driver's life. Somewhat surprisingly, it appears that Q1 does not significantly correlate with later questions on trust on car security, signifying that trust on security must grow even for those who are knowledgeable about the field.

We calculated the Phi coefficients between the answers of question Q3 to determine if there are any associations, i.e. whether there are pairs of categories of personal data that appear together in the answers. The coefficient values are shown in Table 6, and it becomes apparent that there are only two values that may establish a possible association. The Phi Coefficient obtained between the couple "Special categories of personal data" and "Financial data about the driver" is 0.3255, which means that those who think that financial data are collected by modern cars also think that special categories of personal data are collected as well. This exhibits a correct preconception because financial data are routinely grouped with special categories of data. Also, given the 0.3363 value, we notice that drivers who think "Special categories of personal data" are collected from the car, also think that "Personal data about the driver" are collected, emphasising a correct understanding that personal data also include the special categories (of personal data).

Table 6. Phi Coefficients of question 3

ϕ	No data	Fin	Spec	Pub	Pub$_{driver}$	Pers
No data	1					
Fin	−0.0920	1				
Spec	−0.0999	**0.3255**	1			
Pub	−0.2371	0.0004	−0.0624	1		
Pub$_{driver}$	−0.2973	0.1468	0.0759	0.0255	1	
Pers	−0.3136	0.2332	**0.3363**	−0.2099	0.1743	1

Moving on to question Q4, there is a strong statistically significant correlation between question Q4 and question Q5: both the Pearson coefficient and the Spearman coefficient have very high values ($r = 0.55$, $\rho = 0.68$) both with a reliability value $p < 0.001$. In consequence, we can affirm that those who think that it is necessary to collect personal data for the full functioning of their vehicle also think that this data should be transmitted over the Internet. There is also another statistically significant correlation between question Q4 and question Q8 ($r = 0.39$, $\rho = 0.50$, $p < 0.01$ for both), showing that those who agree to the collection of personal data also think that the data are processed legitimately in a manner consistent with the relevant regulations. Both of these can be taken as indications that those with modest privacy concerns show some trust on security, but we are mindful of the generally low agreement with Q4 and Q5 and only fair agreement with Q8 noted above.

Question Q5 correlates only moderately with question Q8 ($\rho = 0.48$, $p < 0.01$) but more significantly with question Q10 ($r = 0.36$, $\rho = 0.52$, $p < 0.01$). It follows that those who think that data should be transmitted over the Internet, also think that this data will be adequately protected during transmission. This shows that trust on security is broad if present.

Spearman's correlation coefficient detects a moderately significant correlation between question Q6 and question Q8 ($\rho = 0.45$, $p < 0.01$), so that it seems that those who think that a modern car safeguards its driver's life also think that the personal data collected are processed legitimately according to the relevant regulations in force. This seems a positive outcome in terms of a spreading of trust on safety over trust on security. It is unfortunate that this correlation is not very strong, and we deem it highly desirable to develop socio-technical security and privacy measures to reinforce it in the future.

There is a statistically significant correlation between question Q7 and question Q10 ($r = 0.38$, $\rho = 0.52$, $p < 0.01$). In fact, those who think that a modern car protects its driver's personal data better than it safeguards its driver's life also think that the personal data are protected by adequate technology when the vehicle transmits it over the Internet. The Spearman's correlation coefficient also shows a significant correlation between question Q7 and question Q8 ($\rho = 0.47$, $p < 0.01$), that is, those who think that a modern car protects its driver's data better than it safeguards its driver's life also think that the personal data collected are processed legitimately according to the relevant regulations. These findings confirm that trust on security is somehow "logical" in the sense that it covers all relevant elements.

There is also a significant correlation between question Q8 and question Q9 ($\rho = 0.41$, $p < 0.01$), it appears that those who think that modern cars carry out a systematic and extensive evaluation of personal data also think that their data are processed in a legitimate way according to relevant regulations. This correlation suggests that drivers who consent to the evaluation of their personal data even consent to profiling—perhaps too lightheartedly, raising concern that the potentially negative consequences of profiling may not be fully understood at present. It may be inferred that drivers are not fully aware that it would be their right to object to profiling, as prescribed by art. 22 of GDPR.

We also noted a moderate correlation between question Q9 and question Q4 ($\rho = 0.45$, $p < 0.01$). Those who think that in order to use the full functionality of the car it is necessary to provide personal data also think that this data is analysed and studied according to automatic processes to evaluate personal aspects of drivers. This reconfirms that profiling is somewhat ill-understood. There is also a statistically significant correlation between question Q9 and question Q5 ($\rho = 0.46$, $p < 0.01$) indicating that those who think that their data are analysed by automatic evaluation processes also think that they are transmitted over the

Internet. This outcome correctly indicates that potential profiling does not take place aboard the car.

There is a statistically significant correlation between question Q10 and question Q4 ($r = 0.37$, $\rho = 0.49$, $p < 0.01$), that is, those who think that the personal data collected by the vehicle is necessary for the full functioning of the car also think that their data is adequately protected when transmitted over the Internet. Once more, modest privacy concerns lead to some trust on security. Finally, there is a statistically significant correlation between question Q10 and question Q8 ($r = 0.51$, $\rho = 0.64$, $p < 0.01$), so we can argue that those who think that their personal data is processed lawfully also think that the data are adequately protected over the Internet. Here is yet another confirmation that trust on security, if at all present, covers all relevant aspects.

5   Conclusions

Our study was designed with care to carve out drivers' privacy concerns and trust perceptions with the ultimate aim of assessing our research hypothesis that low privacy concerns imply high trust perceptions. Crowdsourcing was leveraged to collect a representative sample of participants. Answers were then analysed in isolation as well as statistically correlated, producing very many insights. There would be little use in developing amazing technical security and privacy measures for preserving drivers' privacy and the security of their cars in case drivers are not adequately concerned about the privacy issues bound to their driving and yet do not trust the security of their cars at an appropriate level. That case is confirmed by the results of our study, thus contradicting our research hypothesis. We consider this outcome worthy of further attention.

Precisely, we believe that the privacy concerns that arose are insufficient in the present technological setting. We would have found it more positive if drivers exhibited higher awareness on the personal data involved through their driving, on how treating such data is fundamental for delivering driver-tailored services, and on the fact that such service quality often demands data transmission over the Internet. Unfortunately, the opposite scenario holds. A somewhat logical explanation of low privacy concerns could be a high trust on security, but we were surprised once more that also trust on security was somewhat low. Therefore, the only way to read the general outcome is that privacy is generally ill-understood by drivers, hence we learn that more information must be delivered to them in order to raise awareness and then form correct privacy concerns and correspondingly adequate trust perceptions. We strongly argue that this must be the ultimate effect for the development of more and more advanced technical security and privacy measures.

The correlations among answers could be seen as somewhat logical. For example, knowledge on the field correlates with adequate privacy concerns and well-related trust perceptions. It is noteworthy that the potentially negative implications of profiling on the freedoms of natural persons are far from being well received at the moment. Trust on security is much less represented than trust on safety, arguably because the former derives from a less rooted perception in our society due to the relatively young age of the technologies that should support it. Moreover, trust on cyber-security is normally broad, that is, if it is present to some extent, it then covers all relevant aspects. We ultimately maintain that also correlations justify a need for more awareness and trust building campaigns.

The value of our results is multifaceted. They can be read in support of the ISO/SAE DIS 21434 standard, which is yet to be finalised. They also offer a solid baseline to conduct a cyber-security and privacy risk assessment on cars following standard methodologies such as ISO/IEC 27005. Future work includes tailoring the effort presented in this paper to specific car brands in support of a contrastive analysis among brands. It is clear that the user-level studies in the automotive field that this paper incepted have great potential for growth.

Acknowledgments. This research was funded by COSCA (COnceptualising Secure Cars) [3], a project supported by the European Union's Horizon 2020 research and innovation programme under the NGI TRUST grant agreement no 825618.

References

1. ACKO: Connected Cars: What is it? Features and Benefits (2020). https://www.acko.com/car-guide/connected-cars-features-benefits/
2. Constantin, L.: Researchers hack Tesla Model S with remote attack (2016). https://www.pcworld.com/article/3121999/researchers-demonstrate-remote-attack-against-tesla-model-s.html
3. COSCA Team: COnceptualising Secure CArs (COSCA) Website (2020). https://cosca-project.dmi.unict.it/
4. Derikx, S., de Reuver, M., Kroesen, M.: Can privacy concerns for insurance of connected cars be compensated? Electron. Mark. **26**(1), 73–81 (2016). https://doi.org/10.1007/s12525-015-0211-0
5. European Union: General Data Protection Regulation (EU Regulation 2016/679) (2016). https://eur-lex.europa.eu/legal-content/EN/TXT/PDF/?uri=OJ:L:2016:119:FULL
6. Jeff Crume: OwnStar: Yet another car hack (2015). https://insideinternetsecurity.wordpress.com/2015/08/05/ownstar-yet-another-car-hack/
7. Du, N., Haspiel, J., et al.: Look who's talking now: implications of AV's explanations on driver's trust, AV preference, anxiety and mental workload. Transp. Res. Part C Emerg. Technol. **104**, 428–442 (2019). https://doi.org/10.1016/j.trc.2019.05.025. http://www.sciencedirect.com/science/article/pii/S0968090X18313640
8. Petersen, L., Robert, L., Yang, J., Tilbury, D.: Situational Awareness, Driver's Trust in Automated Driving Systems and Secondary Task Performance, May 2019
9. Schoettle, B., Sivak, M.: A survey of public opinion about connected vehicles in the U.S., the U.K., and Australia. In: 2014 International Conference on Connected Vehicles and Expo (ICCVE), pp. 687–692. IEEE (2014). https://doi.org/10.1109/ICCVE.2014.7297637
10. Valasek, C., Miller, C.: Remote Exploitation of an Unaltered Passenger Vehicle. http://illmatics.com/Remote%20Car%20Hacking.pdf (2015)

AuthGuide: Analyzing Security, Privacy and Usability Trade-Offs in Multi-factor Authentication

Davy Preuveneers[(✉)], Sander Joos, and Wouter Joosen

imec-DistriNet, KU Leuven, Celestijnenlaan 200A, 3001 Heverlee, Belgium
{davy.preuveneers,sander.joos,wouter.joosen}@kuleuven.be,
https://distrinet.cs.kuleuven.be

Abstract. Multi-factor authentication (MFA) reduces the risk of compromised credentials. However, selecting, configuring and combining different authentication factors is a challenge for both security administrators and end-users, as the configuration possibilities are large and the implications of choices on security, privacy and usability are not always well understood. This concern is further aggravated when the security administrator grants the end-user some flexibility for the selection of authentication factors, or when the latter are combined in a risk-adaptive manner. In this work, we present AUTHGUIDE, an authentication knowledge and configuration framework that increases the awareness about these trade-offs. Additionally, it raises the level of abstraction to configure MFA for a given identity and access management (IAM) platform through a series of questions by mapping the responses onto the IAM's workflow of authentication steps for registration and login. We implemented AUTHGUIDE, validated it on top of the open source Keycloak IAM, and evaluated the effectiveness of our framework to analyze the security, privacy and usability trade-offs.

Keywords: Authentication · Security · Privacy · Usability

1 Introduction

Two-factor authentication (2FA) and multi-factor authentication (MFA) [3,10] are effective measures to reduce the impact of breaches caused by stolen credentials and credential stuffing attacks. Yet, configuring an effective multi-factor or multi-modal authentication strategy remains a daunting task due to the non-trivial trade-offs between security, privacy and usability. For example, risk-based MFA solutions that use contextual factors—such as current and previous IP addresses, locations of the end-user, or browser fingerprints [1,4,8]—can help the relying party (RP) to quantify the risk and trigger additional step-up authentication actions. However, the same context factors are exploited for online tracking, and hence harm the privacy of the user [13]. Also, they may be rendered ineffective when web browsers implement countermeasures against such tracking.

© Springer Nature Switzerland AG 2021
S. Fischer-Hübner et al. (Eds.): TrustBus 2021, LNCS 12927, pp. 155–170, 2021.
https://doi.org/10.1007/978-3-030-86586-3_11

Protocols and standards like FIDO2, WebAuthn and CTAP let web browsers authenticate users with public key cryptography, where the private key on the client is protected by a hardware security key or a mobile device implementing biometric authentication (e.g. fingerprint verification). Passwordless authentication sounds convenient, though the uptake of biometric authentication is slow. Previous research [11] on passwordless authentication has demonstrated that usability concerns remain. Furthermore, from a security point of view, the RP offering WebAuthn authentication, must trust the client—e.g. the biometric factor implementation on a mobile phone—used to unlock the private key. For example, the RP may not know the false positive rate (i.e. a security concern) and false negative rate (i.e. a usability concern) of each biometric factor on every mobile device. Furthermore, in 2019 the 'Face Unlock' feature of Google's Pixel 4 was confirmed to work even when asleep[1], and the use of gel-based screen protectors was also reported[2] to fool fingerprint authentication. Last but not least, end-users may understand the privacy benefits of their biometric templates never leaving their mobile device, but not necessarily the extent to which biometric factors can be subject to the above security threats.

When enabling multi-factor authentication in identity and access management (IAM) platforms, the number of configuration options offered to the security administrator is typically large, and the implications of the choices on security, privacy and usability are not always clear, also for end-users, hereby jeopardizing the onboarding of MFA. To address these challenges, we present AUTHGUIDE, an authentication knowledge framework that:

1. Embeds a body of knowledge to inform about the trade-offs of MFA
2. Analyzes the risk of the customization flexibility granted to the end-user
3. Raises the level of abstraction to simplify the configuration of MFA

AUTHGUIDE achieves this through a series of configuration questions with background and threat information on security, privacy and usability. It validates the responses against requirements from NIST SP 800-63B [5], and maps them onto an IAM's workflow of mandatory, optional and alternative authentication steps. This workflow entails both the registration phase (e.g. the enrollment of security keys or OTP authentication factors) and the login phase. We implemented and validated our solution on top of Red Hat Keycloak, a state-of-practice and open source IAM platform. We evaluated the effectiveness of AUTHGUIDE to configure MFA, and its ability to analyze the security, privacy and usability trade-offs.

The remainder of this paper is structured as follows. Section 2 reviews relevant related work on multi-factor authentication strategies. The design and implementation of our solution is explained in Sect. 3. The experimental evaluation and validation of AUTHGUIDE are discussed in Sect. 4. We conclude with a summary of the main contributions of this work and a roadmap for further research in Sect. 5.

---

[1] Google Pixel 4 Face Unlock works if eyes are shut (2019), https://www.bbc.com/news/technology-50085630.

[2] Samsung: Anyone's thumbprint can unlock Galaxy S10 phone (2019), https://www.bbc.co.uk/news/technology-50080586.

2   Related Work

In this section, we review relevant related work on multi-factor authentication, including adaptive and continuous authentication, to illustrate the complexity of understanding the security, privacy and usability trade-offs from the perspective of the different stakeholders, i.e. security administrators and end-users.

Dasgupta et al. [2] discussed adaptive multi-factor authentication strategies as a combination of the calculation of the trustworthiness of different authentication factors, and an adaptive strategy for selecting authentication factors based on their calculated trustworthiness, performance, surroundings and more. It combines a variety of biometric and non-biometric authentication factors, and also avoids repeated selections of the same set of factors in successive re-authentications to reduce the chance of establishing recognizable patterns. The solution was compared with the FIDO and Microsoft Azure MFA frameworks in a user study, and the proposed solution was found to be better. While the usability of the solution was evaluated, the perceived impact on the user's privacy was not assessed. Wang et al. [14] analyzed 5 MFA solutions based on smart cards, passwords and biometrics, and they specifically investigated security failures of their deployment in multi-server environments under the assumption of various threat models (or adversary models). They found critical security and privacy issues in each of them, including vulnerabilities against stolen-verifier attacks, insider attacks, failing to provide forward secrecy, and the loss of user anonymity.

Many security and authentication guidelines—such as websites of governmental agencies[3]—strongly encourage the use of 2FA and MFA, though often only from an end-user perspective to recommend how to better protect online accounts. Other reports, such the NIST Special Publication 800-63B [5] on 'Digital Identity Guidelines: Authentication and Lifecycle Management' offer detailed technical requirements at different authenticator assurance levels, and with consideration of usability and privacy. While those reports are typically targeted towards security administrators, the latter have to consider not only the security, privacy and usability trade-offs of their MFA implementation, but also the degrees of freedom they are willing to offer to end-users to further customize the MFA experience to their personal preferences. Those trade-offs and their impact on the actual implementation and deployment are less straightforward.

Klieme et al. [7] presented FIDOnuous that builds upon the WebAuthn standard to support continuous authentication. While WebAuthn enables user-friendly passwordless authentication, as well as strong authentication methods with biometrics, it fails to detect an attack after a successful login. The authors propose a WebAuthn extension that uses an Android-based authenticator communicating over Bluetooth Low Energy (BLE), such that the relying party and the authenticator can continuously exchange authentication verifications. While the authors did not evaluate any specific continuous or behavioral authentication method, their simulation demonstrates the practical feasibility of the integration

---

[3] Safeonweb, Use two-factor authentication (2020), https://www.safeonweb.be/en/use-two-factor-authentication.

with WebAuthn. From a privacy perspective, the risk assessment is carried out on the client, and no sensitive behavioral information is shared with the relying party. From a security point of view, the strength of the continuous authentication depends on the accuracy of the authentication methods used and their robustness against threats, such observation, spoofing and replay attacks by an active adversary.

Browser fingerprints are often considered in a risk-adaptive authentication strategy. Andriamilanto et al. [1] researched the adequacy of browser fingerprints as an authentication factor. These fingerprints were composed of 216 attributes, and the analysis was carried out on more than 4 million fingerprints. The authors investigated their distinctiveness and stability through time, as well as their collection time and size. Even though they concluded that browser fingerprints are a promising additional web authentication factor due to the unicity rate of 81% for 1,989,365 browsers, caution is required. Their own analysis indicates that the unicity for mobile fingerprints is 39.9% and far lower than the 88.4% for desktop fingerprints. This observation confirms previous results by Spooren et al. [12]. Also, the impact of countermeasures against tracking, such as FP-Block [13], is not discussed. Laperdrix et al. [8] investigated canvas fingerprinting, a subset of browser fingerprinting, as a user-friendly authentication factor. Their solution is not vulnerable to replay attacks due to its parameterization with a challenge/response protocol. They investigated more than 1.1 million fingerprints and found that the technique is sufficiently deterministic for verification even in the presence of some canvas poisoners that add noise to canvas elements as means to mitigate tracking. Nonetheless, the authors consider the option for users to whitelist their solution intended for authentication. As such, they conclude that canvas fingerprinting is a suitable mechanism. From a privacy perspective, the authors argued that browser fingerprinting is intrusive due to its ability to link user visits, a privacy concern that was already raised earlier by Eckersley in the Panopticlick project [4]. However, the proposed method is intended for first-party websites that already use first-party cookies to track users, and as such does not impose any additional linkability threats.

Karegar et al. [6] studied user perceptions on the widely deployed fingerprint recognition on smartphones, often used to unlock the device or to authenticate against remote applications. More specifically, they investigated in an online survey how 100 individuals think that fingerprint recognition works and this in contrast to PIN codes, as well as privacy and possible other issues with this biometric authentication factor. They compared the attitudes of users and non-users. Their user study demonstrated amongst others that even participants reporting a higher level of knowledge in security do not necessarily have a good perception about access to fingerprint patterns and PIN codes of mobile apps.

3   AUTHGUIDE: Design and Implementation

The main use case of AUTHGUIDE is security administrators configuring their IAM platforms by mapping individual options in AUTHGUIDE onto a specific

IAM workflow of authentication steps for registration and login. To configure MFA for different platforms, AUTHGUIDE generates a custom specialized script to be executed by the security administrator. Additionally, AUTHGUIDE provides security administrators and end-users a breakdown of various security, privacy and usability requirements and trade-offs. As such, the goal of AUTHGUIDE is not to improve any particular authentication factor, but rather to analyze (1) the security, privacy and usability implications of different authentication factors, (2) their combination in an MFA configuration, and (3) the consequences of granting some flexibility on authentication factor selection to the end-user. Our solution builds upon the NIST set of technical requirements [5] to evaluate the assurance level of MFA implementations, as well as their impact on privacy and usability. It validates the configuration options of the security administrator with respect to the 'SHALL' and 'SHOULD' requirement notations and conventions (including the negative forms), the degrees of freedom for customization granted to the end-user, as well as influences of external elements beyond control of the security administrator of an IAM and/or end-user.

3.1 Modeling the Configuration Space of Authentication Factors

AUTHGUIDE models the configuration space of a variety of knowledge, possession, inherence, contextual and behavioral authentication factors, and exposes this body of knowledge to the security administrator in the form of an online configuration wizard. The configuration options can be set by the IAM's security administrator, and optionally further customized by the end-user according to personal preferences and the availability of the necessary equipment.

Even for relatively simple authentication factors such as passwords, the security administrator is typically faced with several configuration options that influence the security and usability trade-off. Some of them are listed below:

- *Are passwords a mandatory or an optional authentication factor?*
  TRADE-OFF: Passwords do not need dedicated hardware, but may be reused.
- *What is the minimal length and complexity of a password?*
  TRADE-OFF: Entering long and strong passwords harms the user experience.
- *Does the implementation offer a password strength meter?*
  TRADE-OFF: Users may not be able to reasonably estimate the relative strength of different passwords.
- *Does the implementation offer to display the secret password?*
  TRADE-OFF: Displaying the password may simplify entering the correct password, but make shoulder surfing attacks easier to carry out.
- *What is the maximum limit of failed authentication attempts?*
  TRADE-OFF: A lower limit reduces the security risk, but also the number of attempts to remember and enter a rarely used password.
- *How often should passwords be changed?*
  TRADE-OFF: Regularly changing passwords improves security, but increases the mental burden to remember ever-changing passwords.

Table 1. Amount of requirements (including negative form) by authenticator type.

Authenticator type	SHALL	SHOULD
Memorized secrets	24	15
Look-up secrets	14	0
Out-of-band devices	27	4
Single-factor OTP device	11	1
Multi-factor OTP devices	20	1
Single-factor cryptographic software	3	1
Single-factor cryptographic devices	9	1
Multi-factor cryptographic software	8	2
Multi-factor cryptographic devices	8	1

Table 2. Amount of general requirements (including negative form) for authenticators.

General authenticator requirements	SHALL	SHOULD
Physical authenticators	2	0
Rate limiting	2	1
Use of biometrics	14	2
Attestation	11	1
Verifier impersonation resistance	6	0
Verifier-CSP communications	1	0
Verifier-compromise resistance	5	0
Replay resistance	0	0
Authentication intent	1	0
Restricted authenticators	2	0

The first configuration option is one that can be delegated to the end-users to enable a passwordless authentication experience for those with alternative means of authentication. Others can be decided upon by the security administrator, or be constrained by the underlying authentication platform (e.g. support for the WebAuthn standard) or the availability of certain hardware (e.g. One-Time Password devices). Even if an IAM platform offers the above capabilities, the NIST SP 800-63B [5] guidelines state, for example, that verifiers SHOULD NOT require memorized secrets—such as passwords—to be changed arbitrarily or periodically, but only if there is evidence of compromise of the authenticator.

Note that certain end-user choices can have a positive or negative impact on security and usability over which the security administrator or the MFA implementation have limited control. Examples are the ability of end-users to store their passwords (in an unprotected document versus in a password manager), or the reuse of previous passwords that unknowingly to the end-user and security administrator may have already been compromised[4]. Also security tools like password managers can raise privacy concerns due to the presence of trackers[5].

Table 1 gives an overview of the amount SHALL/SHOULD requirements, including their negative form, for a subset of authenticator types in terms of how often they occur in the NIST SP 800-63B guidelines. The column SHALL indicates the number of requirements to be followed strictly, whereas SHOULD counts the number of preferred but not necessarily required courses of action. We excluded the CAN and MAY requirements in the table as they are less stringent (and also less frequent in the guidelines). Table 2 lists in a similar manner the amount of general requirements for authenticators. From the above two tables, we discard those implementation specific requirements without any configuration option. An example of such a requirement for password authenticators is the fact that the salt SHALL be at least 32 bits in length and be chosen arbitrarily. Such requirements should be validated directly against the IAM implementations or specific biometric authentication factors to possibly prohibit their usage. Of the 198 requirements in Tables 1 and 2, AUTHGUIDE discards 125 requirements that are either irrelevant for the IAM itself (e.g. those targeting end-user devices) or IAM implementation specific (e.g. use of approved cryptography methods). The latter can be validated separately if the IAM feature is non-configurable, or the script generated by AUTHGUIDE directly configures the IAM to meet the requirements. The actual number of requirements being validated depends on the remaining configuration options selected in AUTHGUIDE. For example, a password-less authentication configuration would not check the password-related requirements (minimum length, acceptable characters, etc.). Other requirements are conditionally dependent on the desired authenticator assurance level (the NIST guidelines define 3 levels).

The remaining configuration options for the security administrator and/or end-user are evaluated by a Drools rule engine[6] in AUTHGUIDE. Based on the responses in AUTHGUIDE the list of requirements is further narrowed down to consider only those that are relevant for the selected set of authentication factors. AUTHGUIDE then evaluates (1) the number of relevant requirements and the amount of violations, (2) a base aggregated score for the SHALL and SHOULD requirements, and (3) an upper-bound and lower-bound to account for those options granted to the end-user for customization.

3.2 Registration and Replacement of Authentication Factors

For a given MFA configuration, an authentication factor can be registered or bound to the account of the end-user during enrollment, or later when the end-user adds an acceptable authenticator to strengthen the security of the account.

For each authentication factor, there should be a backup and recovery strategy in case the authenticator is not available, lost, damaged, stolen or compromised due

---

[4] Have I Been Pwned?, https://haveibeenpwned.com/.

[5] Exodus Privacy: LastPass 4.11.18.6150 has 7 trackers (Mar 2021), https://reports. exodus-privacy.eu/en/reports/165465/.

[6] https://www.drools.org.

to a data breach. These recovery mechanisms need to be secure and user-friendly as well. For example, SMS and push notifications on a mobile have been deprecated as authentication factors due to the possibility of phishing or SIM swapping attacks [9] or interception by IMSI-catchers. Therefore, recovery strategies should not rely on them either.

The consequences on the MFA workflow (i.e. the order of different mandatory and alternative authentication steps) are two-fold: (1) not every end-user will have the same MFA configuration and the workflow should be able to adapt to that, and (2) the workflow should support escalation to alternative authentication factors. For example, end-users that opted for a passwordless authentication experience should not be shown a form to fill in both their username and password, but rather only the username.

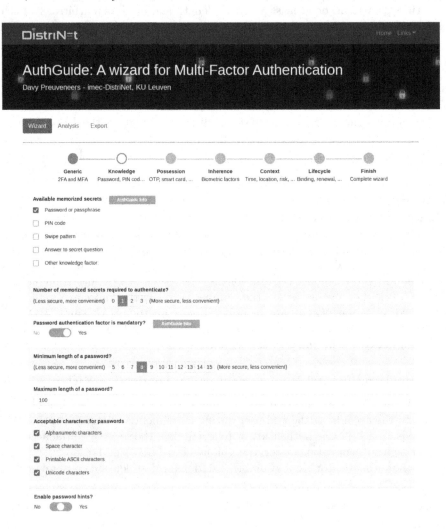

Fig. 1. The AUTHGUIDE wizard for multi-factor authentication configuration and requirement validation.

Fig. 2. The AUTHGUIDE requirement validation summary.

3.3 AUTHGUIDE Implementation

AUTHGUIDE is implemented as an HTML5 dashboard on top of a backend implemented with the Java-based Spring MVC framework. The latter maintains the MFA knowledge base of the wizard to inform the security administrator or end-user about security, privacy and usability concerns. Figure 1 depicts the web-based wizard interface to configure Multi-Factor Authentication configuration and carry out the security, privacy and usability trade-off analysis. The 'AuthGuide Info' button triggers a pop-up window that offers the security administrator or end-user additional background information on possible known threats and trade-offs.

AUTHGUIDE manages the list of configuration options per authentication factor, the mapping onto SHALL/SHOULD requirements, and any dependencies across the choices and requirements. Currently, it manages 73 configuration options in the wizard that are mapped onto a subset of the SHALL/SHOULD requirements of Tables 1 and 2, and that are conditionally exposed in the wizard depending on previously selected options. The requirements are implemented as a ruleset evaluated by the Drools 7.54 rule engine (see Fig. 3 in Appendix for examples of the ruleset). The main reason to rely on a rule engine rather than hardcoding a set of if-then-else rules in the application is to simplify the implementation and evaluation of conditional requirements and dependencies across requirements. Additionally, by managing these rules external to the application, they can be easily updated whenever new recommendations are proposed. As shown in Fig. 2, the outcome of the analysis is a report listing:

– The name of the requirement
– The type of the requirement (i.e. SHALL or SHOULD, or the negative form)
– The outcome of the validation (i.e. PASS or FAIL, and an explanation)
– The name of the Drools rule that produced this result

It also checks for violations against the 3 authentication assurance levels in NIST Special Publication 800-63B [5], though it is not a full compliance analysis tool as AUTHGUIDE does not verify the implementation-specific requirements listed in this report. If certain configuration options can be customized by the end-user, AUTHGUIDE evaluates both a best-case and a worst-case configuration scenario, as depicted in Fig. 2. AUTHGUIDE as such can not only inform the user about security-privacy-usability trade-offs of individual configuration options, but also about trade-offs for configurations as a whole.

The last feature of AUTHGUIDE is its ability to translate the JSON configuration file produced by the wizard into a configuration shell script for state-of-practice IAM platforms (currently only tested with Red Hat's Keycloak 12.0.4) to simplify the configuration of MFA. The remaining customization left for the security administrator before executing this script is to complete the URL end-point of the IAM and the name of the realm for which MFA needs to be configured. After completing these deployment specific details, the security administrator can execute the configuration script to create or update the realm.

4   Evaluation

To evaluate the performance and practical feasibility of AUTHGUIDE, we defined four different MFA scenarios:

1. **Fixed single factor authentication**: This scenario allows for single factor authentication, using as default the password authenticator. This is a typical scenario for sites that do not yet support MFA.
2. **Flexible single factor authentication**: This scenario augments the previous by allowing the end-user to replace the password authentication factor to enable a password-less experience (e.g. token or biometric) after enrollment.
3. **Mandatory 2FA with fixed authentication factors**: The scenario enforces 2FA during enrollment of the end-user with the two authentication factors fixed by the security administrator, i.e. a password combined with a Time-based One-Time Password (TOTP).
4. **Mandatory MFA with flexible authentication factors**: This scenario supports authentication with multiple knowledge, possession, inherence and context factors. The end-user can customize the configuration and select two or more factors, but they must belong to different categories.

Each of the above scenarios allows for multiple configurations, for example, by changing the valid password constraints or the password expiry policy, a 6 or 8 digit TOTP, the number and type of authentication factors in the mandatory MFA scenario, etc. For each scenario, we produced 3 different variants, resulting in 12 variants in total.

4.1   Performance Evaluation

To validate AUTHGUIDE, we first evaluated the efficiency of validating the SHALL and SHOULD requirements. We tested each of the 12 variants 10 times in random order on a machine with an Intel Core i7-7700U CPU running at 3.60 GHz, and with 32 GB of memory. The Spring Boot 2.4.6 application with the embedded Drools 7.54 rule engine runs with OpenJDK 11.0.11 in a Ubuntu 21.04 Linux environment.

We measured the time the Java application needs for the rule-based analysis, i.e. excluding the time to complete the AUTHGUIDE wizard. Overall, the time to evaluate the Drools rules to check the requirements varies between 0.609 and 2.149 ms, which is well below our pre-defined target of 0.1 s. Additionally, the memory used by the Java application (i.e. the maximum resident set size (RSS)) is 678528 kbytes. Based on these results, we believe it would be practically feasible to carry out the requirements validation directly within the browser with support of a proper JavaScript-based rule engine. However, to run AUTHGUIDE's application logic completely in the browser, the code generation for the IAM's configuration script also needs to be refactored and reimplemented.

4.2   Configuration Support for the Security Administrator

For a variant of each of the above 4 scenarios, we compared the time required to configure a realm within a Keycloak 12.0.4 deployment:

1. Manually through the configuration dashboard of Keycloak
2. Using the shell configuration script produced by AUTHGUIDE

For the second approach, the Keycloak's 'kcadm' command-line utility is already configured in advance. Both approaches were executed by an experienced Keycloak user. Additionally, the authentication flows to be manually configured in Keycloak for each of the four authentication variants were defined in advance. The rationale for this decision is the desire to rule out any influences caused by the need to correct misconfigured authentication flows.

The results of this experiment are shown in Table 3. One should compare the time required to configure a variant with the Keycloak Dashboard versus the combined time to achieve the same with the AUTHGUIDE Dashboard and Script. The time for AUTHGUIDE Script is the time required for the security administrator to execute the generated script as AUTHGUIDE does not directly update Keycloak. The time required is less for AUTHGUIDE, and more outspoken for the more sophisticated authentication flows.

Table 3. Time to configure 4 single-factor and multi-factor authentication scenarios.

Scenario	Keycloak dashboard	AuthGuide dashboard	AuthGuide script
Scenario 1	1 min 36 s	35 s	20 s
Scenario 2	2 min 48 s	41 s	23 s
Scenario 3	3 min 51 s	45 s	35 s
Scenario 4	4 min 23 s	59 s	43 s

4.3   Analysis of Security, Privacy and Usability Trade-Off

We evaluated to what extent the different security, privacy and usability requirements in NIST SP 800-63B [5] have been addressed. The result is (a) an indication of the authenticator assurance level achieved, and (b) the number of SHALL and SHOULD requirements that have been met relative to the number of requirements that were assessed (see Fig. 2). The trade-off analysis offers 6 values subdivided by:

- **Category:** Security, privacy and usability
- **Upper- and lower-bound:** Best- and worst-case w.r.t. end-user choices

Within the frame of this research, we did not quantitatively evaluate the level of increased awareness about MFA threats and trade-offs while using AUTHGUIDE, nor did we investigate MFA configuration mistakes when directly using the IAM's configuration interface and AUTHGUIDE's ability to avoid them. This assessment involving stakeholders with different levels of IAM expertise and MFA experience will be part of a future user study.

5   Conclusion

The contribution of this work is AUTHGUIDE, an authentication knowledge and configuration framework. It aims to increase the awareness about security, privacy and usability trade-offs by analyzing to what degree relevant requirements of NIST SP 800-63B [5] have been addressed, while also considering the implications of granting some flexibility on authentication factor selection to the end-user. For the security administrator, it simplifies the process of configuring MFA for a given identity and access management (IAM) platform. Our experimental evaluation demonstrated the practical feasibility and the added benefit of AUTHGUIDE for the security administrator. A user study evaluating the increased awareness about the aforementioned trade-offs and the ability to avoid MFA configuration mistakes is pending.

As future work, we aim for a more balanced weighing of the different types of requirements, as well as enhanced configuration support for alternative IAM platforms with plug-in support for the validation of implementation specific requirements.

Acknowledgments. This research is partially funded by the Research Fund KU Leuven and by the Flemish Government's Cybersecurity Initiative Flanders. Work for this paper was supported by the European Commission through the H2020 project CyberSec4Europe (https://www.cybersec4europe.eu/) under grant No. 830929.

Appendix

```
1   // 8 characters in length
2   rule "password_min_length:1"
3   activation-group "password_min_length"
4   salience 500
5   when
6     MFARequirement($r: req("password_min_length"), $r != null)
7     $config: MFAConfig(
8       "password" memberOf get("knowledge_factor") &&
9       get("password_min_length") < 8
10    )
11    $validate: MFAValidate()
12  then
13    $validate.add(drools.getRule().getName(), "Password too short",
14      MFAValidate.FAIL, $r);
15  end
16
17  rule "password_min_length:2"
18  activation-group "password_min_length"
19  salience 100
20  when
21    MFARequirement($r: req("password_min_length"), $r != null)
22    $config: MFAConfig()
23    $validate: MFAValidate()
24  then
25    $validate.add(drools.getRule().getName(), "Success",
26      MFAValidate.PASS, $r);
27  end
28
29  /************************************************************************/
30
31  // Verifiers SHOULD NOT require memorized secrets to be changed
32  // arbitrarily (e.g., periodically)
33  rule "password_expiry:1"
34  activation-group "password_expiry"
35  salience 500
36  when
37    MFARequirement($r: req("password_expiry"), $r != null)
38    $config: MFAConfig(
39      "password" memberOf get("knowledge_factor") &&
40      get("password_expiry") > 0
41    )
42    $validate: MFAValidate()
43  then
44    $validate.add(drools.getRule().getName(), "Do not set a password
45      expiry policy", MFAValidate.FAIL, $r);
46  end
47
48  rule "password_expiry:2"
49  activation-group "password_expiry"
50  salience 100
51  when
52    MFARequirement($r: req("password_expiry"), $r != null)
53    $config: MFAConfig()
54    $validate: MFAValidate()
55  then
56    $validate.add(drools.getRule().getName(), "Success",
57      MFAValidate.PASS, $r);
58  end
```

Fig. 3. Analyzing MFA requirements with a Drools ruleset, illustrating an example 'SHALL' and 'SHOULD' requirement for passwords from NIST SP 800-63B.

References

1. Andriamilanto, N., Allard, T., Guelvouit, G.L.: "Guess Who?" Large-scale data-centric study of the adequacy of browser fingerprints for web authentication. In: Barolli, L., Poniszewska-Maranda, A., Park, H. (eds.) IMIS 2020. AISC, vol. 1195, pp. 161–172. Springer, Cham (2021). https://doi.org/10.1007/978-3-030-50399-4_16

2. Dasgupta, D., Roy, A., Nag, A.: Toward the design of adaptive selection strategies for multi-factor authentication. Comput. Secur. **63**, 85–116 (2016). https://doi.org/10.1016/j.cose.2016.09.004, https://www.sciencedirect.com/science/article/pii/S016740481630102X

3. Dasgupta, D., Roy, A., Nag, A.: Multi-factor authentication. In: Advances in User Authentication. ISFS, pp. 185–233. Springer, Cham (2017). https://doi.org/10.1007/978-3-319-58808-7_5

4. Eckersley, P.: How unique is your web browser? In: Atallah, M.J., Hopper, N.J. (eds.) PETS 2010. LNCS, vol. 6205, pp. 1–18. Springer, Heidelberg (2010). https://doi.org/10.1007/978-3-642-14527-8_1

5. Grassi, P., et al.: Digital identity guidelines: authentication and lifecycle management [including updates as of 03-02-2020] (01 December 2017). https://doi.org/10.6028/NIST.SP.800-63b

6. Karegar, F., Pettersson, J.S., Fischer-Hübner, S.: Fingerprint recognition on mobile devices: widely deployed, rarely understood. In: Doerr, S., Fischer, M., Schrittwieser, S., Herrmann, D. (eds.) Proceedings of the 13th International Conference on Availability, Reliability and Security, ARES 2018, Hamburg, Germany, August 27–30, 2018, pp. 39:1–39:9. ACM (2018). https://doi.org/10.1145/3230833.3234514

7. Klieme, E., Wilke, J., van Dornick, N., Meinel, C.: FIDOnuous: a FIDO2/WebAuthn extension to support continuous web authentication. In: 2020 IEEE 19th International Conference on Trust, Security and Privacy in Computing and Communications (TrustCom), pp. 1857–1867 (2020). https://doi.org/10.1109/TrustCom50675.2020.00254

8. Laperdrix, P., Avoine, G., Baudry, B., Nikiforakis, N.: Morellian analysis for browsers: making web authentication stronger with canvas fingerprinting. In: Perdisci, R., Maurice, C., Giacinto, G., Almgren, M. (eds.) DIMVA 2019. LNCS, vol. 11543, pp. 43–66. Springer, Cham (2019). https://doi.org/10.1007/978-3-030-22038-9_3

9. Lee, K., Kaiser, B., Mayer, J., Narayanan, A.: An empirical study of wireless carrier authentication for sim swaps. USENIX Association, Virtual Conference (August 2020). https://www.usenix.org/system/files/soups2020-lee.pdf

10. Ometov, A., Bezzateev, S., Mäkitalo, N., Andreev, S., Mikkonen, T., Koucheryavy, Y.: Multi-factor authentication: a survey. Cryptography **2**(1), 1 (2018). https://doi.org/10.3390/cryptography2010001, https://www.mdpi.com/2410-387X/2/1/1

11. Oogami, W., Gomi, H., Yamaguchi, S., Yamanaka, S., Higurashi, T.: Observation study on usability challenges for fingerprint authentication using WebAuthn-enabled android smartphones. In: Symposium on Usable Privacy and Security (SOUPS 2020). USENIX Association (August 2020)

12. Spooren, J., Preuveneers, D., Joosen, W.: Mobile device fingerprinting considered harmful for risk-based authentication. In: Proceedings of the Eighth European Workshop on System Security. EuroSec 2015. Association for Computing Machinery, New York (2015). https://doi.org/10.1145/2751323.2751329

13. Torres, C.F., Jonker, H., Mauw, S.: *FP-Block*: usable web privacy by controlling browser fingerprinting. In: Pernul, G., Ryan, P.Y.A., Weippl, E. (eds.) ESORICS 2015, Part II. LNCS, vol. 9327, pp. 3–19. Springer, Cham (2015). https://doi.org/10.1007/978-3-319-24177-7_1
14. Wang, D., Zhang, X., Zhang, Z., Wang, P.: Understanding security failures of multi-factor authentication schemes for multi-server environments. Comput. Secur. **88**, 101619 (2020). https://doi.org/10.1016/j.cose.2019.101619, https://www.sciencedirect.com/science/article/pii/S016740481930166X

Author Index

Printed in the United States
by Baker & Taylor Publisher Services